Microsoft Security Operations Analyst Exam Ref SC-200 Guide

Second Edition

Achieve SC-200 Certification with Real-World Microsoft Security Operations Insights

Steve Miles

Junaid Mumtaz

Trevor Stuart

Joe Anich

<packt>

Microsoft Security Operations Analyst Exam Ref SC-200 Guide

Second Edition

Portfolio Director: Vijin Boricha
Portfolio Manager: Anindya Sil
Program Manager: Ankita Thakur
Content Engineer: Shubhra Mayuri
Technical Editor: Nithik Cheruvakodan
Copy Editor: Shubhra Mayuri, Swathi Ajaykumar
Indexer: Rekha Nair
Production Designer: Salma Patel
Growth Lead: Ankita Thakur

First published: April 2022
Second edition: June 2026

Production reference: 1190626

Published by Packt Publishing Ltd.
Grosvenor House
11 St Paul's Square
Birmingham
B3 1RB, UK.

ISBN 978-1-83620-441-1
www.packtpub.com

Contributors

About the authors

Steve Miles works in a senior partner technology enablement role for the cloud practice of a multi-billion turnover European IT distributor. He is a Microsoft Most Valuable Professional (MVP), Microsoft Certified Trainer (MCT), and an Alibaba Cloud MVP. He has 25+ years of technology experience in hosted datacenter services, hybrid, and multi-cloud platforms, and a previous military career in engineering, signals, and communications.

Steve is the author and technical reviewer of many books on Microsoft technologies with a focus on security, Azure, AI and data.

Junaid Mumtaz is an experienced Cloud Security Consultant with over 6 years of expertise in cybersecurity and cloud-native defense. He began his career as a Cybersecurity Analyst, where he focused on protecting enterprise infrastructure and developing proactive detection strategies to address evolving threats. As he transitioned into cloud technologies, Junaid specialized in Microsoft Defender XDR and Azure Sentinel, helping organizations modernize their security operations and adopt scalable, resilient solutions. His practical experience spans across complex environments, where he has led initiatives to strengthen detection capabilities and streamline incident response. Currently, Junaid is focused on DevSecOps, risk assessment, and advanced threat hunting. He is also actively exploring Microsoft's latest advancements, including Security Copilot, to drive intelligent automation and enhance security outcomes for modern enterprises.

Trevor Stuart has over 15 years of experience in IT. He started with SMS and Active Directory and maintained exposure in the field through various naming changes and technical additions. Trevor has a passion for IT but more so with cybersecurity. Trevor swiftly moved into Cybersecurity and focused on securing privileged access, hardening operating systems, implementing tiering within AD, tying identities to modern authentication mechanisms, scaling out the identity to the hybrid world, application migration in secure manners in Azure, and leveraging built-in security controls in multiple clouds and platforms to secure workloads. Trevor is a technology enthusiast at heart and the world of cybersecurity only lights the fire of passion inside of him.

Joe Anich has 13 years of experience in the IT industry ranging from endpoint management with a focus in SCCM and Intune, to endpoint security and incident response. As Joe dug deeper into security he realized where his passion resided, and that was in incident response working with the Microsoft Detection and Response Team (DART). Working in incident response has given Joe insight into SOC operations and how to help teams around the world improve their security posture within the Microsoft 365 security stack. Outside of IR, he is in constant pursuit of continued education whether that be SANS courses like the GCED or GCFA, or internal threat hunting training.

About the reviewer

Bee Eng Lau Blewitt is an Identity and Azure Security Architect with nearly three decades of experience across multinational companies. Starting out as a software engineer, she now specializes in digital identity, Azure Security, and DevSecOps. Bee holds a wide portfolio of certifications, including CISSP, CSSLP, CCSP, TOGAF9, Microsoft Certified Cybersecurity Architect Expert, and SC-200 Security Operations Analyst, demonstrating her proven ability to master and pass advanced exams. Bee's expertise spans Entra ID, CIAM, modern authentication, and cloud security, and she has delivered complex identity transformations across industries from financial services to healthcare and retail.

Table of Contents

Preface

Security operations has changed. Analysts are no longer working from a single console, a single alert, or a single source of evidence. Modern incidents move across identities, endpoints, email, cloud apps, data, workloads, and infrastructure. A phishing email may become an identity compromise. An identity compromise may lead to endpoint activity. Endpoint activity may expose data movement, cloud access, lateral movement, or suspicious application behavior. For a security operations analyst, the real skill is not just knowing where each tool lives, but understanding how the evidence connects.

This book provides a practical guide to the Microsoft security operations skills covered by the SC-200: Microsoft Security Operations Analyst exam. It explains how Microsoft Defender XDR, Microsoft Sentinel, Microsoft Entra ID, Microsoft Purview, Microsoft Defender for Endpoint, Microsoft Defender for Office 365, Microsoft Defender for Cloud Apps, Microsoft Defender for Identity, and Microsoft Defender for Cloud workload protections support detection, investigation, response, automation, and threat hunting.

The focus throughout the book is on how security operations actually work. You will learn how data is collected, how detections are created, how alerts become incidents, how entities help explain attacker activity, and how analysts move from triage to investigation and response. You will also see how Kusto Query Language, Advanced Hunting, Microsoft Sentinel hunting, automation rules, playbooks, attack disruption, case management, and agentic AI experiences such as embedded Copilot for Security fit into the wider investigation workflow.

The book is structured to build from exam readiness and SOC foundations into the operational areas tested by SC-200. You will begin by understanding the exam objectives and the evolution of modern security operations. You will then configure Microsoft Sentinel, ingest security data, create detections, investigate threats across Microsoft Defender XDR and Microsoft 365, respond to alerts and incidents, perform endpoint investigation, and configure automation across Microsoft Defender XDR and Microsoft Sentinel.

By the end of the book, you should be able to recognize how Microsoft security tools work together in a real SOC workflow. More importantly, you should be able to make the kind of decisions the SC-200 exam expects: which evidence matters, which tool should be used, which action should be taken, and why that action is the right one for the scenario.

Who this book is for

This book is written for learners preparing for the SC-200: Microsoft Security Operations Analyst exam. It is designed as an exam study guide for readers who need to understand how Microsoft security operations tools are used to detect, investigate, respond to, and hunt for threats across Microsoft cloud, hybrid, and on-premises environments.

The book is especially useful for SOC analysts, security engineers, incident responders, Microsoft 365 administrators, Azure administrators, and security professionals who work with or support Microsoft Defender XDR and Microsoft Sentinel. It is also suitable for readers moving into a security operations role who need a clear, practical path through the SC-200 objectives.

What this book covers

Chapter 1, Preparing for Your Microsoft Exam and SC-200 Objectives, introduces the SC-200 exam structure, the current security operations objectives, and the resources you can use to prepare effectively.

Chapter 2, The Evolution of Security and Security Operations, explains how security operations have moved from traditional perimeter-based models to modern, identity-first, cloud-connected, and automation-driven SOC operations.

Chapter 3, Configure the Microsoft Sentinel SIEM and Platform, covers Sentinel roles, data retention, workbooks, and platform optimization so that Sentinel can support effective security operations.

Chapter 4, Ingest Data into Microsoft Sentinel, explains how to connect and collect security data from Windows events, Syslog, CEF, Azure activity logs, and threat intelligence sources.

Chapter 5, Configure Detections, covers custom detections in Microsoft Defender XDR, analytics rules in Microsoft Sentinel, MITRE ATT&CK coverage, anomaly detection, and machine learning-based detections.

Chapter 6, Detect Threats by Using Microsoft Defender XDR, explains how to use KQL, Advanced Hunting, threat analytics, hunting graphs, blast radius analysis, and entity relationships to identify suspicious activity.

Chapter 7, Detect Threats by Using the Microsoft Sentinel Platform, covers hunting queries, KQL jobs, summary rules, notebooks, and large-scale analysis techniques for proactive threat hunting.

Chapter 8, Investigate Microsoft 365 Activities to Identify Threats, explains how to use Microsoft Purview Audit, Content Search, and Microsoft Graph activity logs to reconstruct activity and validate suspicious behavior.

Chapter 9, Respond to Alerts and Incidents in Microsoft Defender XDR, covers investigation and remediation across Defender XDR workloads, including email, identities, cloud apps, data, cloud workload protections, Sentinel incidents, case management, complex attacks, and Copilot-assisted investigations.

Chapter 10, Respond to Alerts and Incidents in Microsoft Defender for Endpoint, focuses on endpoint investigation using device timelines, evidence and entity analysis, live response, investigation packages, and automated attack disruption.

Chapter 11, Configure Automation for Microsoft Defender XDR and Microsoft Sentinel, covers alert and email notifications, Defender for Endpoint settings, automated investigation and response, attack disruption, device groups, automation rules, and Sentinel playbooks.

To get the most out of this book

- You should have a basic understanding of security operations concepts such as alerts, incidents, logs, identities, endpoints, email threats, cloud services, and incident response. Some exposure to KQL is helpful, but the book explains the query and hunting concepts needed for the exam as they appear in context.
- It is useful to read each chapter alongside the official SC-200 *Skills measured* and use the review questions, exam tips, flashcards, and mock exam content to check your understanding as you progress.
- As you work through the chapters, focus on the investigation flow: how data is collected, how detections create alerts, how alerts become incidents, how entities connect evidence, and how analysts decide which response or hunting action to take.

Download the color images

We also provide a PDF file that has color images of the screenshots/diagrams used in this book. You can download it here: `https://packt.link/gbp/9781836204411`.

Get in touch

Feedback from our readers is always welcome.

General feedback: If you have questions about any aspect of this book or have any general feedback, please email us at `customercare@packt.com` and mention the book's title in the subject of your message.

Errata: Although we have taken every care to ensure the accuracy of our content, mistakes do happen. If you have found a mistake in this book, we would be grateful if you reported this to us. Please visit `http://www.packt.com/submit-errata`, click **Submit Errata**, and fill in the form. All valid errata will be timely updated on GitHub: `https://github.com/PacktPublishing/Microsoft-Security-Operations-Analyst-Exam-Ref-SC-200-Guide`

Piracy: If you come across any illegal copies of our works in any form on the internet, we would be grateful if you would provide us with the location address or website name. Please contact us at `copyright@packt.com` with a link to the material.

If you are interested in becoming an author: If there is a topic that you have expertise in and you are interested in either writing or contributing to a book, please visit `http://authors.packt.com/`.

Share your thoughts

Once you've read *Microsoft Security Operations Analyst Exam Ref SC-200 Guide-Second Edition*, we'd love to hear your thoughts! Scan the QR code below to go straight to the Amazon review page for this book and share your feedback.

https://packt.link/r/1836204418

Your review is important to us and the tech community and will help us make sure we're delivering excellent quality content.

Free benefits with your book

This book comes with free benefits to support your learning. Activate them now for instant access (see the "*How to Unlock*" section for instructions).

Here's a quick overview of what you can instantly unlock with your purchase:

Online Exam-Prep Tools

Ace your certification exam with exam-ready online resources

DRM-Free PDF Version

Download DRM-free PDF and ePub copies of this book.

7-Day Packt Library Access

Get 7-day unlimited access to 8,000+ books and videos. No credit card required.

Available for first-time Packt+ trial users only.

Next-Gen Reader Access

Read this book on Packt Reader with progress sync, dark mode and note-taking.

How to Unlock

Scan the QR code (or go to `packtpub.com/unlock`). Search for this book by name, confirm the edition, and then follow the steps on the page.

UNLOCK NOW

Note: Keep your invoice handy. Purchases made directly from Packt don't require one

Part 1

Readiness and Security Operations Foundations

In this first part of the book, you will build the foundation needed to approach the SC-200 exam and understand the role of a Microsoft Security Operations Analyst.

You will look at the exam structure, the official preparation resources, and how the objectives connect to real SOC work. You'll also explore how security operations has evolved from traditional perimeter-based monitoring to modern, identity-first, cloud-connected, and automation-driven investigation and response.

This part of the book includes the following chapters:

- *Chapter 1, Preparing for Your Microsoft Exam and SC-200 Objectives*
- *Chapter 2, The Evolution of Security and Security Operations*

1

Preparing for Your Microsoft Exam and SC-200 Objectives

This chapter is dedicated to ensuring that you grasp how to prepare for the **Microsoft SC-200 exam** and that you fully understand the objectives, along with how they apply in the real world. Passing the exam is just the beginning. This book's primary aim is to equip you with cybersecurity principles that you can apply in your daily security operations. Prepare for a practical learning experience that goes beyond exam preparation, covering threat detection, incident response, and proactive security measures. Let's get into it!

In both traditional and modern enterprises, the **Microsoft security operations analyst** serves as a central coordinator, facilitating collaboration between individual contributors and enterprise stakeholders to strengthen security operations. This role in most organizations aims toward one goal: to protect against, secure against, detect, and respond to threats present in an enterprise as expeditiously as possible. They are responsible for reducing organizational risk by rapidly remediating active attacks in the environment, advising on improvements to threat protection practices, and escalating violations of organizational policies to appropriate teams and stakeholders. Historically, this level of responsibility has always involved lots of tooling, alert fatigue, human interaction in investigations, and so on.

Security operations have evolved significantly with the shift to cloud-based solutions. Platforms such as **Microsoft Sentinel** have replaced traditional on-premises tools, offering real-time threat detection, automated responses, and improved scalability. AI and automation now play a key role in reducing manual tasks and speeding up incident response. As a result, today's Microsoft Security Operations Analysts must adapt to these modern tools to quickly detect, investigate, and mitigate threats in enterprise environments.

This chapter will cover the following topics:

- Preparing for a Microsoft exam
- Introducing the resources available and accessing Microsoft Learn
- Creating a Microsoft demo tenant

Microsoft terminology, platform names, and platform capabilities have changed as security operations requirements and business demands have evolved over time. The following updates reflect the current Microsoft SOC platform structure, terminology, and operational experience referenced throughout this book:

- Microsoft has consolidated its Defender portals into the *unified* **Microsoft Defender XDR portal,** providing a single investigation and response experience across identities, endpoints, email, applications, and data.
- Microsoft Sentinel is now part of the *unified security operations experience,* where **XDR, SIEM,** and **SOAR** work together in a single platform.
  Microsoft Sentinel is generally available in the **Microsoft Defender portal**, and at a future point will no longer be supported in the Azure portal and will be available only in the Defender portal.

Technical requirements

To get the most value from this book, it helps to have some familiarity with Microsoft security concepts and the core Microsoft security platforms. You do not need expert-level knowledge before starting, as the book will guide you through the key areas required for the SC-200 exam.

A basic understanding of the following areas is helpful:

- **Microsoft Defender XDR** and core security workloads, including identities, email, applications, and data protection
- **Microsoft Defender for Endpoint** and general endpoint security concepts
- **Microsoft Defender for Cloud** and the **Azure** resources it helps protect
- **Microsoft Sentinel** fundamentals, including data collection, detections, investigations, and threat hunting
- Basic familiarity with **Kusto Query Language** (**KQL**)

> Note
>
> **Free Benefits with Your Book**
>
> Your purchase includes a free PDF copy of this book along with access to the online cert prep platform designed to help you ace your SC-200 certification. Check the *Free*

Benefits with Your Book section in the *Preface* to unlock them instantly and maximize your learning experience.

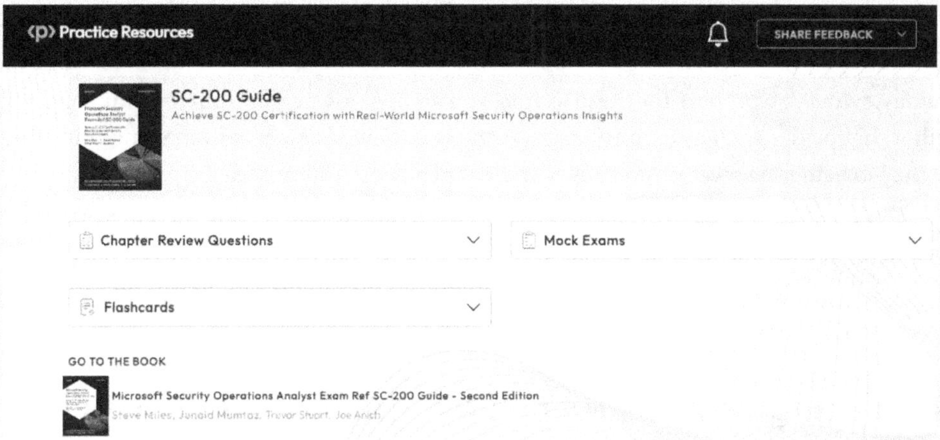

Figure 1.1 – Dashboard interface of the online practice resources

Here's what you'll find on the online platform:

- 2 Mock Exams
- Flashcards
- Exam Tips
- Chapter Review Questions

Preparing for a Microsoft exam

When preparing for a **Microsoft exam**, there are a few things to keep in mind. First, Microsoft always provides the *Skills measured* section on the exam page, which lists everything assessed during the exam. In this *Skills measured* outline, you also get an estimate of the weightage given to each exam domain, that is, the percentage of questions that will appear from a particular domain. These are usually spot on. You can use this outline to check some of the bigger domains and spend more time studying and practicing in the labs on those.

Another thing worth mentioning is that a lot of the sections mentioned in the *Skills measured* outline align with the modules for the **Microsoft Learn SC-200 learning path**. If you incorporate the skills measured into your training, you'll find it easy to prepare for the respective domain of the exam outline. You will understand more about the **learning path modules** in the next section.

If you are curious about learning more outside of the module links provided on the exam page, go to `https://learn.microsoft.com/` and search for more topics of interest.

Generally, when you prepare for these exams, you are looking at all resources available, whether that be the *product documentation, learning path modules*, or testing things out in a lab, with the lab being the most important to me, as they allow you to actively practice what you are learning. You will cover setting up labs for testing in later sections.

Once you are settled on the kind of preparation that suits you best for the exam, it will become a lot clearer what resources you can use to help you prepare. The next section covers some of these resources.

Introducing the resources available and accessing Microsoft Learn

When it comes to training or studying resources, Microsoft does a great job of showing you the exam structure. You should always start with the learning paths for the SC-200 exam available from **Microsoft Learn**: `https://learn.microsoft.com/en-us/training/courses/sc-200t00`

Whether you are looking into everything available to begin your journey toward taking the SC-200 exam or learning the skills needed to be successful in your career as a SOC analyst specializing in the *M365* security stack, remember that it takes time. There is a lot of content for all the features available; therefore, it's beneficial to take your time to pick it all up.

For you, it's best to start in the order of the bullet list provided later in this section, and here's why. It's helpful to go through the learning paths and review the content laid out for you. Basic knowledge checks are included to ensure you're absorbing the material. If you encounter any areas in the modules that are unclear or if you need more information, start by looking for the corresponding Microsoft Learn page. Once you've completed the learning path, set up a lab and begin following the order outlined in the exam.

The next section summarizes some of the larger portions of the learning paths, as they're critical to ensure that you learn, for both the exam and tasks that you may encounter in your career.

Study guide for the SC-200 exam: Microsoft Security Operations Analyst

As of the April 16, 2026 SC-200 Skills Measured update, the exam focuses on three core domains that reflect how modern security operations are performed across Microsoft Defender XDR and Microsoft Sentinel.

Rather than treating each product as a separate area of study, the exam tests how detections, investigations, response actions, and platform operations work together across the full security operations workflow.

The three measured domains are as follows:

- **Manage a security operations environment (40–45%)**
  This includes configuring and maintaining Microsoft Defender XDR and Microsoft Sentinel, managing permissions and access, configuring automation and playbooks, managing data connectors, configuring security controls and detections, and maintaining the overall operational security platform used by the SOC
- **Respond to security incidents (35–40%)**
  This covers alert investigation, incident analysis, evidence review, device and entity investigation, automated investigation and response, remediation actions, and the use of Microsoft Defender XDR and Microsoft Sentinel to contain and resolve security incidents
- **Perform threat hunting (20–25%)**
  This includes threat hunting by using Kusto Query Language (KQL), advanced hunting, threat intelligence, anomaly analysis, identifying malicious behavior across identities, endpoints, cloud apps, and workloads, and validating suspicious activity through deeper investigation

KQL remains a core skill across all three domains. It supports threat hunting, analytics rules, investigation workflows, and detection tuning in both Microsoft Defender XDR and Microsoft Sentinel. Rather than being treated as a separate product area, KQL is used throughout the exam as the operational language behind detection and investigation.

Microsoft Defender XDR and Microsoft Sentinel now operate as part of a unified security operations experience. Microsoft Defender XDR provides cross-domain investigation across identities, endpoints, email, applications, and data, while Microsoft Sentinel extends that capability with SIEM, SOAR, threat intelligence, and broader telemetry correlation. Understanding how these platforms work together is more important than studying them as isolated tools.

This book focuses on the operational decisions behind the exam—where detection happens, how incidents are investigated, and which tools provide the right response at the right time.

There is a lot to cover, especially if you are new to the Microsoft security operations platform, but the concepts build naturally as you progress. Working through the learning paths, reviewing the supporting Microsoft Learn documentation, and validating those concepts inside a demo tenant will make the material far easier to retain. The advantage of hands-on practice is that you can return to each area, follow the investigation flow directly in the platform, and connect the theory to real operational behavior.

The next step is building that demo environment.

Creating a Microsoft demo tenant

One of the absolute best things you can do to get hands-on experience is to build a lab – in this instance, your Microsoft demo tenant! However, without context, you might end up exploring features aimlessly. Once you've completed the learning paths and knowledge checks, you'll be ready to dive in! You'll have a clear structure, knowing where to start, where to end, and what's in between.

To get started with setting up your lab, first bookmark the following URLs:

- `https://learn.microsoft.com/en-us/entra/fundamentals/create-new-tenant`
- `https://learn.microsoft.com/en-us/entra/fundamentals/how-subscriptions-associated-directory`
- `https://learn.microsoft.com/en-us/defender-xdr/get-started`

Summary

There is a lot to take in at the start of SC-200, especially if you are new to the Microsoft 365 security stack, but the good news is that the platforms connect more naturally than they first appear. As you begin working through Microsoft Defender for Endpoint, you also start building familiarity with the wider security portal, which makes learning the rest of the platform much easier.

As you move into areas such as Defender for Office, Defender for Identity, and Microsoft Defender XDR, the investigation flow starts to feel consistent rather than separate. Alerts, incidents, response actions, and investigation paths begin to follow the same logic, which helps reduce the learning curve as you progress.

By the time you move into Microsoft Sentinel, much of the terminology and investigation approach already feels familiar. The same applies to KQL, which becomes useful across advanced hunting, Microsoft Sentinel, and Log Analytics workspaces. The goal is not to memorize products individually, but to understand how detection, investigation, and response work together across the full security operations platform.

In *Chapter 2*, you will continue exploring the evolution of security operations, examining how security practices have shifted from traditional perimeter-based methods to the modern, identity-first, and cloud-driven approaches that define today's SOC. You will understand the limitations of traditional SOC models and how platforms such as Microsoft Sentinel and Microsoft Defender XDR have transformed detection, investigation, and response across modern enterprise environments.

Get this book's PDF version and more

Your purchase includes a PDF copy of this book along with access to online cert prep platform designed to help you ace your SC-200 certification. Scan the QR code (or go to `packtpub.com/unlock`). Search for this book by name, confirm the edition, and then follow the steps on the page.

UNLOCK NOW

Note: Keep your invoice handy. Purchases made directly from Packt don't require an invoice.

2

The Evolution of Security and Security Operations

In order to understand the true importance and impact of the **Microsoft Security Operations Analyst** and their role within an organization, you need to take a quick step back and understand the true evolution of both **security** and **security operations**.

This chapter outlines some important topics to give learners the ability to understand the context a bit. You must understand this because it quickly becomes an important part of your role! The topics you will read about in this chapter include the following:

- Understanding the traditional approach to security
- Introducing the modern approach to security
- Getting to know traditional **security operations center** (**SOC**) issues
- Exploring modern ways to resolve traditional SOC issues

In this chapter, you will explore key topics related to working in a SOC, including common challenges, critical issues, and essential SOC tools. Our goal is to provide you with a deeper understanding of the evolving landscape of security and the critical role that security operations play in it.

Understanding the traditional approach to security

Security has always been important to enterprises worldwide, because without it, the risk factors of compromise, data exfiltration, and overall breach, which may or may not be publicly disclosed, can have a massive financial and trust impact on an enterprise. Historically, if you look back at security, it has been focused on network boundaries, getting feeds, and logging from all network appliances and devices. There has been a **four-wall approach** to any resource access, meaning an employee must be within a known network boundary, such as a **virtual**

private network (**VPN**) connection if they are not within the office, or, of course, within an office subnet or known network segment. While network segmentation and security boundaries do indeed possess their importance in security, it has been an increasingly losing battle, one that comes with many gaps and downfalls. Some downfalls are as follows:

- SOC analysts are completely overwhelmed by alert influx and fatigue
- SOC analysts are struggling to keep traditional values relevant in a modern "remote work" world
- SOC analysts are spending too much time investigating, versus proactively protecting or allowing modern technologies to do the anomalous behavior analysis

Traditionally, SOC analysts spend their day analyzing feed and signal data, collaborating with other teammates to make a disposition on the next steps for alerts that come into their **security incident and event management** (**SIEM**)/security tools. However, with the ever-growing threat landscape, there must be a mechanism in place that decreases the requirement for human interaction and coordination and increases the ability to have tools in an enterprise that include automatic investigation, triaging, comparison, and even remediation of active threats in an enterprise. The issue here is that traditionally, the tools and operations available did not support these new preferred requirements. These are indeed requirements in the world we live in today; there is a ridiculously small chance that keeping such processes in place will allow your enterprise to maintain a healthy and secure environment.

So, what has changed? Is it merely tooling? Or is there more to this story? Let's dive into the next section, review the modern approach to security, and move onward to what has changed in the approach and evolution of security operations.

Introducing the modern approach to security

Many of you would have noticed some noticeably substantial changes in the approach to security. In **modern enterprises**, teams can shift their focus from the traditional approach, as discussed previously, and move toward an approach that fits the requirements and landscape of their enterprises. You have heard of security teams ingesting and analyzing network-level logging details, keeping as much authentication, access, and authorization internal as possible, and approaching service publishing with a block-first mentality (a security approach where the default stance is to block or deny access by default until it is explicitly allowed).

Here is the thing: this approach simply does not fit the mold of how end users and enterprises are required to function anymore. Increasingly, there are online services, such as Office 365, Teams, or Dynamics, that enterprises use that require a shift of security mindset and operations around how enterprise end users can access such online services. Additionally, online services are not the only items that require a shift. Often, there is an increasing number of end users that are working remotely; this can be by design or by situation—either way, remote work has increased tremendously over the past few years, and security needs to provide services to remote workers in a secure manner just like they would if they were in the office.

So, how does a security team shift and meet these newer and more modern requirements? Security teams must understand **zero trust**. There are so many vendors out in the security world that have a zero-trust model defined for enterprises to follow. Here, however, you will be following and referring to the **Microsoft Zero Trust framework**.

The rise of cloud applications and remote work has changed the way we think about security. Employees now frequently access company data from personal devices and remote locations, and often share it with external partners. As enterprise applications transition from on-premises to cloud environments, security needs to focus on every access point, rather than relying solely on traditional network boundaries.

Nowadays, whenever an end user or employee goes to access such resources, the traditional on-premises perimeter is bypassed, and security models that are dependent on network firewalls and VPNs are null and void. Any enterprise that relies on those traditional security models will lack the visibility, solutions, and ability to deliver timely, end-to-end SOC coverage.

So, what is required? What must change? Enterprises need a new security model and approach that adapts to the changes and complexity of the new requirements and new business interactions. This model must embrace and understand the mobile workforce, the remote workforce, and the accessibility of cloud applications that go far beyond the traditional perimeter. This is the absolute core of zero trust.

The following diagram illustrates the shift from the traditional perimeter-based security model to the Zero Trust approach, where every access request is continuously verified, evaluated, and authorized based on identity, device state, location, and risk signals rather than network location alone.

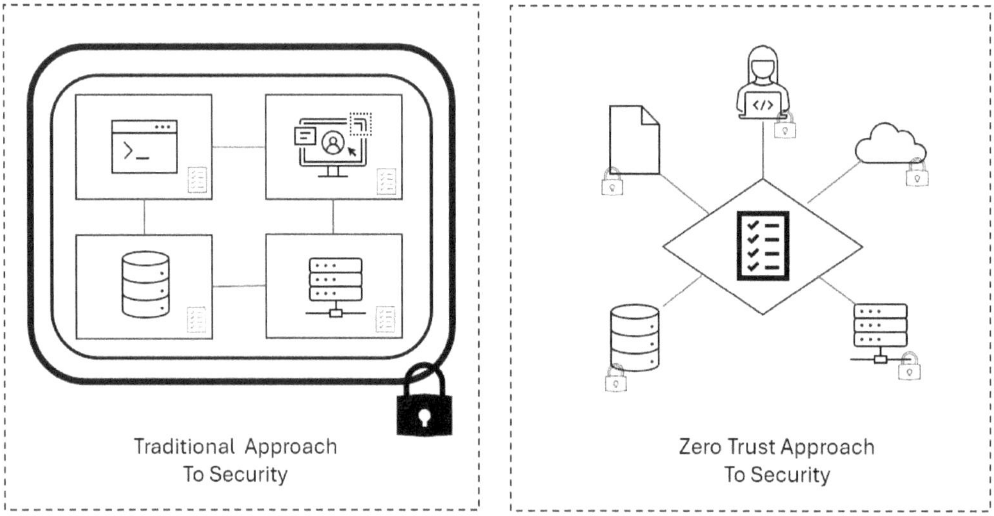

Figure 2.1 – Zero-trust model

So, what is at the core of the zero-trust model? Every single access request by any user (employee, partner, or vendor) must be authenticated, then it must be authorized by an **enterprise policy**, and then inspected for any anomalies before granting access. There are various feeds that will be a part of the inspection process that you will read about later in the book. Again, every single access request, by any user, will be inspected, no matter where that request is coming from; that's the core of zero trust.

Here are the general *guiding principles* of zero trust:

- **Verify explicitly**: Always authenticate and authorize based on all available data points, including user identity, location, device health, service or workload, data classification, and anomalies. This must be done for all requests. Ensure your enterprise policies and discussions fully take this into account.
- **Use least-privilege access**: Limit user access with **just-in-time (JIT)** access and **just-enough access (JEA)**, risk-based adaptive policies, and data protection to protect both data and productivity.
- **Assume breach**: Minimize the blast radius for breaches and prevent lateral movement by segmenting access by network, user, device, and application awareness. Verify all sessions are encrypted from end to end. Use analytics to get visibility, drive threat detection, and improve defenses.

With this model in place, security teams can begin supporting modern access and security needs effectively and efficiently. But with such a shift also comes a shift in how the SOC operates with this new model. You can now take a look at the traditional issues prevalent within a SOC and the modern ways to resolve them.

Getting to know traditional SOC issues

With the **traditional approach** to security being in place for years, it should not be a surprise that, with such an approach, naturally, there are SOC issues. There have been numerous studies conducted by Cisco, Exabeam, Enterprise Strategy Group, and Microsoft that have deeply reviewed how SOC teams work and what the gaps are that bring about issues and security threats. Think about it; with every gap, with every moment wasted on a slow triage process, the security threat increases. You will now spend a little time going over the main issues and sub-issues of traditional operations within a SOC.

Tooling, tooling, and tooling

One of the first gaps that have been assessed in studies comes down to this: what tools do SOC analysts have within their reach to be effective? What we have come to find out is that there are numerous teams without a proper set of tools to secure operations effectively. There might be an enterprise with a centralized logging infrastructure; in addition to the logging infrastructure, there is a monitoring infrastructure; in addition to logging and monitoring, there is another team that manages performance; in addition to logging and monitoring and performance, there is another team that manages tooling for closing out alerts and so on. There are too many tools, doing completely different aspects of management, managed by different teams, which simply causes problems. Imagine having to operate within it and keep it up to date. It becomes increasingly difficult to know what is important to focus on, who needs to be involved, and what tool is triggering the alert or feed.

Alert fatigue

With improper tooling comes another huge issue in traditional SOCs – alert fatigue. Alert fatigue can have an adverse impact on your business's cybersecurity. Usually, over 50% of alerts in any organization are false positives. Most businesses deal with this problem by having a particular threshold that reduces the alerts. Nevertheless, other businesses choose to ignore specific alert categories. This desensitization due to an overabundance of alerts can weaken your security system. However, with effective cybersecurity services, you can address security alert fatigue, minimizing the chances of a successful cybercrime.

Slow triage times

Often, because of improper tooling, there is a slow triage or response time. This is because there are many tools present, none of which integrate or talk to each other, even from an API perspective, and each tool requires a different team to manage it. This quickly brings up confusing and deep communication requirements that many times do not exist within enterprises. With slow triaging and responses comes the increased chance that the security threat will only spread or, at worst, be missed altogether.

So, how do you resolve these traditional SOC issues? You will learn that in the next section.

Exploring modern ways to resolve traditional SOC issues

Keeping in mind the security shift that is required to be successful in the modern world, one of the first things enterprises must do from a security perspective to resolve traditional SOC issues is to review tooling and coverage. As you saw in the previous section, tooling has a drastic impact on the SOC.

The overarching solution to common and traditional SOC issues is to begin integrating enterprise internal security systems into automation, coordination, and other threat intelligence backends. This type of data and integration will allow enterprises to have insight into threats that far surpass what is merely in their environments. Whenever you bring in these vast external data sources (primarily through native tooling, such as your **endpoint detection and response** (**EDR**) or SIEM solution), security teams in enterprises gain much more context into the actual threat that exists in their enterprise and what each alert means, but most importantly, how to act on each alert.

This solution then turns traditional SOC issues into the following remediated key capabilities:

- **Filter out false positives**: Know which alarms can truly be ignored
- **Speed up triage**: Prioritize investigations based on the presence in your enterprise and the severity of the impact the threat already poses
- **Simplify incident analysis**: Determine quickly what has already been impacted, protect other vulnerable assets, and contain the damage

The Microsoft Defender stack (Microsoft Defender for Cloud, Microsoft Defender for Endpoint, Microsoft Defender for Identity, Microsoft Defender Antivirus, Microsoft Defender for Cloud Apps, and Microsoft Sentinel) provides an all-around solution that provides proper tooling, insight, and automation to effectively manage a modern enterprise. This solution helps resolve traditional SOC issues greatly! The rest of the chapters will be dedicated to diving into each of these tools within the solution and explaining their importance in the SOC, what you need to know to deploy and manage them, and then, of course, what you need to know to pass the SC-200 exam!

Summary

To conclude the chapter, security and security operations have evolved vastly over the years. There have been numerous traditional approaches to security, and with that come traditional ways to manage the enterprise SOC – but with the ever-changing technical world and tools that enterprises must operate in and adopt, there needs to be a shift – a shift from the traditional to the modern; a shift from the network to the identity; a shift from manual SOC processes with multiple tools and no integration to fewer tools, more efficiency, automation, and less alert fatigue.

We hope this chapter has provided you with a solid foundation to enhance your understanding and skill set on your learning journey. Now that you've mastered these concepts, it's time to dive deeper. Get ready to level up your expertise in threat detection and incident response. Let's move forward together – there's much more to uncover!

Get this book's PDF version and more

Your purchase includes a PDF copy of this book along with access to online cert prep platform designed to help you ace your SC-200 certification. Scan the QR code (or go to `packtpub.com/unlock`). Search for this book by name, confirm the edition, and then follow the steps on the page.

UNLOCK NOW

Note: Keep your invoice handy. Purchases made directly from Packt don't require an invoice.

Part 2

Manage a Security Operations Environment

In this part of the book, you will configure the Microsoft Sentinel foundation that supports security operations. You will learn how roles, data retention, workbooks, platform optimization, data connectors, collection rules, Windows Security events, Syslog, Common Event Format, Azure activity logs, and threat intelligence ingestion help analysts collect, organize, and use security data during investigations.

This part of the book includes the following chapters:

- *Chapter 3, Configure the Microsoft Sentinel SIEM and platform*
- *Chapter 4, Ingest Data into Microsoft Sentinel*

3

Configure the Microsoft Sentinel SIEM and Platform

Microsoft Sentinel operates as a **SIEM** and **SOAR** platform, but without a clear foundation for roles, data management, visualization, and optimization, it can become inefficient or costly to operate.

This chapter focuses on configuring Sentinel to establish that foundation by introducing the core elements that define how it operates in a SOC environment.

By the end of this chapter, you will understand how configuration decisions affect how much data can be queried, how much it costs to retain, how efficiently analysts can investigate, and how to build a structured, scalable Sentinel environment.

The chapter addresses the following key exam objectives of SC-200:

- Specifying Microsoft Sentinel roles
- Managing data retention for XDR and Microsoft Sentinel tables, including analytics, data lake, and XDR tiers
- Creating and configuring Microsoft Sentinel workbooks
- Optimizing the Microsoft Sentinel platform, including SOC optimization recommendations

Specifying Microsoft Sentinel roles

Security operations break down quickly when access is not intentionally structured. In Microsoft Sentinel, every action, including viewing data, responding to an alert, or changing configuration, is controlled through assigned permissions, so the way access is designed directly shapes how the platform is used day to day.

Roles define what each person can access and change across data, incidents, and configuration, aligning access with responsibility. Without that separation, changes are harder to control, accountability becomes unclear, and enforcing least privilege becomes difficult. Analysts working on incidents read data, investigate alerts, and take response actions as they move through a case. They can close incidents, add context, or isolate a device, but they do not edit analytics rules or disable data ingestion. Updating analytics rules, onboarding data sources, and adjusting detection behavior require broader access and sit outside that investigation flow.

When that separation breaks down, it shows up during live work, particularly in fast-moving environments where broad permissions are sometimes granted to avoid delays and later introduce risk. When roles reflect real responsibilities, investigations move faster, changes stay controlled, and the environment remains auditable even under pressure.

Understanding the Microsoft Sentinel RBAC model

When access needs to be controlled across the SOC, Microsoft Sentinel relies on **role-based access control** (**RBAC**) to define and enforce permissions. **Microsoft Sentinel** does not implement a separate permission model; instead, it uses **Azure RBAC**. Permissions are assigned at the **Log Analytics workspace level**, which acts as the access boundary for Microsoft Sentinel and governs access across all capabilities running on that workspace, rather than to individual Sentinel features.

Permissions are grouped into **roles** and assigned to **identities** such as users, groups, or service principals. Each role represents a predefined set of **allowed actions** that determines what a user can see and do. For example, assigning the Microsoft Sentinel **Responder role** allows you to view incidents, investigate alerts, and take response actions such as updating incident status or isolating a device, but it does not allow them to create or modify analytics rules or change data ingestion settings.

At this level, roles such as **Reader**, **Responder**, or **Contributor** are assigned, and the permissions they grant, such as viewing data, investigating alerts, or making configuration changes, apply across the entire workspace. *Figure 3.1* shows how identities are assigned roles at the Log Analytics workspace level, which defines the access boundary for Microsoft Sentinel.

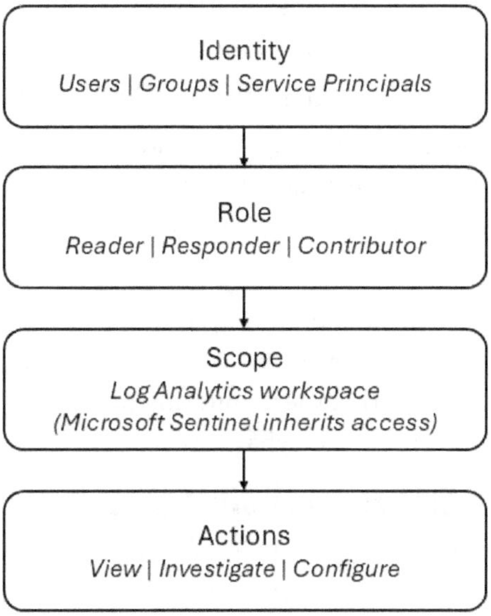

Figure 3.1: Microsoft Sentinel RBAC model and role assignment flow

Assigning roles without fully understanding what they include can easily grant more access than intended, particularly when configuration or response permissions are involved. This is a common source of misconfiguration in many environments.

Using built-in Microsoft Sentinel roles

With responsibilities being split across SOC, Microsoft Sentinel provides **built-in roles** that group permissions into practical access levels aligned to common security operations tasks. For example, a **Reader** role can be used for users who only need to view data and monitor activity, a **Responder** role supports incident investigation and response, and a **Contributor** role is used where configuration changes, such as creating analytics rules or onboarding data sources, are required.

Instead of assigning individual permissions, these roles define what a user can do across the workspace, making access easier to manage and more consistent. They are designed to reflect how work is typically divided within a SOC.

These roles align with different levels of access across the workspace:

- **Visibility**: A **reader** role allows users to view data, alerts, and incidents without making changes

- **Response**: A **responder** role allows analysts to take action on incidents, such as updating status or initiating response actions
- **Configuration**: A **contributor** role provides broader access to configure and manage the Sentinel environment, including settings and data connections

Although RBAC allows **custom roles**, creating them adds complexity. Custom roles should only be used when there is a clear requirement that cannot be met by the predefined roles. These role distinctions only become meaningful when they are applied to real operational responsibilities within the SOC.

For example, someone responsible for monitoring activity may only need to view alerts and data, while someone handling incidents needs to investigate and take response actions. If both are given the same level of access, either the monitoring role gains permissions it does not need, or the investigation role is limited in what it can do.

Aligning roles to SOC responsibilities

Defining roles is only effective when they reflect how SOC actually operates. Permissions on their own do not create structure; they need to be mapped to real responsibilities. Without that alignment, access either becomes too restrictive, slowing down investigations, or too broad, increasing the risk of unintended changes.

Consider an analyst working on an alert involving suspicious sign-in activity. If their role only allows visibility, they can review the alert but cannot investigate related activity or take response actions, delaying the investigation. If the same analyst is given broader permissions, they may be able to modify analytics rules or data collection while handling the incident, affecting how alerts are generated or what data is available during the investigation.

In most environments, responsibilities are split across different functions. Some analysts focus on monitoring and triage, others handle incident response, and a smaller group manages and maintains the platform. Each function requires a different level of access, and role assignment needs to follow that separation.

For instance, monitoring-focused roles typically require visibility into alerts, incidents, and underlying data without the ability to modify configuration. In this case, analysts can assess activity and escalate when needed without introducing unnecessary risk. Similarly, response-focused roles need the ability to take action, such as updating incidents or initiating response actions, but still do not require full administrative control. Platform owners and engineers are responsible for configuring data sources, managing settings, and maintaining the Sentinel environment. These tasks require broader permissions, but those permissions should remain limited to the individuals responsible for maintaining the platform rather than extended across the wider team.

Problems tend to appear when these boundaries are not clearly defined. Granting broad permissions to all analysts may seem convenient, but it increases the likelihood of accidental changes and makes accountability harder to track. Overly restrictive access, however, creates friction by slowing response when analysts must rely on others to perform actions they cannot take themselves.

Extending role assignment across tenants

Security operations are rarely confined to a single tenant. In many environments, a centralized SOC is responsible for monitoring and responding across multiple environments, either within the same organization or across different customers. In these scenarios, access needs to extend beyond a single directory boundary while remaining controlled.

Azure Lighthouse enables this by allowing **delegated access** from one tenant into another. Instead of creating separate accounts in each tenant, access is granted through **delegation**, allowing users in a managing tenant to work with resources in a target managed environment. From a Microsoft Sentinel perspective, this does not introduce a new permission model; it extends the existing **RBAC model** across tenant boundaries.

For example, a security team in a central tenant can be given access to a Sentinel workspace in another tenant. An analyst signs in using their organization's tenant identity, is assigned a role such as **Reader** or **Responder** on the target workspace and can then investigate incidents and take response actions without needing a separate account in that tenant.

Roles are assigned to identities, scoped to the appropriate resource, and enforced consistently across the workspace. Consistent role assignment across tenants helps keep multi-tenant operations manageable, although differences in onboarding and configuration can still introduce variation between environments.

A centralized SOC can operate across multiple Sentinel workspaces using a single, repeatable access model rather than maintaining separate configurations for each environment. At the same time, all role assignments remain visible and auditable through Azure.

Granting overly broad permissions in a delegated scenario can expose multiple environments at once, not just a single workspace, increasing the impact of mistakes. Roles and scope must be applied carefully so delegated access remains limited to SOC requirements. In a multi-tenant setup, the same RBAC principles apply—the boundary is simply wider. When applied correctly, this enables analysts to access multiple environments using the same roles while maintaining controlled access boundaries.

Managing data retention for XDR and Microsoft Sentinel tables, including analytics, data lake, and XDR tiers

Security data only helps if it is still available when an investigation starts. In Microsoft Sentinel, how long data is retained and where it is stored directly determine how far back analysts can look and how much of the incident timeline they can actually reconstruct.

As data is collected and stored over time, Microsoft Sentinel manages it across storage tiers and retention models, each designed for a specific purpose. Some data stays in the analytics tier for active investigation, while older data is moved into lower-cost tiers to support historical analysis, compliance, or retrospective investigations. These choices influence how quickly it can be queried, accessed, and how much it costs to retain.

The complexity increases when multiple data sources are involved. Microsoft Sentinel ingests data from across environments, including Microsoft services such as Microsoft Defender XDR, and each of these sources can follow different retention behaviors. As a result, analysts often work across data that does not exist within the same time window, which can affect how incidents are correlated and understood. A common scenario is an analyst investigating a suspicious sign-in, reviewing recent activity in Microsoft Sentinel, but missing earlier related actions because they fall outside the retention window for one data source while still existing in another. This can result in only part of the activity being visible, making it harder to reconstruct the full sequence of events.

Keeping all data immediately accessible makes investigations faster but increases cost. Moving data into longer-term storage reduces cost at the expense of slower access. For example, recent high-value data such as sign-in logs or endpoint alerts may be kept in the analytics tier for fast investigation over a shorter period, while older data is moved to a lower-cost storage tier for longer retention. You can investigate current activity quickly using readily accessible data and still retrieve older records when needed, without keeping all data in the highest-cost tier.

Retention ultimately defines how much of the incident timeline remains visible during investigation. If data is not retained long enough, critical context may no longer be available when an investigation begins. If it is retained without structure, the environment becomes harder to manage and more expensive to operate. Getting this balance right ensures the SOC can investigate effectively without adding unnecessary cost or complexity.

Configuring log analytics workspace retention

In Microsoft Sentinel, retention is configured through the underlying Log Analytics workspace. Rather than setting retention inside individual features, administrators define how long data is kept at the workspace level, and that setting applies across everything stored within it. The workspace acts as the common data layer for controlling how long security data remains available.

This retention model follows a progression. Data is ingested into the Log Analytics workspace, organized into tiers, and governed by a retention window before moving beyond the active period. This progression is illustrated in the following diagram.

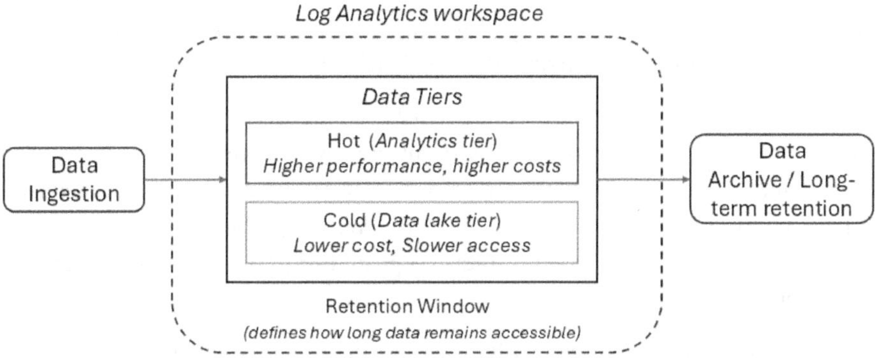

Figure 3.2: Data retention and storage tier model in Microsoft Sentinel

Data is ingested into the workspace and made available in the **analytics tier**, where it can be queried for investigation. As data ages, it can move into lower-cost storage tiers, where access is slower but retention can be extended. Once it moves beyond the active retention window, it is no longer available for direct querying, defining how far back investigations can go.

This configuration controls how much data is retained but requires deliberate decisions about retention length and cost. Setting retention too short reduces the investigation window and can remove important context before it is needed. Setting it too long increases storage and query costs, especially in environments with high ingestion volumes.

If retention is set to **30 days**, an analyst investigating activity that began earlier may no longer have access to the initial events needed to understand how it started. Increasing retention to **90 days** keeps that earlier context available, but also increases storage and query costs, particularly in environments generating large volumes of log data.

In day-to-day SOC work, this setting defines the default investigation window, including how far back analysts can look and how much historical context is available. Getting this balance right ensures investigations are effective while keeping cost and data growth controlled.

Understanding data ingestion and retention relationships

In Microsoft Sentinel, **retention** is configured independently, but **ingestion** volume and data type determine how much data is stored within that retention window over time. The relationship becomes more pronounced in environments with high ingestion volumes. Large volumes of incoming data can quickly increase storage requirements and drive up costs. At the same time, reducing ingestion to control cost can limit visibility, particularly if important data sources are excluded or filtered too aggressively.

Ingestion and **retention** must be managed together, as many environments ingest large volumes of data first and only later optimize, which can lead to unexpected cost increases before retention and table plans are adjusted. Increasing ingestion without adjusting retention quickly grows stored data, while reducing retention without considering ingestion patterns removes context that analysts rely on during investigations.

For example, if a large volume of endpoint telemetry is onboarded without adjusting retention, storage can grow quickly and increase costs without improving investigation outcomes. Reducing retention to control that growth may then remove earlier activity that analysts rely on when tracing how an incident developed. Adjusting both together (retaining high-value data for longer while limiting lower-value data) keeps investigations effective without unnecessary cost.

The type of data being collected directly affects retention decisions. Not all logs provide the same value. Some are critical for investigation and need to remain available for longer periods, while others are primarily useful for short-term monitoring. Differentiating data types allows ingestion and retention to be configured based on investigation value.

For example, sign-in logs, endpoint alerts, and audit activity are needed to trace how an incident began and progressed, so they are typically retained for longer. In contrast, high-volume telemetry, such as performance metrics or routine network traffic, is typically used for short-term monitoring and can be retained for a shorter period.

Managing ingestion and retention together maintains visibility while controlling cost and complexity.

Using Microsoft Sentinel table plans (Analytics, Basic, Auxiliary)

Not all data in Microsoft Sentinel is treated the same way. Different types of data have different operational values, and the platform reflects this by allowing tables to use different plans. These **plans** determine how data is stored, how it can be used, and how much it costs to retain. Choosing the right plan ensures that important data remains accessible without driving unnecessary cost.

For data that needs to be actively investigated, the **Analytics plan** provides full capability. Data in this plan can be **queried interactively**, used in **analytics rules**, and included in investigations. This makes it suitable for high-value data sources that are actively used by the

SOC, where speed and flexibility are more important than cost efficiency. For example, sign-in logs, endpoint alerts, and audit activity are typically kept in **Analytics tables** so they can be queried interactively, used in detection rules, and investigated without delay.

The **Basic** and **Auxiliary plans** are designed for more cost-sensitive scenarios, although they serve slightly different use cases within the platform. **Basic tables** are more commonly used for lower-cost ingestion scenarios. For example, high-volume data such as network flow logs or performance metrics can be placed in **Basic tables**, where they are retained at lower cost and accessed less frequently. **Auxiliary tables** are system-generated, non-security tables used for enrichment, lookups, and metadata, and are not intended for **analytics rules** or **standard investigation queries**.

Only **Analytics tables** support **analytics rules** and detection scenarios, whereas **Basic tables** store data at lower cost but cannot be queried by analytics rules, so they cannot trigger detections. This means data required for detections or active investigations remains in **Analytics tables**, while high-volume data that is not used in detections is better suited to **Basic tables**.

This guides how different types of data should be handled. For instance, high-value security data should remain in the **Analytics plan**. Lower-value or high-volume data that is primarily retained for reference or compliance purposes can be placed in lower-cost plans to reduce overall cost impact.

Table plans align data value with how it is stored and accessed. Treating all data the same increases cost without improving visibility. Selecting the appropriate plan for each data type allows the SOC to maintain effective operations while controlling storage and query cost. Table plans define how data can be used, while data tiers define where data is stored over time.

Working with data tiers (analytics tier and data lake tier)

As data ages, it moves into tiers optimized for different use cases within Microsoft Sentinel.

Data tiers separate actively used data from data retained for longer-term purposes, shaping how data moves through the platform over time.

The **analytics tier** is designed for information that is frequently queried and used in investigations. It provides fast access and full query capability, making it the primary tier for day-to-day operations.

The **data Lake tier** (*long-term or archive storage*) is intended for longer-term storage. Data in this tier is kept at a lower cost but is not optimized for the same level of interactive use. It is used to retain historical data for compliance, audit, or retrospective investigations where immediate access is less critical.

Keeping everything in the **analytics tier** provides maximum flexibility, but it can quickly increase costs. Moving older or less frequently used data into the **data lake** tier reduces storage cost while still preserving it for future use.

Data in the **data lake tier** is not designed to be queried interactively using **standard KQL queries** and instead requires asynchronous search jobs or query acceleration, with results returned asynchronously, meaning it cannot be used in the same way as analytics tier data during real-time investigation. For example, an analyst investigating a recent alert can query data in the analytics tier and get immediate results. If the investigation needs to go further back, the same analyst retrieves older data from the data lake tier, where retrieval takes longer and results are returned asynchronously.

When investigations span longer timeframes, analysts need to be aware of where the data resides, as this affects how quickly results can be obtained. Data tiers define which data remains immediately accessible and which can move to lower-cost storage over time. Using both tiers appropriately allows organizations to maintain a strong investigative capability while managing long-term storage efficiently.

Understanding Microsoft Defender XDR data retention

In investigations, activity often spans multiple platforms, which means Microsoft Sentinel operates alongside Microsoft Defender XDR rather than in isolation.

Defender XDR generates and stores its own telemetry, with retention defined within the service itself. By default, Defender XDR retains data for **30 days**, and this can be extended using the **Defender XDR Storage Add-on**. Importantly, ingesting Defender data into Microsoft Sentinel does not extend Defender's native retention period, so retention must be managed separately across both platforms during investigation. In addition, not all Defender data is ingested into Sentinel by default; some tables, such as **DeviceEvents**, must be explicitly configured before they become available for analysis.

When this data is ingested into Microsoft Sentinel, it follows the retention configured in the Log Analytics workspace. Defender XDR continues to enforce its own separate retention within its platform. This affects investigations. Some activity may be visible in Microsoft Sentinel based on workspace retention, while related activity may only exist in Defender XDR if it falls outside that window. If this is not understood, investigations can appear incomplete, even though the activity still exists in another location.

For example, an analyst investigating suspicious sign-in activity may see recent events in Microsoft Sentinel within the configured workspace retention period, but earlier related activity may only be available in Defender XDR. If the analyst only queries Sentinel, the timeline appears incomplete, even though the full activity still exists in Defender XDR.

There is also a difference in how information is accessed. Microsoft Sentinel provides centralized querying and analysis through the workspace, while Defender XDR offers its own investigation and hunting experiences. Although these platforms are integrated, they do not share a single retention model, which means analysts need to be aware of where they are working from.

Sentinel defines visibility based on workspace configuration and data tiers, while Defender XDR maintains its own retention for the telemetry it generates. Both contribute to the overall investigative view.

Investigating across Sentinel and Defender XDR requires knowing where data originates and how long it is retained in each platform. This enables analysts to identify where data resides and retrieve it during investigations.

If retention is not configured appropriately, investigations are constrained by missing historical data. Analysts may be unable to correlate activity across time, resulting in incomplete investigations. Retention settings ultimately define the practical limits of incident analysis, shaping how far investigations can go and how much context remains available.

Creating and configuring Microsoft Sentinel workbooks

Security data on its own is difficult to interpret. In Microsoft Sentinel, large volumes of logs and alerts are collected continuously, and without structure, it becomes hard to understand what is actually happening across the environment.

To make sense of large volumes of data, **workbooks** transform raw log data into query-driven visualizations that analysts use to identify patterns and investigate activity. They present security data through dashboards, charts, and interactive views, reducing reliance on raw queries and outputs. This positions workbooks as a core method that analysts use to interpret data during investigations.

Figure 3.3 focuses on how collected data is transformed into visual insight through queries and visualizations:

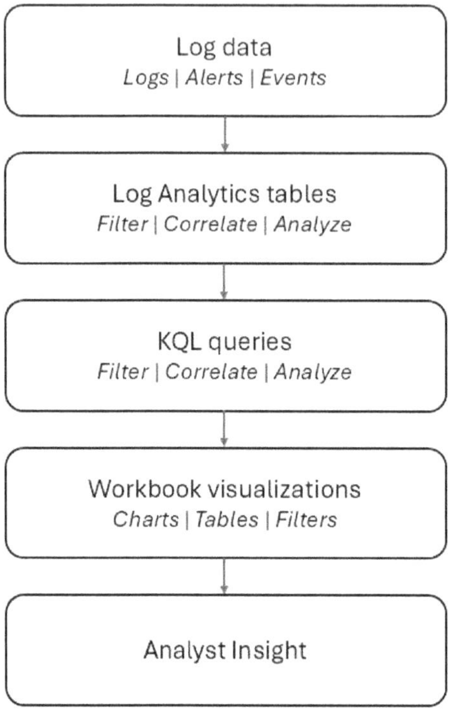

Figure 3.3: Workbook data flow from ingestion to visualization

The flow starts with log data such as alerts, events, and telemetry being ingested into the workspace. This data is stored in Log Analytics tables, where it can be filtered, correlated, and analyzed. Analysts then use KQL queries to explore the data in more detail, identify patterns, and refine their investigation. The results of these queries can be visualized in workbooks using charts, tables, and filters, helping to present the data in a way that supports analysis. This progression transforms raw telemetry into structured query results used during investigation and response.

Understanding the purpose of workbooks

In day-to-day operations, workbooks make security data usable by presenting it in a structured and accessible way. While queries and logs provide details, they are not always the fastest way to understand what is happening across the environment.

For example, an analyst investigating unusual sign-in activity can use a workbook to view sign-in patterns across users and locations over time, rather than reviewing individual log entries. The workbook highlights spikes, repeated failures, or activity from unfamiliar locations, helping the analyst quickly identify what stands out. From there, the same view can be used to focus the investigation on specific users or timeframes and to present the findings clearly when escalating or reporting on the incident.

Workbooks act as a visualization layer on top of Microsoft Sentinel data. With the help of charts, tables, and interactive elements, analysts can move from raw input to a clearer view of activity without having to rebuild queries each time. One of their key purposes is to allow analysts to see patterns across users, devices, and time that are not visible in individual logs. This exposes trends that are not visible when reviewing individual alerts or logs.

Workbooks support investigation by providing a consistent starting point, allowing analysts to begin with a high-level view and drill into specific areas as needed, while also making it easier to present findings to other teams who do not work directly in Microsoft Sentinel. This reduces the effort required to interpret security data during investigation.

If ingestion is incomplete or retention is misconfigured, visualizations will reflect those gaps. Workbooks do not create insight on their own; they expose what the platform already contains.

Connecting workbooks to data sources

Workbooks do not store data and rely entirely on what is available in Microsoft Sentinel. Every visualization, chart, or table is driven by queries that pull information from underlying data sources. As a result, the quality of a workbook is directly tied to the data it is built on.

Workbooks connect data through the Log Analytics workspace that underpins Microsoft Sentinel. Queries retrieve information from the workspace, and the results are presented visually. This makes the workspace the central point of integration between raw telemetry and the insights shown in a workbook.

Because workbooks combine data from multiple sources, gaps caused by missing ingestion or retention limits directly affect the results they display. Poorly structured queries can lead to incomplete or misleading views, while well-designed queries provide accurate insight.

Consider a case where a workbook is designed to show failed sign-in activity. It may use a query that filters only specific event types or time ranges. If that query is too narrow, it may exclude related activity and give the impression that the issue is limited. Expanding the query to include additional event types or a broader timeframe can reveal a larger pattern, providing a more accurate view of what is happening.

Connecting workbooks to data sources requires ensuring the right data is available and queried correctly, as gaps or poor query design result in incomplete or misleading views.

Using built-in workbook templates

Microsoft Sentinel provides built-in **workbook templates** that act as a starting point for visualization and analysis. Instead of building everything from scratch, these templates include predefined layouts, queries, and visual components aligned to common security scenarios.

Many templates focus on specific areas such as security monitoring, user activity, or threat visibility, providing structured views that highlight key information such as sign-in trends, alert volumes by severity, and activity across users and devices over time. This standardizes how analysts interpret and review data across investigations.

However, templates are not intended to be used without adjustment. The data available, how it is structured, and the priorities of the SOC all influence how useful a template is in its original form. In most cases, they are adapted to better reflect the environment in which they are used. For example, a workbook template designed for sign-in monitoring may be adjusted to focus on specific users, locations, or applications relevant to the environment, allowing analysts to highlight the activity that matters most rather than using a generic view. Using consistent workbook templates ensures analysts interpret data in the same structure, making it easier to analyze results and collaborate during investigations.

Workbooks are made up of several core components that determine how data is filtered and presented. Parameters allow analysts to define inputs such as time ranges, users, or specific resources. This enables the same workbook to be reused across different investigations without modifying the underlying structure. Custom queries, typically written in KQL, control how data is retrieved and shaped before it is displayed, allowing templates to be adapted to reflect specific detection or investigation requirements. Visual types define how query results are presented, including tables, charts, timelines, and maps. Choosing the right visual type helps analysts quickly identify patterns, trends, or anomalies without needing to interpret raw query output.

Access to workbooks is controlled through Azure RBAC at the Log Analytics workspace level, meaning permissions are inherited from the workspace, which defines the access boundary for all workbook data and actions. This restricts workbook access based on assigned roles, controlling who can view or modify data.

It is also important to distinguish between workbooks and dashboards. Workbooks are interactive and query-driven, allowing analysts to explore data dynamically, apply filters, and drill into results. Dashboards are typically used for high-level monitoring views, while workbooks support interactive, query-driven investigation.

Built-in templates introduce visualization into Microsoft Sentinel with predefined queries and layouts. They reduce setup effort, standardize analysis across the SOC, and provide a base that can be extended for specific requirements.

Deploying workbooks through Content Hub

In many cases, workbooks are deployed alongside solutions rather than being created individually. They are delivered as part of broader solutions through the **Content Hub**. This brings in prebuilt content, including workbooks, aligned to specific data sources and security scenarios.

Content Hub acts as a central location for managing solutions within Microsoft Sentinel. These solutions often include a combination of components such as analytics rules, connectors, and workbooks designed to work together. When a solution is deployed, any associated workbooks are installed alongside it and made available for use. For example, deploying a Microsoft Sentinel solution for a specific data source, such as **Microsoft Entra** ID, can install prebuilt workbooks that provide immediate visibility into sign-in activity, user behavior, and potential risks, without requiring analysts to create those views manually.

This groups related content into a single deployment. Instead of manually building or importing individual workbooks, analysts can install a solution and immediately access visualizations aligned to a particular use case, especially when onboarding data sources that include supporting content.

For example, when onboarding a new data source such as Microsoft Defender for Endpoint, the associated solution can include workbooks that immediately show device activity, alerts, and investigation trends, allowing analysts to start using the data without first building custom visualizations.

Workbooks deployed through Content Hub follow consistent structures aligned to the solution they belong to. This ties visualizations directly to collected data, so workbooks reflect actual ingestion and follow a consistent structure. These workbooks remain part of the Sentinel environment and can be modified after deployment. While they provide a ready-to-use starting point, they often need to be adjusted to reflect specific organizational requirements, including data availability, naming conventions, or operational priorities.

Optimizing the Microsoft Sentinel platform, including SOC optimization recommendations

Over time, as the environment changes, Microsoft Sentinel does not remain optimal without ongoing review. As data sources are onboarded and detection capabilities expand, the platform needs continuous review to prevent inefficiencies such as excessive ingestion, noisy alerts, or unused capabilities.

As the environment evolves, data collection, detection configuration, and how analysts work with alerts start to drift, which is where optimization focuses. For example, recommendations can identify unused or low-value analytics rules or gaps in data collection where key sources have not been onboarded.

Understanding SOC optimization recommendations

SOC optimization recommendations in Microsoft Sentinel provide guidance on how the platform is currently being used and where improvements can be made. Analysts use these recommendations to identify configuration gaps across the environment.

They are platform-generated by evaluating ingestion patterns, analytics rule activity, and workspace configuration. They are not triggered by alerts or manually defined rules. They can highlight gaps such as missing data sources, underused capabilities, or configurations that do not align with expected practices. For example, recommendations may highlight that key data sources such as identity or endpoint telemetry have not been onboarded, preventing analysts from querying specific activity such as sign-ins or endpoint events. They may also identify analytics rules that generate large volumes of alerts but are rarely acted on, indicating a need for tuning. In other cases, they can point to tables that are not being queried or used in detections, suggesting that collected data is not contributing to investigations.

These recommendations highlight configuration or coverage gaps and require analyst interpretation rather than direct execution. Not every recommendation will be relevant and applying them without context can lead to unnecessary or ineffective changes.

Prioritization is also important. Multiple recommendations are often presented, but they do not all have the same impact. Some directly affect detection coverage or investigation capability, while others relate to efficiency or cost. Understanding this difference allows the SOC to prioritize changes that affect detection coverage over those that only reduce alert volume. For example, a recommendation highlighting a missing data source, such as endpoint telemetry, should be prioritized because it limits detection coverage. In contrast, tuning a noisy analytics rule improves efficiency by reducing alert volume without changing what can be detected. Both are useful, but they address different problems and should be handled accordingly.

SOC optimization recommendations identify gaps such as missing data sources, underused capabilities, and analytics rules that generate high volumes of low-value alerts. As the environment evolves, these recommendations update continuously and require regular review to prioritize actions that improve detection coverage and reduce alert noise.

Summary

This chapter focused on how you configure Microsoft Sentinel to establish a working foundation for the SOC. You covered how roles control access to data, response, and configuration, and how aligning those roles to real responsibilities keeps operations structured and controlled. You learned how data retention defines how far back you can investigate and how workspace settings, ingestion, table plans, and data tiers affect both visibility and cost.

You also covered how Microsoft Defender XDR retention sits alongside Sentinel and how that affects where you look during investigations. You also covered how workbooks are used to turn collected data into usable insight, including how they connect to underlying data, how templates and Content Hub are used, and how data quality directly affects what they show. Finally, you covered how the platform is optimized over time using SOC optimization recommendations. These identify gaps, reduce noise, and keep the environment aligned to SOC operations.

In the next chapter, you move into data ingestion, where Microsoft Sentinel begins receiving the security events, logs, and threat intelligence needed to support detection and investigation.

Exam Readiness Drill – Chapter Review Questions

Apart from mastering key concepts, strong test-taking skills under time pressure are essential for acing your certification exam. That's why developing these abilities early in your learning journey is critical.

Exam readiness drills, using the free online practice resources provided with this book, help you progressively improve your time management and test-taking skills while reinforcing the key concepts you've learned.

HOW TO GET STARTED

- Open the link or scan the QR code at the bottom of this page
- If you have unlocked the practice resources already, log in to your registered account. If you haven't, follow the instructions in *Free Benefits with Your Book* section in this book's *Preface* and come back to this page.
- Once you log in, click the START button to start this chapter's quiz
- We recommend attempting a quiz multiple times till you're able to answer most of the questions correctly and well within the time limit.
- You can use the following practice template to help you plan your attempts:

Working On Accuracy		
Attempt	**Target**	**Time Limit**
Attempt 1	40% or more	Till the timer runs out
Attempt 2	60% or more	Till the timer runs out
Attempt 3	75% or more	Till the timer runs out
Working On Timing		
Attempt 4	75% or more	1 minute before time limit
Attempt 5	75% or more	2 minutes before time limit
Attempt 6	75% or more	3 minutes before time limit

The above drill is just an example. Design your drills based on your own goals and make the most out of the online quizzes accompanying this book.

Link to this Chapter's Quiz

You need to unlock the online practice resources to access the link below. Check the *Free Benefits with Your Book* section in the *Preface* for detailed instructions on how to do this. You only need to unlock the resources once.

Open Quiz `https://packt.link/sc200js-ch3` or scan the QR code:

4

Ingest Data into Microsoft Sentinel

Data onboarding into Microsoft Sentinel determines whether detection, investigation, and response can occur. Security events that are not ingested into the Log Analytics workspace are not available for query or detection. This makes it a core focus of this chapter, which covers selecting data connectors, configuring ingestion, and ensuring data reaches the workspace. By the end of this chapter, you will be able to select appropriate data connectors, configure data collection across different environments, and ensure that relevant security data is ingested into Microsoft Sentinel for analysis.

This chapter addresses the following exam objectives of SC-200:

- Selecting data connectors based on data source requirements, including Windows logs and security events
- Configuring collection of Windows Security events by using Windows Security Events via AMA, including data collection rules
- Planning and configuring collection of Windows Security events by using Windows Event Forwarding (WEF)
- Planning and configuring Syslog via AMA and Common Event Format (CEF) via AMA connectors
- Configuring collection of Azure activities by using Azure Policy and resource diagnostic settings
- Ingesting threat indicators into Microsoft Sentinel
- Creating custom log tables in the workspace to store ingested data

These skills align with the **Configure the Microsoft Sentinel environment and connect data sources** skill area of the SC-200 exam.

Selecting data connectors based on data source requirements, including Windows logs and security events

Data connectors control how data is brought into Microsoft Sentinel, and every query, incident, or investigation depends on what has been ingested. Each connector is tied to a specific type of data source, including Microsoft services, Windows systems, Linux and network devices, Azure resources, threat intelligence platforms, and third-party systems.

The selected connector defines whether data is collected using the correct ingestion method for that source, such as Windows event collection, Syslog, or CEF for network and device logs. Service-based integration is used for cloud activity. Some connectors integrate directly with services, while others rely on agents or intermediary systems to collect and forward data, which means configuration alone does not guarantee data flow if those requirements are not met.

Once ingested, all data is written to a Log Analytics workspace, where it becomes available for analysis. Connector configuration determines what data is collected. Unconnected sources do not appear in the workspace. Data sources generate different types of telemetry, and Microsoft Sentinel organizes connectors around these groupings so that each source follows a predictable ingestion path.

Figure 2.1 shows how each data source category follows a different ingestion path (*and pipeline*) into the workspace.

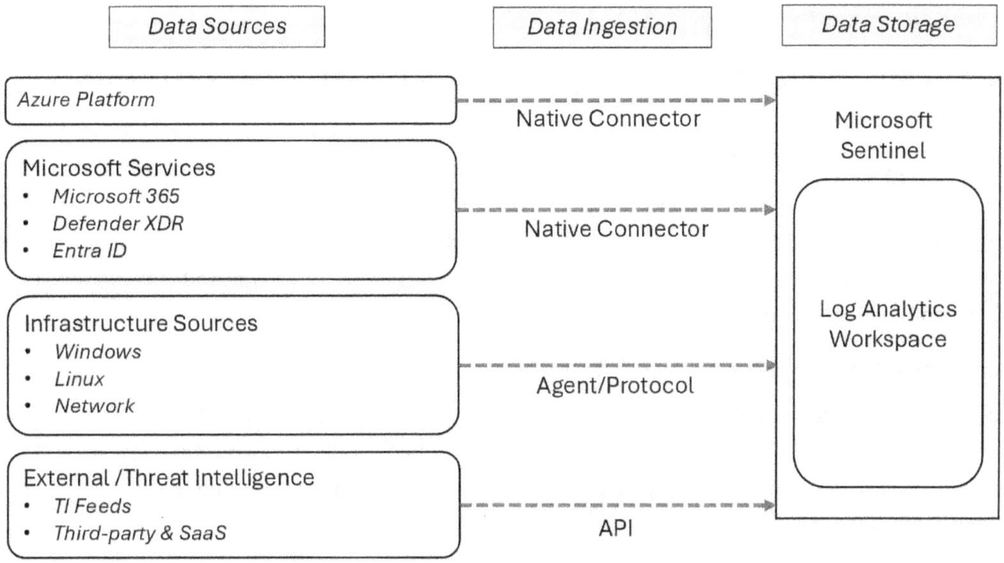

Figure 4.1 – Data ingestion paths into Microsoft Sentinel

Each category uses a different ingestion model, which determines how connectors are selected and configured. Selecting the correct data connector depends on two key factors: where the data originates and what type of data is required.

Microsoft services integrate directly at the platform service level, allowing access to activity generated natively within the platform without requiring collection from individual systems. Azure platform resources produce logs generated at both the subscription and resource level that must be explicitly configured using diagnostic settings or Azure Policy before being sent to the workspace, although they still use a native platform connector.

In contrast, Windows systems generate security events at the operating system level, collected via agent level as event log data including authentication and system activity, and other security-relevant operations. Linux systems and network devices follow a different model, where logs are typically forwarded at the protocol level using Syslog, including **Common Event Format (CEF)**, to a Linux-based collector running the AMA.

Threat intelligence platforms represent a different type of data, where the focus is not on activity but on indicators such as IP addresses, domains, URLs, and file hashes. These indicators enrich and correlate collected data rather than generating it.

For example, a security team may want to monitor authentication activity on Windows servers. Selecting the Windows Security Events connector with AMA ensures that relevant security events, such as logons and account changes, are collected. If the connector is configured but the required event set is not selected through the data collection rule, the expected events are not ingested, creating a visibility gap.

Understanding connector prerequisites and configuration requirements

Data ingestion fails when connector-specific requirements are not in place, and these requirements vary depending on how the data is collected. A consistent pattern in Microsoft Sentinel is that a connector appears enabled but produces no data. In most cases, this is not a connector failure, but a prerequisite issue. When connector collection methods are not clear, ingestion failures are often misidentified.

Service-to-service connector prerequisites

Some connectors rely on direct service-to-service integration. For example, Microsoft 365 and Microsoft Defender connectors use permissions to access data directly from the service. If those permissions are not correctly configured, the connector may appear enabled, but it does not retrieve any data.

Each connector type depends on a different prerequisite model, so these requirements must be understood in relation to how the connector collects data. In these service-to-service scenarios, prerequisites fall into clearly defined categories that must all be satisfied for data ingestion to succeed:

- **Required roles** determine whether the connector has sufficient access within the source service. If the assigned role does not grant visibility over the relevant data, the connector can authenticate successfully but still return no results.
- **API permissions** control whether the connector is allowed to retrieve data through the service interface. If permissions are missing or not consented, the connection can appear valid while data retrieval silently fails.
- **Microsoft Defender connector requirements** extend beyond access. The relevant Defender workload must be deployed, licensed, and actively generating telemetry. If Defender for Endpoint, Identity, or Office 365 is not producing data, there is nothing available for Sentinel to ingest. Microsoft Sentinel does not generate this telemetry itself and only ingests data that is already produced by the connected service.
- **Microsoft 365 connector requirements** follow a similar pattern. Unified audit logging must be enabled, and activity must already exist within the tenant. Without audit data being generated, the connector has no data source to retrieve from, even when roles and permissions are correctly configured.

These roles and API permission dependencies are specific to service-to-service connectors and do not apply to connectors that rely on agents, collectors, or diagnostic settings. Each connector model has its own prerequisite chain, and applying the wrong assumption is a common cause of ingestion failures during investigation. Other connector types, such as agent-based, collector-based, and diagnostic settings-based connectors, follow different prerequisite chains.

Azure resource connector prerequisites

Azure resource logs follow a different pattern through diagnostic settings. Data is generated at the resource level but must be explicitly configured to be sent to the Log Analytics workspace. Data remains within the resource and never reaches the workspace when diagnostic settings are not enabled, creating a visibility gap.

Agent-based connector prerequisites

Some connectors rely on agents to collect data from systems. For example, Windows Security Events collected through the Azure Monitor Agent (AMA) require the agent to be installed on each system and connected to the Log Analytics workspace.

Data collection is also governed by Data Collection Rules, which define what events are collected and sent. If the agent is missing, not connected, or the Data Collection Rule is not configured correctly, the system continues to generate events locally, but no data is sent to the workspace.

Collector-based connector prerequisites

In scenarios where logs are forwarded, a collector is used as an intermediary. For example, Syslog and CEF connectors rely on a Linux-based collector to receive logs from network devices and forward them using the Azure Monitor Agent. Logs fail to reach the workspace when the collector is misconfigured or forwarding is incomplete. This breaks the ingestion chain, even though individual components may appear to be functioning.

Data ingestion follows a consistent process (pipeline): data is generated at the source, collected by a connector or agent, forwarded through any required intermediary systems, and written to the Log Analytics workspace. Data ingestion may be subject to latency depending on the source and connector type, but a complete absence of data typically indicates a configuration or prerequisite issue rather than a normal delay.

Understanding data ingestion destination and workspace roles

Microsoft Sentinel does not store data directly and operates on data that resides in the Log Analytics workspace. The connector and its configuration determine what data is sent, and once that data is ingested, it is organized into tables based on its type, allowing different kinds of data to be stored consistently and queried together.

Each data source contributes to specific tables that reflect the structure of the information rather than the origin itself. As a result, the workspace reflects only the data successfully delivered by connectors, determining how analysis is performed.

For example, a security team needs to investigate failed login activity on a set of Windows servers. The Windows Security Events connector is selected, the **Azure Monitor Agent (AMA)** is deployed to the servers, and a data collection rule is configured to collect the required event set. If the connector is selected but the agent is not connected, or the workspace is not correctly configured, the data never becomes available for analysis. As a result, no relevant events are available for querying, and the investigation cannot proceed.

Data ingestion targets a single workspace, and each connector sends data to one workspace at a time, while queries can still span multiple workspaces. Connector selection, prerequisites, and ingestion configuration must align, or expected data is not ingested into the Log Analytics workspace.

In more complex environments, organizations may operate across multiple Log Analytics workspaces or even across multiple tenants. These scenarios are common in larger enterprises or managed service environments where data is segmented for administrative, geographic, or regulatory reasons.

Multi-workspace and multi-tenant considerations

Cross-workspace queries, multi-tenant boundaries, and Azure Lighthouse define how analysis extends across environments without changing ingestion. While data ingestion always targets a specific Log Analytics workspace, security operations often extend beyond a single workspace or tenant. In these scenarios, understanding how analysis is performed across boundaries becomes critical.

Cross-workspace queries allow analysts to search and correlate data across multiple Log Analytics workspaces without moving or duplicating data. This is particularly important in distributed environments where different business units, regions, or environments maintain separate workspaces. Instead of centralizing all data, analysts can query across these workspaces to build a complete view of activity during an investigation.

In multi-tenant scenarios, ingestion remains scoped to the tenant where the connector is configured. Data is not ingested across tenants, and each tenant maintains its own Log Analytics workspace and data boundaries. This means that while analysis can span environments, data collection does not. Azure Lighthouse supports this model by enabling centralized access to Microsoft Sentinel across multiple tenants, which is commonly used by **managed security service providers (MSSPs)**. It allows analysts to access and manage workspaces across tenants from a single context, without requiring separate sign-ins or manual context switching.

These capabilities are introduced in *Chapter 3* and are referenced here to reinforce how analysis can extend across environments without changing how data is ingested. Importantly, these capabilities do not alter the ingestion model. Connectors, agents, and data collection rules continue to send data to their configured workspace, reinforcing the principle that ingestion is always workspace-specific and tenant-scoped, even when analysis spans multiple environments.

Once data sources are onboarded and data is flowing into the workspace, the focus shifts to controlling ingestion volume and cost over time.

Understanding connector types and data mapping

Microsoft Sentinel connectors differ in how they integrate with data sources and how data is delivered into the workspace. These differences determine how connectors are selected and whether the expected data is collected and available for analysis. This section covers how connectors are categorized and how the data they collect is written into tables within the workspace.

Types of Microsoft Sentinel connectors

Microsoft Sentinel connectors fall into defined categories based on how they integrate with data sources and how data is collected and delivered into the workspace. Understanding these patterns helps when selecting connectors in more complex environments; they are explained below:

- **Built-in connectors** provide direct integration with supported Microsoft services and Azure resources, typically requiring minimal configuration beyond enabling access
- **Microsoft 365 connectors** ingest data from services such as Microsoft Entra ID, Exchange, SharePoint, and Teams, using service-to-service integration based on permissions rather than agents
- **Microsoft Defender connectors** integrate security telemetry from Microsoft Defender products, including alerts and advanced threat signals, and are tightly coupled with Microsoft security services
- **Agent-based connectors** are used for operating systems and devices, such as Windows Security Events and Syslog or CEF, where data is collected locally and forwarded using the Azure Monitor Agent
- **API-based connectors** allow external systems to send data programmatically into Microsoft Sentinel and are commonly used for integrating third-party platforms

- **Custom connectors** are used when no predefined connector exists and rely on custom ingestion methods to onboard data into custom tables
- **Azure-native connectors** such as Activity Logs and resource logs rely on platform-level configuration through diagnostic settings to route data into the workspace

The connector type is determined by how the data source integrates with Microsoft Sentinel, whether through direct service integration, agents, collectors, or APIs.

How connectors map to tables in the workspace

Each connector determines not only how data is collected, but also where that data is stored in the Log Analytics workspace. Rather than organizing data by source alone, Microsoft Sentinel writes data into tables based on structure and purpose, which allows different data types to be queried and correlated consistently.

For example, Microsoft Entra ID sign-in activity is written to the **SigninLogs** table, Azure Activity Logs are stored in the **AzureActivity** table, and security alerts from Microsoft Defender are written to the **SecurityAlert** table. Endpoint telemetry may populate tables such as **DeviceEvents**, depending on the connected data source.

Analytics rules, queries, and investigations operate on these tables, so incorrect mapping results in missing detection. Selecting a connector is therefore not just about enabling data collection, but about ensuring that the expected data is available in the correct table for detection and analysis.

If a connector is enabled but its prerequisites are not met, the expected tables may remain empty even though the configuration appears correct. This creates a visibility gap where data is assumed to exist but is not actually available for querying or detection. Connector-to-table mapping determines which data is available for queries and analytics rules, and whether analysts can validate ingestion, troubleshoot missing data, and align detection logic with the data present in the workspace. Analytics rules form the detection layer in Microsoft Sentinel, generating alerts when defined conditions are met.

Managing data ingestion volume and cost considerations

Data ingestion decisions directly determine both the volume of data collected and the cost of storing and analyzing that data. These controls fall into three areas: how data is ingested, how much data is ingested, and how long it is retained, which together define ingestion volume, cost, and whether data remains available for detection.

Basic logs vs. analytics logs

Not all data in Microsoft Sentinel is treated the same once it arrives, and that distinction directly shapes both cost and detection capability. This distinction is applied at the table level, where each table is configured to use either the Analytics or Basic log plan. Analytics Logs form the foundation for detection and alert generation in Microsoft Sentinel. They support analytics rules, alert generation, correlation, and all the detection logic that turns raw data into actionable signals. When a suspicious sign-in is flagged or a rule is triggered based on a sequence of events, it is because that data exists in Analytics Logs.

Basic Logs sit outside of that detection pipeline. They are designed for high-volume data where the likelihood of needing real-time detection is low but where retaining the data for occasional investigation still has value. They can be queried when needed, but they do not participate in analytics rules and cannot generate alerts. This reduces costs but also removes them from the core detection flow.

If a data source is required for detection, correlation, or alerting, it must be ingested as Analytics Logs. If it is only useful for retrospective investigation or compliance visibility, it may be suitable for Basic Logs. Misclassifying this is where problems emerge—placing critical security data into Basic Logs reduces cost but silently removes detection coverage.

Basic Logs cannot be used for detection and are limited to query-based investigation. Log type selection (Basic Logs versus Analytics Logs) is independent of retention configuration, and these controls must not be confused.

Data caps and daily ingestion limits

As ingestion increases, so does cost, and without control, this can become unpredictable. Daily caps provide a hard limit on how much data can be ingested into a workspace within a 24-hour period. Once that limit is reached, ingestion stops, and events generated after that point are dropped and are not recoverable. From a SOC perspective, this creates blind spots that are difficult to detect until after an incident has already been missed.

In a stable environment, daily caps can act as a safeguard against unexpected spikes, such as misconfigured connectors or sudden log surges. However, they are not a true optimization strategy. They are a protective boundary, not a tuning mechanism. Relying on them as primary cost control shifts the problem from cost management to visibility loss, which is rarely an acceptable trade-off in security operations.

Commitment tiers and pricing models

While ingestion volume can fluctuate, many environments settle into predictable patterns over time. Commitment tiers take advantage of this by allowing organizations to commit to a fixed daily ingestion level in exchange for a reduced cost per gigabyte.

This is not technical control within Sentinel itself, but a pricing model decision that influences how ingestion is billed. When the committed level aligns closely with actual usage, it provides consistent, and optimized pricing. When it does not, either over-commitment leads to wasted spending, or under-commitment results in higher costs for excess data.

Commitment tiers reduce cost when ingestion volume is stable. In rapidly changing environments, where new data sources are still being onboarded or where log volume varies significantly, committing too early can lock in inefficiencies rather than reduce them. Commitment tiers do not change how data is ingested, processed, or used for detection; they only affect how ingestion is billed.

Cost optimization techniques in data ingestion

Effective cost optimization is achieved by controlling how data enters and is retained within the system. The most effective optimization occurs before ingestion, where data volume can be reduced before cost is incurred, rather than after data has already been stored.

Data Collection Rules (DCRs) allow filtering at the source, ensuring that only relevant events are sent to the workspace. For example, instead of ingesting all Windows Security Events, a DCR can limit collection to only the event IDs that contribute to detection or investigation. This reduces volume without sacrificing meaningful visibility, provided the filtering is aligned to actual security use cases. Poorly designed filtering, however, can remove critical signals and weaken detection.

Once data is ingested, table-level retention becomes the next control. Not all data needs to be stored for the same duration. High-value security logs may require extended retention for investigation or compliance, while lower-value data can be retained for shorter periods. Adjusting retention at the table level ensures that storage cost reflects the actual value of the data.

Selecting Basic Logs for appropriate data sources is another optimization layer, but it must be applied carefully. Moving high-volume, low-signal data into Basic Logs reduces cost, but as established earlier, it also removes that data from the detection pipeline. The decision is not purely financial—it is a trade-off between cost and capability.

When these techniques are applied together, filtering before ingestion, aligning retention to value, and choosing the appropriate log type, the result is a controlled ingestion model that directly controls ingestion volume, storage duration, and detection capability. Cost is reduced not by limiting visibility, but by ensuring that only meaningful, usable data is retained and processed within the SOC.

Configuring collection of Windows security events by using Windows Security Events via Azure Monitor Agent, including data collection rules

Windows Security events provide visibility into activity occurring on Windows systems. To make this data available in the Log Analytics workspace used by Microsoft Sentinel, collection must be enabled using the AMA and controlled through data collection rules.

This collection process follows a defined flow between the system, agent, and workspace, as shown in *Figure 4.2*.

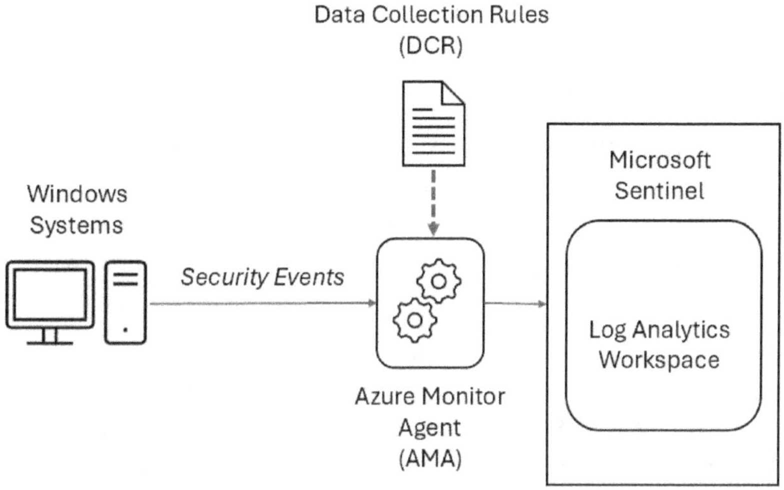

Figure 4.2 – Windows Security event collection using AMA and Data Collection Rules

Events are collected according to the data collection rules applied to each system. Data collection rules determine what is collected by selecting specific event sets rather than ingesting everything, allowing the scope of collection to align with monitoring requirements. Together with the agent, they determine whether data is collected and how much of it is available, since both the AMA and an associated data collection rule are required.

The following sections break down how the agent is deployed, how data collection rules are configured, and how event collection is defined.

Deploying AMA to Windows systems

Deployment of the AMA to Windows systems involves installing the agent on each target system and ensuring it is connected to the correct workspace. This connection enables data to be forwarded from the operating system to the Log Analytics workspace used by Microsoft Sentinel. If that connection is missing or incorrect, the system is effectively isolated, even though the agent may appear to be installed.

The AMA acts as the entry point for Windows Security event collection, determining whether a system contributes data to the Log Analytics workspace used by Microsoft Sentinel. Once the agent is in place, it reads event data from the Security log and prepares it for transmission. It does not determine which events are collected but enables that data to leave the system and reach the workspace.

Even when the agent appears healthy, issues in the connection path or workspace association can prevent data from reaching the intended destination, creating the appearance that no data is being collected. For example, the Azure Monitor Agent is deployed across Windows systems, and a data collection rule is defined, but the rule is not associated with all machines or does not include the required event set. Some systems send data while others do not, resulting in inconsistent visibility during investigation.

Creating and configuring Data Collection Rules

Data Collection Rules (DCRs) determine which Windows Security events are actually collected once the AMA is in place. While the agent establishes the ability to send data, the rule determines what data is included in that process, making it the control point for event selection.

Rather than collecting every available event from the Security log, DCRs are used to limit collection to specific event sets. This allows the scope of data ingestion to be aligned with monitoring requirements, ensuring that the data being collected is relevant while avoiding unnecessary volume. This decision directly affects how much visibility is available during an investigation.

These rules are not applied automatically. A DCR must be associated with the systems from which data is to be collected. Until that association is in place, the agent remains active but does not collect any events because it has no defined instruction. This often creates confusion, as systems appear correctly configured but produce no data.

Event selection is based on predefined event sets, which group Security log entries into categories such as minimal, common, or all events. Choosing between these sets determines how much detail is captured. A minimal set reduces data volume but may omit important signals, while a broader set increases coverage at the cost of higher ingestion. This choice has a direct operational impact. If the selected event set does not include the required events, they will not be captured.

Another common scenario is when the rule is correctly defined but not associated with all relevant systems. For example, a data collection rule may be configured to collect security events from a group of Windows servers but only associated with a subset of those systems. In this case, some systems contribute data while others do not, creating inconsistent visibility across the environment.

Configuring Windows Security event collection

Windows Security event collection determines which entries from the Security log are actually sent to the Log Analytics workspace used by Microsoft Sentinel once the agent and data collection rules are in place. This determines the actual content of the ingested data and, therefore, what activity can be analyzed.

Event collection is configured through predefined event sets that group Security log entries by level of detail, providing a structured way to control collection without selecting individual events. For example, selecting the "Common" event set collects a standard set of security events such as logon activity and account changes, while the "Minimal" set captures a smaller subset focused on essential events.

Selecting an event set directly affects both the volume of data collected and the depth of coverage. A minimal set reduces data volume but may exclude important events, while a broader set increases coverage at the cost of higher ingestion. The selected event set is enforced through the data collection rule, ensuring that all associated systems follow the same collection pattern. This consistency is important because differences in event collection between systems can result in uneven coverage across the environment.

If the scope is too narrow, only a subset of activity is captured, which can limit the ability to detect or investigate certain behaviors.

Planning and configuring collection of Windows Security events by using Windows Event Forwarding (WEF)

Windows Event Forwarding (WEF) collects Windows Security events by forwarding them from source systems to a central collector before ingestion. In contrast, AMA-based collection sends events directly to the Log Analytics workspace used by Microsoft Sentinel.

In this model, systems continue to generate Security log events locally, but only selected events are forwarded, creating a separation between where events are generated and where they are collected. Control is applied at the forwarding layer rather than on each individual system. This separation introduces a forwarding path between source systems, a collector, and the Log Analytics workspace used by Microsoft Sentinel, as shown in *Figure 4.3*.

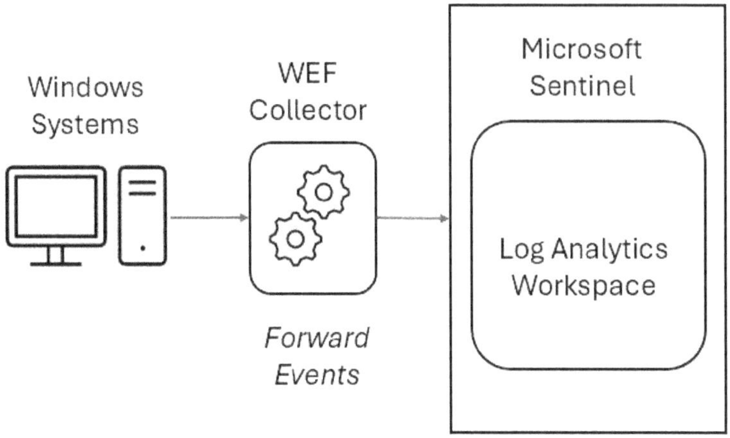

Figure 4.3 – Windows Event Forwarding (WEF) collection architecture

This flow shows how selected events are aggregated at the collector before ingestion. This differs from AMA-based collection, where data is sent directly from each system to the Log Analytics workspace without a collector.

The forwarding process depends on a defined relationship between source systems and the collector, where source systems send selected events to the collector before ingestion. This relationship is configured through subscriptions, which define both the events that are forwarded and the systems that participate. This determines the scope of collected data.

Because data is routed through a collector, the reliability of collection depends on the forwarding configuration rather than direct collection from each system. If forwarding is not configured correctly, events remain on the source systems and are not available for ingestion into Microsoft Sentinel.

The next sections break down how the forwarding architecture works, how subscriptions control data flow, and how forwarding behaves in practice.

Designing Windows Event Forwarding architecture

Designing WEF architecture defines how events move from source systems to a collector. It also determines how that data is organized before ingestion. The architecture is built around two roles: source systems and the collector. Source systems generate Security log events and forward selected entries, while the collector receives those events and stores them in a centralized location. The separation introduces a collection model in which event generation and aggregation occur in different places, which means the reliability of the process depends on multiple stages working together.

Failures can occur at the source, during transmission, or at the collector, resulting in gaps in collected data. Designing this architecture, therefore, requires identifying which systems act as sources and selecting a system to function as the collector. The collector must be able to receive events from multiple systems and maintain a consolidated view of forwarded activity. The configuration then defines how source systems are associated with the collector and how events are routed between them. If the collector cannot consistently receive events, gaps appear in the data that may only become apparent during investigation.

Configuring WEF subscriptions

WEF subscriptions determine how event forwarding actually behaves by specifying which events are sent and which systems participate. They act as the configuration layer that determines what data leaves source systems and reaches the collector, effectively controlling both the scope and coverage of collected data.

Configuration begins with selecting the events to be forwarded, while all other activities remain on the source systems. It also defines which systems are associated with the subscription, meaning only those systems contribute data to the collector. Together, these settings determine both the content of the data and where it comes from.

When subscriptions are not configured correctly, the result is incomplete or inconsistent data. Selecting the wrong events can exclude expected activity, while incorrect or inconsistent system associations can lead to uneven coverage across the environment. Because subscriptions control both what is forwarded and which systems participate, they define how reliably event data is collected before ingestion into Microsoft Sentinel.

Configuring event forwarding to collector systems

Event forwarding determines whether selected events are transferred from source systems to the collector once subscriptions are in place. While subscriptions determine what should be forwarded, this configuration ensures that those events are delivered to the central system.

Source systems must be configured to send events to the collector, establishing the path that allows activity to move from individual machines into a centralized location. The collector then receives events from multiple systems and stores them before they are ingested into the Log Analytics workspace used by Microsoft Sentinel. This process depends on communication between systems, and its reliability directly affects whether data is successfully collected.

For example, a WEF collector is configured to receive events from multiple systems, but subscriptions are only applied to a subset of those machines. Some events are forwarded while others are not, creating gaps that are only identified during investigation.

Planning and configuring Syslog via AMA and CEF via AMA connectors

Syslog and CEF enable the collection of log data from Linux systems and network devices, extending visibility beyond Windows-based environments. Because these sources generate logs in formats that differ from Windows event logs, they require a different collection approach before the data can be ingested into Microsoft Sentinel.

Syslog provides a standard method for capturing log data from Linux systems and supported devices, defining how messages are transmitted, while CEF standardizes how security products represent their log data by defining a consistent structure.

This data is collected through a Linux-based collector, as shown in *Figure 4.4*, which receives Syslog or CEF messages from Linux systems and network devices. The collector then forwards them to the Log Analytics workspace associated with Microsoft Sentinel using the AMA. The collector sits between the data sources and the Log Analytics workspace.

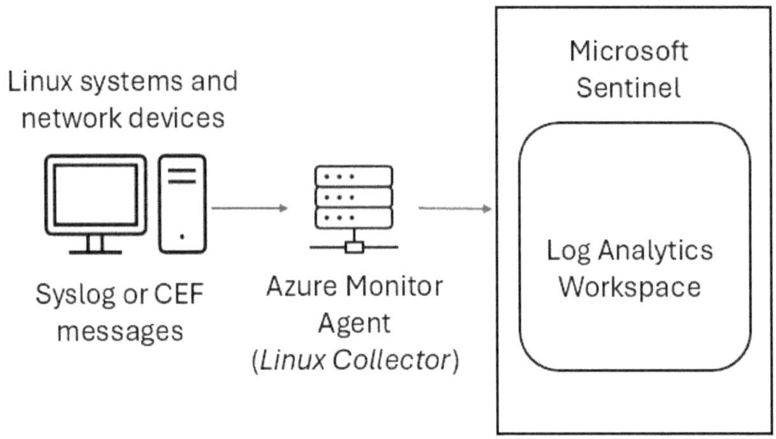

Figure 4.4 – Syslog and CEF data collection through a Linux-based collector

The configuration of this process determines which logs are received and how they are categorized. Syslog uses facilities and severity levels to define what is collected, while CEF relies on a consistent event structure so that data can be processed correctly. If the collector is not configured correctly, or if forwarding is incomplete, logs do not reach the Log Analytics workspace.

Configuring Syslog data collection using AMA

Syslog data collection defines how log messages from Linux systems and supported devices are received and sent to the Log Analytics workspace using the AMA on a Linux-based collector. The collector receives messages from multiple sources, including Linux hosts and network devices, and prepares them for forwarding to the Log Analytics workspace used by Microsoft Sentinel. This defines the entry point for non-Windows data.

The configuration determines which messages are accepted by the collector, controlling what data enters the collection pipeline and therefore which activity becomes visible. For example, a configuration may be set to collect only authentication-related messages with a higher severity level, such as warnings and errors, while excluding informational system logs. This ensures that only relevant security events are forwarded to the workspace.

Once those messages are received, AMA forwards the data to the workspace, completing the path into Microsoft Sentinel. Because this process depends on both receiving and forwarding, any break in that path prevents data from being collected. For example, if network devices are not configured to send Syslog messages to the collector, or if the collector is not correctly configured to receive those messages, no data is collected. Similarly, if the Azure Monitor Agent is not properly connected to the workspace, messages may be received but not forwarded, resulting in incomplete or missing data.

Configuring Syslog facilities and severity levels

Syslog facilities and severity levels determine how log messages are categorized and filtered before they are sent to the Log Analytics workspace used by Microsoft Sentinel, determining both which messages are collected and how much detail is included. Facilities represent the source or category of the log message, such as authentication, system processes, or other system components, while severity levels indicate the importance of each message, ranging from informational entries to higher-priority events.

Together, these settings control how incoming messages are filtered at the collector, allowing collection to be targeted to specific types of activity. A broader configuration increases coverage but also generates more data, while a narrower configuration reduces volume but may exclude relevant signals if the required messages are not included. For example, a broader configuration may collect messages across multiple facilities and include all severity levels, capturing both informational and critical events. In contrast, a narrower configuration may limit collection to authentication-related facilities and higher severity levels, such as warnings, and errors, reducing data volume but focusing on security-relevant activity.

Consistency is required because differences in facility or severity configuration across systems can result in varying levels of detail, making it harder to compare activity or correlate events across the environment.

Configuring Linux-based collectors for Syslog and CEF

Linux-based collectors act as the central point for receiving Syslog and CEF messages before they are forwarded to the Log Analytics workspace used by Microsoft Sentinel. They provide a system that accepts incoming log data from multiple sources and prepares it for ingestion, forming the core of the collection pipeline for non-Windows environments. This ensures that logs from different systems are received and organized before being forwarded.

Once the data is received, the AMA on the collector sends it to the Log Analytics workspace, completing the path into Microsoft Sentinel. The collector sits between the data sources and the workspace, making it a critical dependency that must receive both incoming messages and forward them successfully.

When this does not function correctly, issues typically appear as partial or inconsistent data, where some sources contribute logs while others do not, or where data is received but never forwarded to the workspace. Because all Syslog and CEF data pass through the collector, its configuration directly affects the reliability of the entire pipeline.

Configuring Linux-based collectors correctly ensures that log data is consistently centralized and delivered to Microsoft Sentinel for analysis. This creates a consistent pattern for non-Windows ingestion: data is received by a collector, processed, and then forwarded to the Log Analytics workspace.

Configuring CEF data connectors

CEF data connectors define how standardized log data from security products is received and processed in the Log Analytics workspace used by Microsoft Sentinel. They provide the configuration that allows CEF-formatted events to be recognized and ingested correctly once they reach the collector, ensuring that data from different vendors can be handled in a consistent way.

Because CEF enforces a common structure, the connector relies on that structure to interpret incoming events rather than having to process multiple formats. The connector then accepts these structured events from the collector and makes them available in the Log Analytics workspace, completing the ingestion path. This makes alignment between the data format and the connector configuration essential because if incoming data does not match the expected structure, events may reach the collector but cannot be processed or ingested in a usable form within Microsoft Sentinel.

For example, network devices are configured to send logs, but the collector or agent forwarding path is incomplete. Some messages are received while others are not forwarded to the workspace, resulting in partial visibility across network activity.

Configuring collection of Azure activities by using Azure Policy and resource diagnostic settings

Beyond system and network-based data sources, Azure introduces platform-level activity that must also be captured. Azure Activity Logs capture subscription-level events without requiring configuration, while resource logs are resource-level and must be enabled using diagnostic settings. This data is only useful when it is correctly collected and delivered to Microsoft Sentinel.

Diagnostic settings are used to route resource logs to the Log Analytics workspace, defining which logs are sent. Azure Policy can be used to enforce this configuration at scale so that logging is applied consistently as resources are created or updated. As a result, both subscription-level and resource-level activity become available in a single location for analysis.

The next sections break down how subscription-level activity is collected and how resource-level logs are actually routed to the workspace.

Configuring Azure Activity Log ingestion

Azure Activity Log ingestion defines how subscription-level events are brought into Microsoft Sentinel. These logs capture operations that affect the Azure environment, including administrative actions and changes to resources, providing a high-level view of activity across the entire subscription.

Azure Activity Logs are generated automatically at the subscription level, but they are not available in Microsoft Sentinel until they are explicitly connected to a Log Analytics workspace. This connection establishes how those events become available for querying and detection. If ingestion is not configured, the events are still generated by Azure but are not available within Microsoft Sentinel.

Configuring resource logs using diagnostic settings

Resource logs provide detailed visibility into the internal operations of individual Azure services. They capture events within specific resources rather than across the subscription as a whole. Because they are generated at the resource level, they must be explicitly configured before they are available in Microsoft Sentinel. Their collection, therefore, depends on a correct setup.

The configuration determines which categories of logs are enabled and ensures that the selected data is routed to the Log Analytics workspace. The choice of log categories must align with the activity being monitored, because selecting the wrong categories can make logging appear enabled while still missing critical data.

Consistency across resources also becomes important, as differences in configuration can lead to uneven visibility where some resources provide detailed logs while others provide little or none. In addition, because diagnostic settings apply only from the point they are configured, activities that occurred before configuration are not captured, creating gaps in the timeline. This behavior applies across all data sources in Microsoft Sentinel, where data is only ingested from the point at which collection is enabled and previously generated events are not ingested retroactively.

As environments grow, maintaining a consistent configuration across all resources becomes more difficult, increasing the risk of blind spots. Configuring resource logs through diagnostic settings ensures that internal service activity is collected and delivered in a consistent way so it can be analyzed effectively in Microsoft Sentinel. Resource logs are not collected by default and must be explicitly enabled using diagnostic settings before they are sent to the workspace.

Routing logs to Microsoft Sentinel through workspace

Routing logs to Microsoft Sentinel depends on the Log Analytics workspace, which serves as the central destination for all collected data. Both Azure Activity Logs and resource logs must be directed to this workspace, so they can be used for analysis.

This routing is defined during configuration, with Activity Logs connected at the subscription level and resource logs sent through diagnostic settings. In both cases, the configuration determines whether generated data is actually delivered to the workspace. If logs are not routed correctly, they are still generated by Azure but are not available within Microsoft Sentinel. Routing, therefore, defines the point at which Azure activity becomes visible and usable.

Enforcing logging using Azure Policy

Azure Policy ensures logging configurations are applied consistently across the environment, rather than relying on individual resource configurations. As environments scale, manually enabling diagnostic settings becomes difficult to maintain. This leads to gaps in log collection.

Policy addresses this by defining required configurations and applying them automatically, ensuring that logging is enabled and that logs are routed to the Log Analytics workspace as resources are created or updated. This shifts logging from a manual task to an enforced standard, allowing new and existing resources to remain aligned without additional intervention.

As a result, coverage is maintained over time even as resources change or are redeployed, reducing the risk of gaps and ensuring that activity generated by Azure resources continues to be collected consistently. For example, Azure Activity Logs are available, but resource logs are only enabled for selected resources and not enforced using Azure Policy. As new resources are created, they do not send logs to the workspace, leading to inconsistent visibility across the environment.

Ingesting threat indicators into Microsoft Sentinel

Threat indicators allow observed activity to be matched against known malicious patterns such as IP addresses, domains, URLs, and file hashes.

Indicators are ingested from threat intelligence platforms and integrated into the workspace, becoming part of the available data set and used to identify matches between known indicators and observed activity. Because they are used for correlation, their value depends on being present and up to date; if they are missing or outdated, relevant activity may not be identified.

Connecting threat intelligence platforms

Connecting threat intelligence platforms establishes how external indicator data is brought into Microsoft Sentinel. These platforms provide known indicators such as IP addresses, domains, URLs, and file hashes, which are then integrated into the workspace as part of the overall data set.

Once the connection is configured, indicators can be ingested automatically from connected platforms or added manually, and their effectiveness depends on being kept up to date over time. These indicators are then ingested and managed through several mechanisms, each affecting how they are brought into the workspace, maintained over time, and used during detection.

TAXII connectors

TAXII connectors provide an automated method for ingesting threat intelligence into Microsoft Sentinel from external platforms. These connectors continuously retrieve indicators such as IP addresses, domains, URLs, and file hashes, ensuring that the workspace is populated with current intelligence without requiring manual updates. This allows detection and correlation to operate on up-to-date threat data as new indicators are published.

Manual indicator upload

Manual indicator upload provides a direct way for analysts to add indicators into Microsoft Sentinel without relying on external feeds. This is typically used during investigations, where newly identified indicators can be added immediately to support correlation and detection. Once added, these indicators behave in the same way as those ingested through automated sources, so they can participate in matching and enrichment across the workspace.

Indicator expiration

Indicator expiration determines how long an indicator remains usable during correlation and detection. Each indicator includes a time-bound lifecycle, and once it expires, it is no longer used for correlation or detection matching. If expiration is not managed correctly, outdated indicators may continue to generate noise, or valid indicators may no longer be used, reducing detection effectiveness.

Indicator scoring

Indicator scoring determines how much weight an indicator carries during correlation and investigation. Higher-scored indicators are treated as more trustworthy, allowing analytics rules and investigations to prioritize matches based on confidence rather than treating all indicators equally. This prioritizes high-confidence indicator matches over low-confidence ones.

Threat intelligence table structure

All indicators, regardless of how they are ingested, are stored in the Threat Intelligence table structure, specifically within the **ThreatIntelligenceIndicator** table. This table defines how indicator data is represented in the workspace, including attributes such as indicator type, value, confidence, and expiration. This consistent structure allows indicators to be queried and correlated effectively against observed activity across the environment.

Once indicators are ingested and maintained, their value is realized when they are applied during detection and investigation.

Using threat indicators in analytics and detection

Threat indicators are used in analytics and detection to identify activity that aligns with known malicious patterns. Once ingested into Microsoft Sentinel, these indicators become part of the data set and can be applied across multiple sources, allowing activity from different systems to be assessed against the same set of known patterns. For example, an indicator containing a known malicious IP address can be matched against sign-in logs from Microsoft Entra ID, network device logs collected via Syslog, and endpoint telemetry from Microsoft Defender. If the same IP appears across these sources, it highlights coordinated activity that may indicate a broader attack.

This cross-source correlation exposes activity that would otherwise appear unrelated, making it easier to identify relevant signals across the environment. The effectiveness of this process depends on the availability and accuracy of the indicators, because if they are missing or outdated, relevant activity may not be identified.

A match between observed data and an indicator does not confirm malicious activity but instead signals a potential association that requires further analysis to determine its significance. Threat indicators provide context and are used within queries, analytics rules, and correlation logic to identify matches within collected data. Further, indicators do not generate alerts on their own and only produce detection outcomes when used within analytics rules or queries. For example, if threat indicators are outdated or incomplete, activity that matches those indicators will not be flagged, even though the data is present in the workspace.

Creating custom log tables in the workspace to store ingested data

Custom log tables are used to store data that does not fit into standard Microsoft Sentinel tables. This allows data from non-standard sources to be included in the workspace instead of being excluded. When a custom log table is created, it defines how incoming data is structured once it is ingested, which determines how that data can be interpreted and queried. Since this data does not follow predefined formats, the structure of the table becomes critical to ensuring it can be used consistently alongside other data.

Custom tables integrate with the Log Analytics workspace in the same way as standard tables, allowing this data to be queried alongside existing logs. If a custom table is not created for an unsupported data source, that data remains outside the workspace and cannot be used in analysis.

Ingesting custom log data into a workspace

Ingesting custom log data into the workspace determines whether externally sourced or non-standard data actually becomes usable in Microsoft Sentinel. Once a schema has been defined, the ingestion process maps incoming data to it so it can be written into the custom table in a consistent and usable format. Because this data does not follow predefined formats, the structure of the incoming data must align with the expected schema; otherwise, it cannot be interpreted correctly. If this alignment is not in place, data may fail ingestion or be rejected, preventing it from being written to the table.

Once ingestion is successful, it becomes part of the Log Analytics workspace and can be queried alongside other data sources. For example, data from a custom application is collected, but no custom log table or ingestion configuration is defined. As a result, the data is never ingested into the workspace, preventing it from being queried alongside other logs and limiting its use in detection and investigation.

Methods for ingesting custom log data

Custom log data can be ingested into Microsoft Sentinel through several methods, depending on how the data is generated and how it needs to be processed before ingestion. The following points explicitly cover the Log Ingestion API, HTTP Data Collector API, Azure Functions, Logic Apps, and CSV-based ingestion through the workspace:

- The Log Ingestion API provides a structured and scalable approach and is the modern ingestion method for sending data into custom tables. It uses Data Collection Rules to define how incoming data is transformed and mapped into the target table, making it suitable for ingestion scenarios where schema control and transformation are required.
- The HTTP Data Collector API offers a simpler ingestion method, typically used for legacy integrations or lightweight scenarios where full transformation via Data Collection Rules is not required. This allows data to be sent directly to a Log Analytics workspace over HTTPS.
- Azure Functions can be used to process and transform incoming data before sending it to the workspace. This is particularly useful when data requires enrichment, filtering, or restructuring prior to ingestion into a custom table.
- Logic Apps provide a workflow-based approach to ingestion, allowing data to be collected from external systems and routed into the workspace through connectors and automation logic. This is commonly used for integrating SaaS platforms or triggering ingestion based on events.
- CSV ingestion via the workspace UI provides a manual method for uploading structured data directly into a custom table. If a custom table or ingestion method is not defined, externally generated data cannot be stored in the workspace or used for analysis.

The following methods provide ways to define that ingestion and structure. This is typically used for one-time or ad hoc ingestion scenarios rather than continuous data collection, where other ingestion methods are more appropriate.

Summary

This chapter focused on how data is brought into Microsoft Sentinel and how that directly affects detection and investigation outcomes. The most critical areas are selecting the correct data connector based on the data source and data type, understanding how ingestion methods differ across Windows, Linux, and Azure sources, and recognizing the prerequisites required for each connector to successfully collect data.

You should be able to identify when AMA-based collection is required versus Windows Event Forwarding and understand how Syslog and CEF collection rely on a collector and the correct configuration of facilities and severity levels. It is also important to recognize how diagnostic settings and Azure Policy are used to ensure Azure resource logs are consistently collected.

Next, you move into detection, where ingested data is used to create analytics rules, generate alerts, and drive investigations.

Exam Readiness Drill – Chapter Review Questions

Apart from mastering key concepts, strong test-taking skills under time pressure are essential for acing your certification exam. That's why developing these abilities early in your learning journey is critical.

Exam readiness drills, using the free online practice resources provided with this book, help you progressively improve your time management and test-taking skills while reinforcing the key concepts you've learned.

HOW TO GET STARTED

- Open the link or scan the QR code at the bottom of this page
- If you have unlocked the practice resources already, log in to your registered account. If you haven't, follow the instructions in *Free Benefits with Your Book* section in this book's *Preface* and come back to this page.
- Once you log in, click the START button to start this chapter's quiz
- We recommend attempting a quiz multiple times till you're able to answer most of the questions correctly and well within the time limit.
- You can use the following practice template to help you plan your attempts:

Working On Accuracy		
Attempt	**Target**	**Time Limit**
Attempt 1	40% or more	Till the timer runs out
Attempt 2	60% or more	Till the timer runs out
Attempt 3	75% or more	Till the timer runs out
Working On Timing		
Attempt 4	75% or more	1 minute before time limit
Attempt 5	75% or more	2 minutes before time limit
Attempt 6	75% or more	3 minutes before time limit

The above drill is just an example. Design your drills based on your own goals and make the most out of the online quizzes accompanying this book.

Link to this Chapter's Quiz

You need to unlock the online practice resources to access the link below. Check the *Free Benefits with Your Book* section in the *Preface* for detailed instructions on how to do this. You only need to unlock the resources once.

Open Quiz `https://packt.link/sc200js-ch4` or scan the QR code

Part 3

Configure and Detect Threats

In this part of the book, you will move from platform setup into detection and investigation. You will learn how detections are created across Microsoft Defender XDR and Microsoft Sentinel, how Kusto Query Language supports threat detection, and how hunting and analytics capabilities help analysts identify suspicious activity before it becomes a wider incident.

This part of the book includes the following chapters:

5

Configure Detections

You now have data flowing into the platform and have visibility across security events, logs, and telemetry collected from the environment. The next step is identifying activity that stands out and requires investigation. The chapter explains how detections are created and managed across Microsoft Defender XDR and Microsoft Sentinel.

It addresses the following exam objectives of SC-200:

- Creating custom detection rules using advanced hunting in Microsoft Defender XDR
- Managing custom detection rules in Microsoft Defender XDR
- Configuring and managing analytics rules in Microsoft Sentinel SIEM
- Analyzing attack vector coverage using MITRE ATT&CK matrix
- Configuring anomalies in Microsoft Sentinel

This chapter explains how detections are built from queries and how they run over time to produce alerts. Different analytics rule types apply detection depending on the scenario. Detections connect into investigation through alert context and incidents, while coverage is evaluated using MITRE ATT&CK. Anomaly detection highlights activity that does not match known patterns. By the end of this chapter, you will be able to create and manage detection rules, understand how analytics rules operate, and evaluate detection coverage using MITRE ATT&CK.

Creating custom detection rules using advanced hunting in Microsoft Defender XDR

Advanced hunting exists to expose activity that has not yet been defined as a detection rule. It provides access to telemetry across Microsoft Defender XDR so behavior can be examined directly, rather than relying on predefined rules. At this stage, the focus here is not alerting, but identifying patterns that represent something worth detecting, such as unusual sign-in activity, repeated failed logons, or suspicious process execution.

A custom detection begins when the observed behavior becomes repeatable. The same query used to explore activity is converted into a detection rule that the system runs continuously. The query itself does not change. What changes is how the result is used. What was previously an investigation tool becomes part of the detection layer.

A typical example is identifying repeated PowerShell execution across multiple devices where the commands are obfuscated. During hunting, this may appear as a pattern across several devices and users. Once confirmed as suspicious, the same query can be converted into a detection so that future occurrences automatically generate alerts instead of requiring manual investigation.

For that transition to work, the output must carry enough context to be understood outside the query itself, such as the device, user account, process, and timestamp involved. Rather than just being a result test, the detection becomes a signal that feeds into the wider system. This is what allows it to contribute to alerting and investigation, rather than remaining an isolated query.

That separation matters because advanced hunting defines the logic behind a detection, while the detection rule defines how that logic is applied. Understanding that boundary keeps the detection accurate and prevents it from becoming noise when it is later executed as part of the platform. A detection rule is what generates alerts; advanced hunting itself does not produce alerts unless the query is converted into a detection.

Advanced hunting data and query model

Telemetry in advanced hunting is exposed in a structured way so it can be queried consistently across Microsoft Defender XDR. Instead of a single log stream, the data is separated into tables. Each table represents a different part of the environment, such as device activity, identity events, and email interactions. This structure allows activity to be followed across domains without changing tools or context. Each table contains events that share a common schema, which makes them predictable to query.

In Microsoft Sentinel, a similar consistency is achieved through the **Advanced SIEM Information Model** (**ASIM**), which uses parsers to map data from different sources, including Syslog and CEF, into a normalized common schema so analytics rules can operate consistently across them.

Fields such as timestamps, device identifiers, and account information act as linking points between different types of activity. Without that consistency, correlating behavior across sources would require separate queries and manual alignment. The structure enables those relationships to be expressed directly in the query, for example linking a user sign-in event to a device process execution through shared account and device identifiers.

Kusto Query Language (KQL) is used to shape this data into something meaningful. Rather than pulling raw events, queries define conditions that filter, join, and refine the dataset until only relevant activity remains. The signal begins to separate from noise, and the effectiveness of a detection later depends on how well this step is handled because the query defines exactly what the system will evaluate when it runs automatically.

For example, a query can join sign-in logs with device activity to identify users who sign in from an unusual location and then execute suspicious processes on a device, such as:

```
SigninLogs | join DeviceProcessEvents on UserPrincipalName | where Location !=
"expected" and ProcessCommandLine contains "powershell"
```

As queries move beyond a single table, they begin to express relationships between events. A process execution can be tied to a user, which can then be linked to a sign-in or an email action, allowing behavior to be correlated across the environment and ultimately turned into a detection.

Converting hunting queries into detection rules

In advanced hunting, queries are exploratory and help you understand activity. Converting a query into a detection changes the expectation, as the output must now represent a condition that can be evaluated repeatedly without manual interpretation, for example detecting repeated failed sign-ins from a single account.

A stricter structure is required at this stage. The query can no longer return loosely related results, and it must define a clear condition that represents something actionable. When the logic is too broad, the detection generates excessive alerts, while overly narrow logic causes relevant activity to be missed. Balance is established before the rule is ever created. For example, a broad query might flag all sign-ins, while a narrow query might only detect a specific rare condition and miss related activity. This is commonly tested when queries produce broad or inconsistent results. If a query returns too many unrelated results, it should not be converted directly into a detection. Instead, it must be refined until it defines a clear and repeatable condition, such as a specific process behavior, sign-in pattern, or file activity that consistently indicates risk.

To function within Microsoft Defender XDR, a detection must produce identifiable entities, such as devices, user accounts, files, or IP addresses. Results that include a device, user account, or file allow the system to associate the detection with activity and support correlation during investigation. Without these entities, the detection may still run, but the resulting alert lacks the context needed to be useful. Detections commonly fail at this point. Queries that do not return entities such as devices, users, or files can execute successfully but fail to produce actionable alerts.

Once these conditions are met, the query can be promoted into a detection rule. At that point, it becomes part of the system's detection logic rather than an analyst-driven tool, and its effectiveness depends on how reliably it produces consistent, meaningful signals.

Detection rule execution configuration

Once converted into a detection, the focus moves from what is detected to how it runs. The same logic is now evaluated automatically, which means its effectiveness depends on how it is executed over time, not just what it looks for.

Execution is controlled through scheduling. The detection runs at defined intervals, and each run evaluates data over a specified time window. These two elements (how often the rule runs and how far back it looks) must align. This relationship can be visualized, as shown in *Figure 5.1*, to show how alignment affects detection coverage.

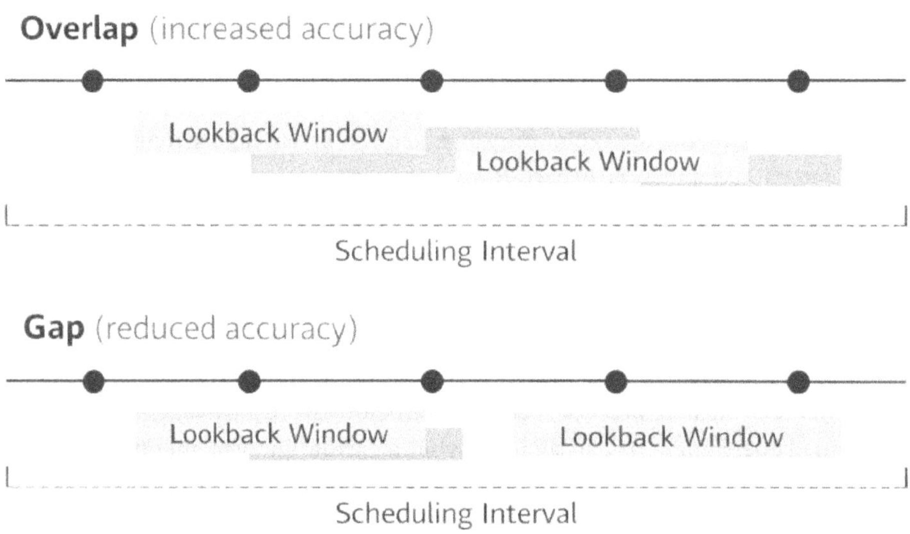

Figure 5.1 – Impact of scheduling interval and lookback window alignment on detection accuracy

The figure illustrates how alignment between the scheduling interval and the lookback window determines whether activity is consistently captured or missed. In the first example, the lookback windows overlap between each execution point. This ensures that activity occurring between runs is captured by at least one evaluation cycle. No events are missed and detection coverage remains continuous. In the second example, there is a gap between lookback windows. Activity that occurs within this gap is not included in any evaluation cycle and is therefore not detected. This creates blind spots in monitoring and reduces detection accuracy.

A typical situation involves a rule running every 10 minutes but only evaluating the last 5 minutes of data. The key point is that evaluating only the last 5 minutes of data creates gaps where activity is never assessed. Scheduling interval and lookback window must be aligned so that coverage is continuous. Overlap is acceptable and ensures reliability, while gaps introduce missed events and weaken detection. If the lookback window is shorter than the schedule interval, events are missed; if it is longer, duplicate alerts can be generated.

Detection now moves from logic into runtime behavior. A well-written query can still fail if the execution model does not match the pattern of activity it is designed to detect. High-frequency activity may require shorter intervals to remain relevant, while broader patterns may need longer windows to be visible. The configuration determines whether the detection captures the intended signal or distorts it through timing.

While the rule runs, it evaluates incoming telemetry based on its configured execution model. At this point, the detection is no longer dependent on manual execution. Its reliability is tied to whether the execution model consistently captures the activity it was designed to identify, without creating gaps or duplication in the results.

Alert generation and investigation context

A detection only becomes useful when it produces an alert that can be understood and acted on. So far, you have learned how to define and execute logic. When that logic evaluates to a match, the outcome is no longer a query result—it becomes an alert that enters the investigation workflow. The pipeline in *Figure 5.2* shows how detection logic progresses through execution into alerting, where signals are correlated into incidents and drive response.

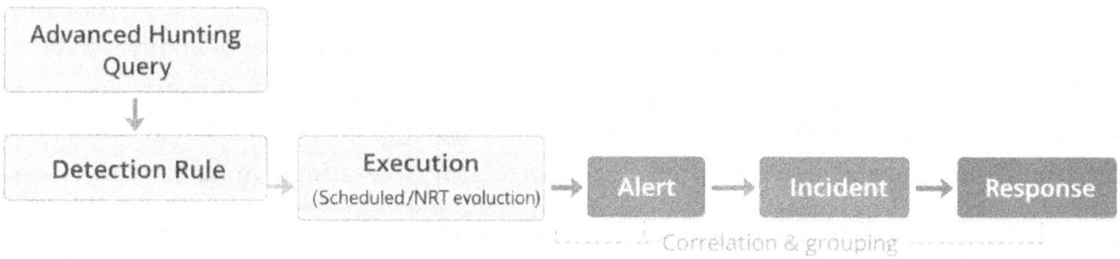

Figure 5.2 – Detection pipeline from query execution to incident response

A detection generates an alert, and alerts are then grouped into incidents based on shared entities and context. These are distinct stages in the detection pipeline. An alert carries context that a raw result does not. The detection includes the entities and data identified in the query, allowing the system to associate the alert with a specific device, user, or file. This context enables correlation. Without it, the alert remains isolated and cannot be effectively linked to other activity across Microsoft Defender XDR. For instance, an alert identifying a suspicious process becomes more useful when it includes the user account and originating IP address, allowing the alert to be correlated with sign-in activity or email events, forming part of a larger incident rather than remaining a single, isolated signal.

Detections align with attacker behavior models at this stage. When alerts are associated with known techniques, they can be interpreted as part of a broader pattern rather than as isolated events. This does not change how the detection operates, but it improves how the alert is understood during investigation.

From there, alerts feed into incidents, where related signals are combined to represent a sequence of activity. The value of a detection is not whether it triggers, but whether the alert it produces can be correlated, interpreted, and used to move an investigation forward. If that context is missing, the detection may function technically but fail operationally. For example, a detection may generate an alert for suspicious sign-in activity, which is grouped into an incident with related alerts and then investigated to trace the user's activity across devices and services.

Automated response actions in Microsoft Defender XDR

A detection does not have to stop at alerting. In Microsoft Defender XDR, it can also trigger predefined actions that respond to the activity as it is identified. The detection moves from passive signaling to active containment, where the system takes immediate steps based on the condition that was matched. Response actions are tied directly to the detection and execute when the rule produces an alert. Instead of waiting for an analyst to interpret the signal, the platform can isolate a device after detecting suspicious process activity, initiate an antivirus scan, or collect additional data for investigation.

Detection confidence becomes critical at this stage. A detection that produces highly reliable results can safely trigger more automated actions, while one that generates uncertain or variable output should remain limited to alerting. If that balance is not maintained, automated actions can disrupt normal activity or introduce unnecessary operational impact.

Response actions extend the detection into the response phase of the SOC workflow. The detection identifies the condition, and the response acts on it immediately. The effectiveness of this model depends on how accurately the detection reflects real activity, because the system will execute those actions without requiring further validation once the detection is triggered.

Managing custom detection rules in Microsoft Defender XDR

Creating a detection is only the starting point. Once a rule is active, it becomes part of a live system where its behavior directly affects alert volume, investigation quality, and overall signal reliability. Managing custom detections is therefore not about maintaining configuration, but about controlling how those detections behave over time.

While detections run continuously, their output reflects both the logic defined during creation and the conditions of the environment. A rule that initially produces useful signals can become noisy as activity patterns change, while another may stop triggering entirely if its conditions no longer align with real behavior. This ongoing management keeps detections aligned with actual activity rather than the original assumptions they were based on.

However, not all hunting queries can be converted into detection rules, as custom detections have limitations such as restrictions on how data can be joined across certain tables and how results must be structured to produce consistent, actionable alerts. They also have limits on supported advanced hunting tables, joins across certain data sources, some KQL operators, long-running queries, and dynamic schema expansion, and their results must be structured to produce consistent, actionable alerts.

An ongoing cycle of adjustment is introduced, for example refining a noisy detection rule, disabling it if it produces excessive alerts, and re-enabling it once the logic is improved. Rules may need to be modified, temporarily disabled, or removed entirely depending on how they perform. The goal is not to preserve the original detection, but to maintain a set of detections that produce reliable, high-confidence signals. If a rule cannot meet that standard, it becomes a liability. The outcome of this process is a detection layer that remains accurate as the environment evolves.

Ongoing management by SOC analysts ensures that detections continue to generate signals that can be trusted, reducing unnecessary noise while preserving visibility into relevant activity. Without this, even well-designed detections degrade over time and lose their operational value. In Microsoft Defender XDR, custom detection rules must also produce identifiable entities such as users, devices, or IP addresses so alerts can be correlated during investigation. Each detection is assigned a severity level that reflects its impact and can optionally trigger automated response actions such as isolating a device or collecting additional investigation data. These elements define how the detection operates within the wider investigation and response workflow.

Detection rule lifecycle management

Once a detection is created, it enters a lifecycle where it must be maintained as conditions change. The rule continues to run, but its relevance depends on whether its logic still reflects real activity. Management begins by adjusting the detection logic, so it remains aligned with the environment it is monitoring.

Changes to a detection define how it behaves going forward. Modifying the query alters what is detected, while adjusting its configuration changes how that detection is applied, such as refining a query to focus on a specific process instead of all activity. These updates do not correct past results but redefine future output. Management is forward-looking rather than corrective. Tuning refines how a detection identifies activity, while lifecycle actions such as disabling or deleting control whether the detection continues to operate at all.

There are also situations where a detection should remain in place but temporarily stop producing alerts. Disabling a rule allows it to be taken out of active use without removing it entirely. This is often used when evaluating its impact or when conditions make its output unreliable. The detection remains available, but it no longer contributes to alert generation until it is re-enabled. If a detection no longer provides value, it can be removed from the system. Deleting a rule eliminates it completely, ensuring it does not continue to influence the detection logic. This is the final stage of the lifecycle, where the focus shifts from maintaining the rule to maintaining the overall quality of detections within the environment.

Detection tuning and optimization

As detections run in a live environment, their output reflects how accurately logic captures real activity. Over time, this exposes gaps. Some detections generate too many alerts, while others fail to trigger as expected. Tuning exists to correct that imbalance, so the detection produces signals that are both relevant and consistent.

Adjustment happens within the query itself. Refining filters, narrowing conditions, or introducing thresholds changes how the detection interprets activity. The goal is precision, not added complexity. A detection that triggers less often but with higher confidence is more valuable than one that produces frequent but low-quality alerts.

The effect of tuning is directly visible in the alert output. As the logic is refined, noise is reduced, and the remaining alerts represent more meaningful activity. This improves how detections contribute to investigation, because you can focus on signals that are more likely to require action rather than filtering out irrelevant results. If tuning is not applied, detections degrade over time as patterns in the environment change. What was once an accurate signal becomes either too noisy or too quiet. Optimization keeps the detection aligned with current behavior, ensuring that it continues to function as a reliable part of the detection layer rather than becoming a source of inconsistency.

In exam scenarios, tuning is often assessed by recognizing whether a detection is too broad or too narrow based on its output. Candidates may be required to identify which detection logic produces meaningful, actionable alerts rather than excessive noise or missed activity.

Monitoring detection effectiveness

With detections active and tuned, their value is determined by how they perform over time. Monitoring focuses on observing the output of each rule to understand whether it is producing meaningful signals or unnecessary noise. Alert output is the primary indicator of effectiveness. A detection that triggers too frequently without clear investigative value indicates that its logic is still too broad, while one that rarely or never triggers may no longer align with actual activity. Monitoring makes these patterns visible, allowing adjustments to be made based on how the detection performs rather than how it was originally designed.

This process also reveals how detections contribute to the overall signal within the system. Some rules may consistently produce alerts that lead to useful investigation outcomes, while others generate signals that are repeatedly dismissed. Over time, this distinction becomes clear through observation, helping to identify which detections are adding value and which are degrading the quality of the alert stream.

If monitoring is neglected, detections drift out of alignment with the environment. Changes in user behavior, system activity, or attack patterns can reduce their effectiveness without any change to the rule itself. Monitoring ensures that these shifts are identified early, allowing detections to be adjusted before they become either a source of noise or a gap in visibility.

Configuring and managing analytics rules in Microsoft Sentinel SIEM

Microsoft Sentinel uses multiple detection approaches. **Fusion rules** is a built-in analytics approach that correlates alerts across different sources to identify multi-stage attacks without requiring manually defined query logic. Fusion rules are enabled by default in Microsoft Sentinel and operate automatically, requiring minimal configuration beyond ensuring that relevant data sources are connected. Fusion correlates alerts across sources to detect multi-stage attacks, while machine learning rules identify anomalies within specific datasets and UEBA identifies behavioral anomalies across users and entities.

Analytics rules evaluate data differently depending on the activity being identified. The choice of rule type depends on whether detection requires pattern-based evaluation over time, immediate event detection, known indicator matching, or behavioral analysis. This enables detection to operate across different conditions, from structured queries to behavioral models, without relying on a single method. For example, scheduled rules evaluate data over time using queries, **near-real-time** (**NRT**) rules detect events almost immediately, threat intelligence rules match known indicators, and machine learning rules identify anomalous behavior.

The data stored in the Log Analytics workspace sits at the center of this model. Analytics rules evaluate this data automatically based on their execution model to identify potential security activity. Unlike exploratory queries, these rules are designed to run as part of the detection layer, producing alerts that feed directly into investigation workflows.

The distinction between rule types reflects how detection is applied. Some rules evaluate data at defined intervals using query logic, while others operate with minimal delay to identify activity as it occurs. Additional rule types rely on known indicators or behavioral models rather than query conditions. Each approach addresses a different aspect of detection, ensuring that both known patterns and unexpected activity can be identified.

This structure allows detection coverage to be expanded without overloading a single method. By separating how detections are defined and executed, Microsoft Sentinel maintains flexibility in how signals are generated. This model determines how detection is applied, because managing analytics rules is not just about configuration, but about selecting the appropriate detection approach for the type of activity being monitored.

Analytics rule detection model in Microsoft Sentinel

In Microsoft Sentinel, analytics rules operate by evaluating data that has already been collected and stored in the Log Analytics workspace. Unlike exploratory queries, these rules are part of the system, meaning they run automatically and continuously assess incoming data for conditions that represent potential security activity. For example, an analytics rule might use a query to detect repeated failed sign-ins from a single account or suspicious process execution on a device.

The model depends on how data is structured within the workspace. Events from different sources are stored in tables, and analytics rules operate against those tables to identify patterns. The rule evaluates existing data rather than generating additional data. This separation between data collection and detection ensures that the same dataset can support multiple detection approaches without duplication.

> **Note**
>
> In exam scenarios, the focus is on understanding how analytics rules operate, when to use different rule types, and how detection logic is applied to identify meaningful activity. Candidates are not typically required to write full queries but should be able to interpret query logic and identify how it detects specific conditions.

When a rule identifies a match, it produces an alert that represents the condition defined by its logic. That alert carries context from the underlying data, allowing it to be associated with entities such as users, hosts, or IP addresses. This context is what allows alerts to be correlated with other activity and incorporated into incidents for investigation.

The effectiveness of this model depends on the relationship between the rule and the data it evaluates. If the underlying data is incomplete or inconsistent, the detection will reflect those gaps. Analytics rules do not operate in isolation as they rely on the quality and structure of the data they evaluate.

Scheduled analytics rules (KQL-based)

Scheduled analytics rules use query logic to evaluate data at defined intervals. Instead of continuously reacting to individual events, they assess activity in batches, applying KQL to identify patterns that emerge over a period. That makes them suitable for detections that rely on correlation, aggregation, or trends rather than single events.

Running on a schedule, the rule evaluates data within a specified time window. The schedule and the evaluation window define how the detection behaves. The interval determines how often the rule runs, while the evaluation window determines how much data is considered during each run. If these are not aligned, the detection can either miss activity or evaluate the same data multiple times.

Because detection is driven by a query, the structure of that query defines what is identified. Filtering, aggregation, and thresholds are used to shape the output so that only meaningful conditions result in alerts. For example, filtering sign-in events, aggregating failed attempts by user, and applying a threshold to trigger when a limit is exceeded. The rule can detect patterns such as repeated activity, unusual volumes, or relationships between events that would not be visible in a single record.

As the rule executes, it produces alerts based on the results of each evaluation cycle. These alerts carry the context defined by the query and become part of the broader investigation process, for instance, like an alert showing a user account with multiple failed sign-ins across different locations within a short time. The reliability of the detection, therefore, depends on both the query logic and how it is applied over time through the rule schedule (how often it runs) and the evaluation window (how much data it evaluates).

Near-real-time (NRT) analytics rules

Near-real-time rules are designed to detect activity with minimal delay. Instead of evaluating data in scheduled batches, they operate on events as they arrive, allowing the system to respond to conditions almost immediately. This makes them suitable for scenarios where timing is critical and waiting for a scheduled evaluation would reduce the value of the detection. For example, detecting the creation of a new administrative account or the disabling of security controls requires immediate visibility.

Detection shifts toward immediate event evaluation. Rather than looking for patterns across a time window, the rule evaluates individual events or very short sequences of activity. The focus shifts from aggregation to immediacy, where the goal is to identify a condition at the point it occurs rather than after it has accumulated. Because of this, the logic used in near-real-time rules must be precise. There is less opportunity to refine results through aggregation or extended correlation, so the condition being evaluated must clearly represent something that requires attention. If the logic is too broad, alerts will be generated rapidly and continuously. If it is too narrow, relevant activity may pass without detection.

For example, consider a rule that triggers on any PowerShell execution across all devices; it is too broad and will generate a high volume of alerts, many of which are benign administrative activity. In contrast, a rule that only triggers when PowerShell is executed with a highly specific encoded command string may be too narrow and miss variations of the same technique. A well-tuned rule instead focuses on suspicious patterns, such as PowerShell execution with encoded commands initiated from unusual parent processes, balancing coverage with precision.

As these rules execute, they produce alerts that enter the investigation workflow alongside other detections. Their value lies in how quickly they surface activity, providing early visibility into conditions that may require immediate response. The effectiveness of near-real-time detection is therefore defined by how accurately it identifies meaningful events without relying on extended evaluation.

Threat intelligence analytics rules

Threat intelligence analytics rules match known indicators against the data stored in Microsoft Sentinel. These indicators, such as IP addresses, domains, or file hashes, represent activity that has already been identified as suspicious or malicious. Instead of discovering new patterns, the rule evaluates whether known indicators appear within the environment.

Rather than defining conditions through query logic alone, the rule relies on a comparison between ingested indicators and observed activity. The detection is driven by whether a match occurs, not by building a pattern from raw events. That makes it effective for identifying known threats that may otherwise blend into normal activity.

The accuracy of this approach depends on the quality and relevance of the indicators being used. If the indicator set is outdated or overly broad, the rule may generate alerts that do not reflect current risk. If it is too limited, known threats may pass undetected. The detection is therefore only as reliable as the intelligence it is based on.

When a match is found, the rule generates an alert that reflects the presence of that indicator within the environment. This alert carries context from both the observed activity and the associated intelligence, allowing it to be investigated as part of the broader incident workflow. The value of the detection lies in its ability to surface known threats quickly, without requiring the pattern to be rediscovered through query logic. This often appears when an IP address associated with known malicious activity appears in sign-in logs or network traffic, triggering an alert immediately.

Machine learning analytics rules

Machine learning analytics rules identify deviations from established behavior rather than matching predefined conditions. User and Entity Behavior Analytics (UEBA) extends this by analyzing activity across users and entities over time, integrating multiple data sources to identify anomalous behavior that may indicate compromise. UEBA uses signals from multiple data sources such as sign-in activity, device behavior, and alerts, and integrates with incidents to provide behavioral context during investigation. While machine learning analytics rules detect anomalies within specific datasets, UEBA focuses on behavior across users and entities over time, providing a broader behavioral context.

Instead of relying on query logic to define what is suspicious, these rules use models that learn patterns over time and highlight activity that falls outside those patterns. There is no requirement to define detailed conditions in KQL, because the model evaluates behavior automatically. The detection is based on comparison of what is normal versus what is not rather than explicitly describing every scenario that should trigger an alert. This allows activity to be identified even when it does not match a known pattern.

Because detection is driven by learned behavior, the results are probabilistic rather than absolute. Not every anomaly represents malicious activity, and some legitimate behavior may appear unusual depending on the baseline. This introduces a level of interpretation that does not exist in deterministic rules, where conditions either match or do not.

When these rules generate alerts, they provide visibility into activity that may otherwise go undetected by query-based or indicator-based approaches. Their value lies in extending detection beyond known conditions, allowing unexpected or emerging behavior to be surfaced.

The effectiveness of this approach depends on how well the model reflects the environment it is observing, because that baseline defines what is considered normal. A typical situation involves a user suddenly downloading significantly more data than their established baseline, which may not match a predefined rule but is detected because it deviates from established patterns.

Entity mapping and investigation context

For analytics rules to contribute meaningfully to investigation, the alerts they generate must carry identifiable context. This is achieved through **entity mapping**, where elements within the data such as accounts, hosts, or IP addresses are associated with the alert. Without this linkage, the alert remains a standalone signal with limited investigative value.

Through entity mapping, the system relates alerts to other activity across Microsoft Sentinel. When multiple alerts reference the same entities, they can be correlated to form a more complete picture of what is happening. Therefore, individual detections contribute to a broader understanding of activity rather than being treated in isolation.

It defines how the result is interpreted once a match occurs. An alert that includes clearly defined entities can be enriched, correlated, and investigated more effectively, while one without that context requires additional effort to understand and may not align cleanly with other signals. As a result, entity mapping acts as the connection between detection and investigation. It ensures that when a rule generates an alert, that alert can be placed within the wider context of the environment. The quality of this mapping directly influences how easily activity can be traced and understood during an investigation.

Alert grouping and incident configuration

Grouping determines how alerts are combined based on shared context. When alerts reference the same entities or occur within a related timeframe, they can be associated to reflect a single sequence of activity. For example, multiple alerts showing repeated failed sign-ins for the same user account, followed by a successful sign-in from a new location and a suspicious process execution on a device, can be grouped into a single incident. Instead of investigating each alert separately, the analyst sees a coordinated sequence of activity that may indicate account compromise. This allows an investigation to focus on the overall pattern instead of handling each alert independently, which improves clarity and reduces fragmentation.

The way alerts are grouped directly influences how incidents are formed. When grouping is too broad, unrelated activity can be combined, making incidents harder to interpret. If it is too narrow, related alerts remain separate, requiring you to manually connect them. The effectiveness of grouping depends on how well it reflects actual relationships between events.

Using the same example, if grouping is too broad, those sign-in and device alerts could be combined with unrelated activity from other users or devices, making the incident difficult to interpret. If grouping is too narrow, each alert (failed sign-ins, successful sign-in, and process execution) would remain separate, requiring the analyst to manually correlate them. Effective grouping ensures these related signals are combined into a single, coherent incident. As a result, incident quality is shaped by how alerts are combined. Well-grouped alerts produce incidents that accurately represent activity and support efficient investigation.

Rule management and tuning

Once analytics rules are active, their behavior must be adjusted to remain aligned with the data they evaluate. The rule continues to run as defined, but its output reflects how accurately its logic matches current activity. Management focuses on modifying that logic and its application, so the detection remains relevant over time.

Changes to a rule affect how future data is interpreted. Adjusting the query alters what conditions are detected, while changes to thresholds or timing influence how often those conditions result in alerts. These updates do not change past results, rather, they redefine how the rule behaves moving forward. For example, a rule designed to detect repeated failed sign-ins may initially trigger on any account with more than five failures in a short period. In practice, this can generate noise from normal user behavior or service accounts. Tuning the rule to exclude known service accounts and require failures from multiple geographic locations reduces false positives while preserving meaningful alerts. If the threshold is set too high or exclusions are too broad, however, real attack activity may no longer trigger, showing how tuning directly impacts detection effectiveness.

Tuning is applied when the output does not reflect meaningful activity. If alerts are generated too frequently, the rule may be too broad. If alerts are rare or absent, the conditions may be too restrictive. Refining the logic balances these outcomes so that alerts represent activity that requires attention without overwhelming the system.

As these adjustments are made, the quality of the alert stream changes. Effective tuning reduces unnecessary signals while preserving visibility into relevant behavior. Without it, rules drift out of alignment with the environment, either contributing to noise or creating gaps in detection. Management ensures that analytics rules continue to function as reliable components of the detection layer.

Automation integration (automation rules and playbooks)

Analytics rules do not operate in isolation once an alert is generated. In Microsoft Sentinel, those alerts can trigger automation that acts on the incident as it is created. This extends detection into response, allowing predefined actions to be applied without waiting for manual intervention.

At the point where alerts become incidents, automation is applied. When a rule produces an alert, automation rules can evaluate that event and determine what should happen next. This might include assigning the incident, updating its severity, or initiating further actions through playbooks. The detection identifies the condition, but automation defines how the system reacts to it.

Automation depends on how accurately the detection reflects meaningful activity. If the underlying rule produces reliable alerts, automation can be used to accelerate response. If the detection is noisy or inconsistent, automation can amplify that problem by acting on signals that do not require intervention. The quality of the detection, therefore, directly influences the effectiveness of the response. As a result, automation becomes part of the overall detection workflow rather than a separate function. The rule generates the alert, the alert forms the incident, and automation acts on that incident.

Analyzing attack vector coverage using MITRE ATT&CK matrix

Detection on its own does not show what is missing. Individual alerts can confirm that certain activity is being identified, but they do not reveal whether entire areas of attacker behavior remain uncovered. The MITRE ATT&CK matrix (`https://attack.mitre.org/`) addresses this by providing a structured way to understand detection coverage across the attack lifecycle.

The matrix organizes attacker activity into tactics and techniques, representing how an attack progresses rather than focusing on isolated events. When detections are aligned to this model, they can be viewed in terms of which stages of an attack are visible and which are not. The focus moves from individual signals to overall coverage.

In Microsoft Sentinel, this alignment allows analytics rules to be associated with specific techniques. For example, if multiple detections are mapped to techniques under Initial Access and Credential Access, but no detections are mapped to Persistence or Lateral Movement, those gaps become immediately visible. This allows you to identify which stages of the attack lifecycle are covered and where additional detections are required.

The result is a coverage view that reflects which parts of the matrix are supported by existing detections. Instead of evaluating rules individually, the focus becomes how those rules collectively represent visibility across attacker behavior. Coverage analysis, therefore, identifies what is not being detected, guiding where new detections are required or where existing ones need to be adjusted to improve visibility.

MITRE ATT&CK mapping and coverage model

When analytics rules are aligned to the MITRE ATT&CK model in Microsoft Sentinel, each detection can be associated with one or more specific techniques. This association is configured when the analytics rule is created or updated, where relevant MITRE ATT&CK techniques are selected to reflect the behavior, the rule is designed to detect. This mapping does not change how the rule operates, but it defines how its output is interpreted within the context of attacker behavior.

In practice, this alignment is used to evaluate detection coverage. For example, if multiple rules are mapped to Credential Access techniques but none are mapped to Persistence, this indicates a gap where attacker activity may occur without being detected. Instead of asking whether a single rule is effective, you assess whether the detection layer reflects how attacks actually progress.

As a result, MITRE ATT&CK mapping supports decisions on where new detections are required, where existing rules should be refined, and whether critical techniques are being monitored. It provides a structured way to identify gaps, reduce overlaps, and ensure that detection aligns with real attacker behavior.

Coverage visualization in Microsoft Sentinel

Once detections are mapped to techniques, the next step is understanding how that mapping appears across the environment. Microsoft Sentinel provides a coverage view that presents this relationship visually, allowing detections to be seen as part of the MITRE ATT&CK matrix rather than as individual rules. For example, a coverage view may show multiple detections mapped to Credential Access techniques, while areas such as Persistence or Lateral Movement have little or no coverage. This allows you to quickly identify where detection is concentrated and where gaps exist.

This view shows which techniques are covered and where gaps remain. Instead of reviewing rules one by one, the matrix shows coverage across the full attack lifecycle, making it possible to see where visibility exists and where it is missing. The emphasis shifts from rule configuration to overall detection posture.

The value of this visualization lies in how it exposes imbalance. Some areas of the matrix may be densely covered, with multiple rules aligned to similar techniques, while others may have no coverage at all. This shows whether detection is evenly distributed across attacker behavior. Visualization becomes a tool for assessing detection completeness. It allows coverage to be evaluated at a glance, highlighting areas that require attention without needing to inspect each rule in detail. The accuracy of this view depends on how well detections have been mapped, as the visualization reflects the structure defined by that mapping.

Identifying and addressing coverage gaps

Once coverage is visible, attention shifts to what is missing. Gaps appear where no detections are mapped to specific techniques, indicating that certain types of attacker behavior would not generate alerts. These gaps are not the result of a failure in existing detections, but the absence of detections in those areas. Identifying a gap does not automatically mean that a new rule must be created. The first step is understanding whether the gap represents relevant activity for the environment. Some techniques may not apply based on how systems are configured or used. Others may represent meaningful risk and require detection coverage. The decision is driven by relevance, not completeness alone.

Where coverage is required, gaps are addressed by extending the detection layer. Addressing this may involve creating new analytics rules or refining existing ones so they align with the missing techniques. The goal is not to duplicate coverage, but to ensure that each relevant area of attacker behavior is represented by at least one effective detection.

As these gaps are addressed, the coverage model evolves. New detections fill previously unmonitored areas, and the matrix becomes a more accurate reflection of visibility across the environment. This process is continuous, as changes in the environment or threat landscape can introduce new gaps over time, requiring ongoing adjustment to maintain effective coverage.

Operational use of MITRE mapping

Once detections are mapped and coverage is understood, the model begins to influence how investigations are approached. MITRE mapping provides a way to interpret alerts in the context of attacker behavior, allowing individual signals to be viewed as part of a sequence rather than isolated events.

When an alert is associated with a technique, it indicates not just what was detected, but how that activity fits within a broader pattern. This allows you to anticipate related behavior, as techniques are rarely used in isolation. The mapping provides direction, helping to guide the investigation toward what is likely to occur before or after the detected activity.

When alerts are analyzed, instead of evaluating each signal independently, they are considered in relation to other techniques within the same tactic or across the attack lifecycle. This creates a more structured investigation process, where activity can be followed through its progression rather than reconstructed from disconnected events.

As a result, MITRE mapping becomes part of how investigations are conducted, not just how detections are organized. It provides a consistent reference for understanding attacker behavior, allowing you to move from detection to analysis with a clearer view of what the activity represents and how it may evolve.

Configuring anomalies in Microsoft Sentinel

Not all suspicious activity follows a known pattern. Some behaviors only become visible when they are compared against what is considered normal. Anomaly-based detection exists to surface those deviations, identifying activity that stands out rather than activity that matches a predefined condition.

Within Microsoft Sentinel, anomaly detections are driven by models that establish baselines over time. Rather than defining exact criteria, these models learn how entities behave and highlight changes that fall outside those patterns. This allows detection to extend beyond what can be explicitly described in a query, capturing activity that would otherwise remain unnoticed.

The approach focuses on deviations from normal behavior rather than known patterns. The output represents a deviation, not a confirmed condition. Anomaly-based alerts require context and validation to determine whether the activity is expected or represents a potential threat. The detection identifies something unusual, but it does not define intent on its own. A user signing in from a new location may trigger an anomaly. This could represent legitimate travel or a potential compromise. The anomaly highlights the deviation, but further investigation is required to determine whether the activity is expected.

Anomalies do not replace rule-based detections; they complement them. While deterministic rules identify known patterns, anomaly detections provide visibility into unexpected behavior, expanding the overall detection capability without relying on predefined logic.

Anomaly detection model in Microsoft Sentinel

Anomaly detection in Microsoft Sentinel is based on identifying deviations from established behavior rather than matching predefined conditions. Instead of defining what activity should look like, the system builds an understanding of what is normal and then highlights activity that falls outside that pattern. This allows detection to operate without requiring every scenario to be explicitly described.

The model is built by observing behavior over time. This requires sufficient historical data to establish an accurate baseline, as limited or inconsistent data reduces the reliability of anomaly detection. As data is collected, patterns begin to form around how users, devices, and other entities typically operate. These patterns become the baseline against which new activity is compared. When activity differs significantly from that baseline, it is flagged as an anomaly.

Unlike Fusion, which uses machine learning to correlate alerts across multiple sources to detect multi-stage attacks, anomaly detection uses behavioral machine learning models to identify deviations from established patterns and depends on sufficient historical data to establish a reliable baseline. The output is not a direct match against a condition, but a deviation from expected behavior. Because of this, the results are probabilistic. An anomaly indicates that something is unusual, but it does not confirm whether the activity is malicious or benign.

As detections generate alerts, they provide visibility into activity that may not be captured by rule-based detections. The effectiveness of the model depends on how accurately the baseline reflects the environment, as that baseline defines what is considered normal and therefore what is treated as an anomaly.

Anomaly alert generation and investigation context

When an anomaly is detected, the result is an alert that represents a deviation from expected behavior. Unlike rule-based detections, this alert is not tied to a predefined condition but to a change in how an entity is behaving. The alert signals that something is unusual, rather than confirming that a specific activity has occurred.

The context carried with the alert is what makes it usable. Information about the entity involved such as a user, device, or activity provides the starting point for investigation. This context allows the anomaly to be examined alongside other signals, helping to determine whether the deviation is part of a broader pattern or an isolated occurrence. The system highlights deviation, but it does not determine intent. Some anomalies will reflect legitimate changes in behavior, while others may indicate emerging threats. The role of the alert is to surface that difference so it can be evaluated within the wider investigation.

As these alerts are generated, they become part of the incident workflow alongside other detections. Their value lies in how they complement rule-based alerts, providing visibility into activity that may not match known patterns. When combined with other signals, anomaly alerts help build a more complete view of what is happening in the environment.

Interpreting anomaly results

An anomaly highlights a deviation, but the meaning of that deviation is not defined by the detection itself. Interpretation starts with understanding how the observed behavior differs from what is expected. The alert indicates a change in pattern but does not explain why.

The anomaly must be evaluated in context. The same deviation can have different implications depending on the environment, the role of the entity involved, and recent activity. What appears unusual for one user or system may be normal for another. Interpretation, therefore, depends on comparing the anomaly to surrounding behavior rather than assessing it in isolation. For example, a user signing in from a new location late at night may be flagged as anomalous. For a standard employee, this could indicate potential account compromise. However, for an administrator performing out-of-hours maintenance, the same activity may be expected. Interpreting the anomaly requires understanding the role, recent activity, and operational context.

Because the detection is based on probability, there is always uncertainty in the result. Some anomalies will reflect legitimate changes, such as new processes, shifts in usage patterns, or administrative activity. Others may indicate early signs of compromise. The distinction is made through investigation, not by the detection model itself.

As a result, anomaly interpretation becomes part of the investigative process rather than a separate step. The alert provides the starting point, but its value depends on how it is assessed alongside other signals. This allows anomalies to contribute meaningfully to detection without being treated as definitive indicators on their own.

Summary

This chapter focused on how detections operate within Microsoft Sentinel and Microsoft Defender XDR, with emphasis on how analytics rules generate alerts and how those alerts are used in investigation. From an exam perspective, the key areas to understand are how different analytics rule types behave (scheduled, near-real-time, threat intelligence, and machine learning), how scheduling and query logic affect detection outcomes, and how alerts are grouped into incidents. This includes recognizing how MITRE ATT&CK mapping is used to evaluate detection coverage and identify gaps.

Questions are typically scenario-based, requiring you to determine which rule type, configuration, or tuning approach best fits a given situation. This includes understanding when detection depends on correlation over time, when immediate evaluation is required, and how tuning affects alert quality and reliability. When revising, focus on how detections behave in practice rather than how they are configured. Be prepared to identify correct detection approaches based on patterns, timing, and expected outcomes.

In the next chapter, you will build on this by focusing on investigation workflows, including how incidents are analyzed, how entities are used to expand investigations, and how you move from detection to response.

Exam Readiness Drill – Chapter Review Questions

Apart from mastering key concepts, strong test-taking skills under time pressure are essential for acing your certification exam. That's why developing these abilities early in your learning journey is critical.

Exam readiness drills, using the free online practice resources provided with this book, help you progressively improve your time management and test-taking skills while reinforcing the key concepts you've learned.

HOW TO GET STARTED

- Open the link or scan the QR code at the bottom of this page
- If you have unlocked the practice resources already, log in to your registered account. If you haven't, follow the instructions in *Free Benefits with Your Book* section in this book's *Preface* and come back to this page.

- Once you log in, click the START button to start this chapter's quiz
- We recommend attempting a quiz multiple times till you're able to answer most of the questions correctly and well within the time limit.
- You can use the following practice template to help you plan your attempts:

Working On Accuracy		
Attempt	**Target**	**Time Limit**
Attempt 1	40% or more	Till the timer runs out
Attempt 2	60% or more	Till the timer runs out
Attempt 3	75% or more	Till the timer runs out
Working On Timing		
Attempt 4	75% or more	1 minute before time limit
Attempt 5	75% or more	2 minutes before time limit
Attempt 6	75% or more	3 minutes before time limit

The above drill is just an example. Design your drills based on your own goals and make the most out of the online quizzes accompanying this book.

Link to this Chapter's Quiz

You need to unlock the online practice resources to access the link below. Check the *Free Benefits with Your Book* section in the *Preface* for detailed instructions on how to do this. You only need to unlock the resources once.

Open Quiz `https://packt.link/sc200js-ch5` or scan the QR code

6

Detect Threats by Using Microsoft Defender XDR

At this stage, detections are already in place and generating alerts based on observed activity. The focus now shifts to working with that output, using the data behind alerts to understand what actually happened and how activity connects. This chapter focuses on investigating threats using Microsoft Defender XDR and Microsoft Sentinel.

It addresses the following exam objectives of SC-200:

- Identifying appropriate table to use in a KQL query
- Identifying threats by using KQL
- Creating advanced hunting queries
- Interpreting threat analytics in Microsoft Defender XDR
- Creating hunting graphs, including blast radius
- Analyzing relationships between entities by using Sentinel Graph

Investigation starts with the data behind the alert and depends on working from the correct source. Once that data is identified, it needs to be reduced and shaped so the activity can be understood, using filtering to narrow the scope, aggregation to highlight patterns, and correlation to connect events across users, devices, and services. Alongside this, threat analytics and graph views add context, helping explain what the activity represents and how far it extends beyond the initial alert.

By the end of this chapter, you will be able to examine an alert, work through the underlying data, and understand how the activity unfolded across the environment.

Identifying appropriate table to use in a KQL query

Every query in advanced hunting begins with a question that is easy to overlook but determines everything that follows: where the data comes from. Microsoft Defender XDR does not expose activity as a single dataset. Instead, it separates telemetry into distinct tables, each representing a different type of behavior across the environment. The question being asked must be translated into the correct data source before any filtering or analysis can take place.

Microsoft Defender XDR organizes telemetry into distinct tables; each aligned to a specific type of activity. Understanding what each table represents allows the investigation to begin with the correct data source:

- **DeviceProcessEvents** – process creation and execution on endpoints (for example, identifying suspicious PowerShell or command-line activity)
- **DeviceNetworkEvents** – outbound and inbound network connections from devices (for example, connections to malicious IPs or domains)
- **DeviceFileEvents** – file creation, modification, and deletion activity (for example, dropped payloads or modified system files)
- **DeviceRegistryEvents** – registry changes on endpoints (for example, persistence mechanisms such as autoruns)
- **DeviceLogonEvents** – logon activity on devices (for example, local or remote sign-ins)
- **DeviceEvents** – additional device-level security events (for example, security control triggers or system activity)
- **IdentityLogonEvents** – authentication activity across identity services (for example, Azure AD sign-ins)
- **EmailEvents** – email message activity (for example, delivery status, sender, recipient)
- **EmailUrlInfo** – URLs embedded within emails (for example, phishing links)
- **EmailAttachmentInfo** – file attachments in emails (for example, malicious attachments)
- **CloudAppEvents** – activity across SaaS and cloud applications (for example, file access in SharePoint or OneDrive)
- **AlertInfo** – high-level alert metadata (for example, alert name, severity, status)
- **AlertEvidence** – entities associated with alerts (for example, affected users, devices, or files)

Alert tables contain detection results and associated entities, not raw telemetry such as process, network, or logon events. These tables are not interchangeable. Each one represents a different layer of activity, and selecting the correct table determines whether the query reflects the behavior being investigated or produces unrelated results.

> Note
>
> Table selection becomes critical at this point. The query itself can be perfectly written, but if it starts from the wrong table, the results will not reflect the activity being investigated. This distinction determines the correct answer in the exam—the ability to recognize which data source aligns with the scenario being described.

A common scenario is **suspicious sign-in activity**. The correct starting point is an **identity-related table** such as **IdentityLogonEvents** in Microsoft Defender XDR. In Microsoft Sentinel, the equivalent data would be found in **SigninLogs**, but these are separate data sources and are not interchangeable. Advanced hunting queries in Microsoft Defender XDR cannot access Microsoft Sentinel tables such as SigninLogs, and Sentinel queries cannot access Defender Advanced Hunting tables; these data sources are not interchangeable.

In the exam, this decision is based on recognizing the type of activity being described and mapping it directly to the correct table. Endpoint activity, identity events, email activity, and alerts are not interchangeable, and each exist in its own context. Choosing the correct table is not about memorizing syntax or structure; it is about recognizing what type of activity is being examined and aligning the query to that source from the outset.

Advanced hunting schema and table structure

Behind every query in advanced hunting is a structured dataset that separates activity into distinct tables. This structure reflects how data is collected across the environment. Rather than combining all events into a single stream, Microsoft Defender XDR organizes telemetry by type, allowing each category of activity to be queried independently.

Each table represents a specific perspective of activity within the environment:

Table category	**What it represents**	**Example activity**
Device tables	Activity occurring on endpoints	Process execution, network connections
Identity tables	Authentication and access behavior	Sign-ins, account activity

Table category	What it represents	Example activity
Email tables	Message flow and communication activity	Email delivery, URLs, attachments
Alert tables	Detected security events	Alert metadata and associated evidence

Table 6.1 – Table activities in Microsoft Defender XDR

These are not interchangeable views of the same data. They are different slices of activity, each designed to answer a different type of question. Alert tables exist in their own context, representing detections that have already been generated. This structure enables targeted querying. When a query starts from the correct table, the data already aligns with the scenario being investigated. When it does not, the query becomes disconnected from the activity it is trying to analyze. In practice, understanding the role of each table is less about memorizing names and more about recognizing what kind of behavior each one represents.

Mapping investigation scenarios to tables

Once the structure of the data is understood, the next step is applying it to real scenarios. Every query begins with a question, which determines where the data should come from. For example, the question might be "*Which user signed in from an unfamiliar location?*" or "*Which process initiated this network connection?*", and each lead to a different data source. The task is not to think in terms of tables first, but to recognize the type of activity and align it with the correct source.

Each type of investigation aligns with a specific data source:

Investigation focus	Data source (table category)	What it captures
Process/device activity	Device tables	Process execution, device behavior
Authentication/ access	Identity tables	Sign-ins, account activity
Email investigation	Email tables	Message flow, URLs, attachments

Investigation focus	Data source (table category)	What it captures
Alerts/detections	Alert tables	Existing detections and alert context

Table 6.2 – Investigation and data source

Selecting the correct data source keeps the investigation grounded. When the activity and the data source are aligned, the query starts with relevant information and can be refined effectively. When they are not aligned, the query may still return results, but those results will not reflect the behavior being examined. This often results in plausible but incorrect answers, where the query logic is sound, but the starting point is wrong. For example, when investigating suspicious process execution on a device, starting with device tables ensures the query returns activity that directly reflects the behavior being examined.

Multi-table scope in advanced hunting

Not every investigation can be answered from a single source. Many scenarios involve activity that moves between users, devices, and services. This means the data needed to understand it is spread across multiple tables. Looking at only one table in these cases provides a partial view, often missing the connections that explain what actually happened.

Expanding the scope of a query allows those connections to come into focus. When data from different tables are considered together, relationships between events emerge. A sign-in can be linked to device activity, or a process can be associated with a user account. This broader view turns isolated events into something that can be understood as part of a larger pattern. At this stage, the goal is not to define how those tables are combined, but to recognize when a single data source is not enough. The moment a scenario involves more than one type of activity, the investigation must move beyond a single table. That shift in scope enables a complete view of the behavior being analyzed.

For instance, a compromised account may involve a suspicious sign-in (identity table), followed by process execution on a device (device table), and outbound communication (network activity). A single table cannot capture this sequence, making multi-table investigation necessary to understand the full attack path. In practice, this requires combining data across tables using joins so related activity can be analyzed together. For example:

- **Identity + Device activity:** Links a user sign-in to process execution on a device.

```
IdentityLogonEvents
| join kind=inner DeviceProcessEvents on AccountObjectId
```

- **Alerts + Evidence:** Expands an alert to show the associated users, devices, or files involved.

```
AlertInfo
| join kind=inner AlertEvidence on AlertId
```

Cloud application + Identity activity: Links cloud activity to the user account responsible for it.

```
CloudAppEvents
| join kind=inner IdentityLogonEvents on AccountObjectId
```

These joins are not about syntax complexity, but about recognizing which data sources must be combined to reflect the scenario being investigated. In the exam, this appears as selecting the correct tables and join logic to connect related activity across domains.

Identifying threats by using KQL

Once the correct data source is selected, the focus shifts from the data source to how it is examined. In Microsoft Defender XDR, this is done through **Kusto Query Language** (**KQL**), which provides the ability to search, filter, and analyze large volumes of telemetry. The goal is not to retrieve data, but to isolate activity that stands out from normal behavior.

The most important KQL operators define how data is filtered, shaped, and correlated during investigation:

- **where** – filters records to match a condition, such as a specific user, device, IP address, or timeframe
- **project** – selects only the columns needed for investigation
- **extend** – creates a calculated or derived column
- **summarize** – groups data to identify counts, trends, or repeated activity
- **count** – returns the number of matching records
- **dcount** – counts distinct values, such as unique devices or users

- **join** – combines related activity across tables
- **join kind=inner** – returns only matching records from both tables
- **join kind=leftouter** – keeps all records from the left table and adds matching records from the right table when available
- **parse** – extracts structured values from text
- **parse_json** – reads JSON-formatted data so nested fields can be queried
- **mv-expand** – expands multi-value fields into separate rows
- **let** – stores a reusable value or query fragment
- **bin()** – groups time values into intervals for trend analysis
- **in~** – performs case-insensitive matching against a set of values
- **has, contains, startswith** – search text fields using different matching behaviors

These definitions explain what each operator does. In the exam, the focus shifts to recognizing when each operator should be used.

In SC-200, KQL is tested by matching the operator to the investigation goal. The following operators are the most commonly tested:

Investigation goal	Operator	What it does
Filter specific activity	where	Reduces data to matching conditions (user, IP, time, device)
Select relevant fields	project	Returns only the required columns
Create new values	extend	Adds calculated or derived columns
Identify patterns/ trends	summarize	Groups data to show counts or trends
Count activity	count/dcount	Counts total or distinct values
Correlate activity across tables	join	Combines related data from multiple tables

Investigation goal	Operator	What it does
Control join results	join kind=inner/leftouter	Inner = matching only, Leftouter = keep all from left
Extract structured data	parse / parse_json	Pulls fields from text or JSON
Expand multi-value data	mv-expand	Splits arrays into separate rows
Reuse logic	let	Stores values or query parts
Analyze time patterns	bin()	Groups time into intervals
Match values (case-insensitive)	in~	Matches against a list, ignoring case
Search text fields	has/contains / startswith	Finds text patterns in different ways

Table 6.3 – Matching operator to investigation goal

In the exam, the correct answer is determined by matching the operator to the investigation goal, such as filtering (where), grouping (summarize), or correlating data across tables (join), not on writing a complex query.

At this stage, recognition becomes critical. Threats are identified by narrowing the dataset so only relevant activity remains. A broad query returns excessive data that hides meaningful signals, while a targeted query isolates patterns that reveal suspicious behavior. In the exam, this appears as choosing the query that applies specific filtering rather than one that returns all available data.

KQL does not define what is malicious on its own. Instead, it shapes data so that meaningful patterns can be identified. When the query aligns with the behavior being investigated, relevant signals become visible; when it does not, those signals are buried in the overall data volume.

Filtering and time scoping in KQL

Working with raw telemetry means starting with more data than can be reasonably interpreted. Filtering reduces that volume into something usable. By narrowing the dataset to only the activity that matches a specific condition, the query shifts from broad visibility to focused analysis.

Time plays an equally important role. Without a defined time range, a query can return results that are too large to process or include activity that is no longer relevant. Scoping the query to a specific period keeps the results aligned to the scenario being investigated and prevents unrelated data from diluting the outcome.

In practice, if an alert occurred within the last hour but the query is scoped to the past seven days, the results may include a large volume of unrelated activity. Narrowing the timeframe to match the alert ensures the query reflects the relevant activity and avoids unnecessary noise. Together, filtering and time scoping determine how much data is examined and how relevant that data is.

Aggregation and pattern detection

Filtering reduces the dataset to relevant activity, but it does not explain how that activity behaves over time or at scale. Aggregation turns individual events into patterns by grouping data and revealing how often something occurs. Instead of looking at isolated records, the focus shifts to trends, frequency, and repetition.

Patterns begin to emerge at this stage. Repeated sign-in attempts, multiple process executions, or a spike in activity within a short period are not always obvious when viewed as single events. When those events are grouped together, they form a shape that can indicate abnormal behavior. Aggregation makes that shape visible by summarizing activity into counts and trends that can be compared and evaluated.

Aggregation highlights what stands out by exposing how activity behaves over time. Normal activity tends to follow predictable patterns, while suspicious behavior often introduces irregularity. By grouping and summarizing data, aggregation exposes those irregularities, allowing them to be examined more closely. Without it, the investigation remains at the level of individual events, where patterns are easy to miss.

This becomes visible when activity is viewed as a pattern rather than as isolated events. For example, multiple failed sign-in attempts from the same account within a short period may appear insignificant individually, but when aggregated, they reveal a pattern that can indicate a brute-force attempt.

Correlation for threat identification

Some activity only becomes meaningful when it is viewed in relation to something else. A single event may appear normal on its own, but when it is connected to other activity, a pattern begins to form. Correlation brings those relationships together, linking events across users, devices, and services so that behavior can be understood in context.

This becomes especially important when activity spans more than one domain. A user signs in, a process runs on a device, and a connection is established elsewhere. Each of those actions exists in a different part of the data, but they are part of the same sequence. Correlation connects them, allowing the investigation to move from isolated events to a chain of related activity.

The value of correlation lies in its ability to reveal intent. While filtering and aggregation highlight what is happening, correlation shows how those actions are connected. When those connections are visible, it becomes possible to recognize patterns that indicate suspicious behavior. Without that linkage, important relationships remain hidden, and the investigation stays fragmented.

This becomes clear when a successful sign-in is followed by process execution and a network connection. Viewed together, these events show how activity initiated by the same user can span multiple systems and form a single sequence of behavior.

In the exam, aggregation (summarize) is used to identify patterns within a dataset, while correlation (join) is used to connect activity across multiple datasets.

Creating advanced hunting queries

Once suspicious activity has been identified, the next step is shaping that investigation into something repeatable. In Microsoft Defender XDR, this is done by building advanced hunting queries that go beyond one-off searches and consistently surface the same type of behavior when it appears again.

The focus moves from observing activity to defining how it should be found. The query expresses what matters in the data, using structure to isolate patterns such as repeated failed sign-ins, unusual process activity, or unexpected network connections that may indicate a threat. Rather than scanning results manually each time, the same logic can be reused consistently, ensuring that similar activity does not go unnoticed.

Query performance also plays a role in how results can be used effectively during an investigation. Queries that return excessive data or scan large time ranges may be slow or difficult to interpret, which can delay analysis. This is influenced by how data is ingested and available, as some tables may have ingestion latency, meaning recent activity might not appear immediately when investigating near real-time alerts. Performance can be improved by narrowing the scope of the query. Applying filters early, limiting the time range, and selecting only required fields reduce the volume of data processed and produce faster, more relevant results.

Query construction flow in advanced hunting

Building an effective query is not a random process. It follows a sequence that shapes how data is selected, reduced, and presented. That sequence begins with choosing the correct table, then narrowing the data to what is relevant, and finally shaping the output so the results can be interpreted. Each stage depends on the one before it and skipping or misordering them leads to results that are either incomplete or difficult to use.

The starting point defines the context of the query. From there, filtering reduces the dataset so only meaningful activity remains. Once that reduction is in place, the results are shaped to highlight what matters, removing unnecessary detail and focusing attention on the behavior being examined. This progression turns a large volume of raw data into something that can be analyzed with intent.

In practice, this flow keeps queries predictable and repeatable. When the sequence is followed, the output consistently reflects the scenario being investigated. When it is not, the query may still run, but the results will be harder to interpret or may not represent the intended activity. The structure of the query, therefore, makes it reliable, not just the logic within it.

This sequence is used to ensure queries reflect the intended activity and produce reliable results. The correct approach is to start with the appropriate table, apply filtering and time scoping, and then refine or summarize the results. Reversing this order leads to inefficient or incorrect queries.

For example, if the scenario is to identify devices making repeated connections to a suspicious IP address, the query would begin with a device-related table such as DeviceNetworkEvents. Filtering would then narrow the results to the specific IP address and timeframe of interest. Once reduced, the output can be shaped to highlight counts or repeated connections, making the pattern visible. Following this sequence ensures the results directly reflect the activity being investigated rather than returning unrelated network data.

Building multi-stage hunting queries

As investigations become more complex, a single step is rarely enough to expose meaningful behavior. Queries evolve into multi-stage structures, where each stage refines the data further and builds on the results of the previous step. Instead of returning raw activity, the query progressively shapes that activity into something that reflects the scenario being examined.

Layering allows different aspects of the data to be handled in sequence. Initial stages reduce the dataset, while later stages combine and relate activity across sources. By structuring the query in stages, it becomes possible to move from simple filtering to a more complete view of how events connect and interact. Each stage adds context, turning individual pieces of data into a cohesive pattern.

The result is a query that reflects the complexity of the activity being investigated. Rather than attempting to capture everything at once, the logic is applied step by step, making the output easier to interpret and more aligned with the investigation. This approach ensures that even complex scenarios can be broken down into manageable parts without losing the relationships between them.

Shaping query output for investigations

Once the data has been filtered and refined, the final step is deciding how that data is presented. Even when a query correctly identifies relevant activity, the results can still be difficult to interpret if they include too much detail or lack focus. Shaping the output ensures that what is returned is both readable and aligned to the investigation.

Narrowing the results to the information that actually matters ensures clarity. Rather than returning every available field, the query focuses on the key details that describe the behavior being examined. It can also limit the number of results so that patterns are visible without being lost in volume. The goal is not to reduce accuracy, but to remove unnecessary noise so the important signals stand out.

Effective analysis depends on shaping the output correctly. A well-shaped output allows the analyst to quickly understand what is happening and decide what to do next. Without that structure, even correct results can be difficult to interpret, slowing down the investigation and increasing the risk that important details are overlooked.

For example, after identifying network activity to a suspicious IP address, the initial results may include many fields and entries that are not relevant to the investigation. By selecting only key fields such as device name, remote IP, and connection count, and summarizing repeated connections, the output becomes easier to interpret. This allows patterns to stand out clearly, making it possible to quickly identify devices that are repeatedly communicating with the suspicious address.

Interpreting threat analytics in Microsoft Defender XDR

Not all insights come from querying raw data. In Microsoft Defender XDR, some of the most valuable information is already analyzed and presented as part of Threat Analytics. Instead of searching for activity, this shifts the focus to understanding threats that have already been identified and studied.

Threat analytics provides a different perspective. It provides curated intelligence about known threats and does not perform detection, querying, or alert generation. Rather than working through individual events, it brings together intelligence about active threats, showing how they operate and what impact they may have. It enables the analyst to move beyond isolated signals and see the broader context behind them.

A typical situation involves threat analytics highlighting an active phishing campaign targeting specific users. Instead of discovering these through queries, the analyst can use this insight to prioritize investigation of related alerts and focus on affected accounts. At this level, the goal is not to detect activity, but to interpret it. The information provided helps prioritize what matters, identify what is at risk, and understand how a threat fits into the wider environment. This makes it a complementary capability to hunting, offering insight that guides investigation rather than replacing it.

Purpose and scope of threat analytics

Threat analytics exist to provide a level of understanding that raw data alone cannot offer. Instead of presenting individual events, it brings together information about active threats and organizes it into a form that explains how those threats operate. This shifts the focus from searching for activity to understanding what has already been identified as significant.

The scope of this capability is defined by the type of insight it delivers. It focuses on known threats, campaigns, and techniques, presenting them in a way that highlights their relevance to the environment. This is not a collection of alerts or query results. It is a curated view that connects activity to a broader threat context, making it easier to understand what the activity represents.

This defines how the information is used. Threat analytics does not replace investigation or detection; it provides context that helps guide those processes, allowing decisions to be based on a clearer understanding of the threat rather than isolated observations.

Threat context and exposure analysis

Understanding a threat is not only about knowing that it exists, but also about seeing how it affects the environment. Threat analytics provides this by linking identified threats to the assets and activities they relate to. Instead of viewing a threat in isolation, it becomes possible to see where it has an impact and how it interacts with systems, users, and services.

This context turns abstract threat information into actionable insight. By identifying which assets are exposed and how they are involved, the analysis moves from general awareness to specific relevance. It highlights where attention should be focused, showing not just that a threat is present, but how it applies to the environment being monitored.

Exposure analysis also introduces a sense of priority. Not all threats carry the same level of risk, and not all assets are affected equally. By connecting threats to specific parts of the environment, it becomes possible to distinguish between what requires immediate attention and what can be addressed later. This allows investigations and responses to be guided by impact rather than assumption.

Mitigation guidance and prioritization

Once the impact of a threat is understood, the next step is deciding what should be done about it. Threat analytics provides guidance that translates insight into action by identifying recommended mitigation steps and highlighting their priority based on impact. This shifts the focus from understanding the threat to determining how it should be addressed.

The value of this guidance lies in how it prioritizes effort. Not every recommendation carries the same urgency, and not every threat requires immediate response. By linking suggested actions to the level of impact, threat analytics helps direct attention toward what matters most. It prevents resources from being spent on lower-risk issues, while more significant exposures remain unaddressed.

At this stage, the role of threat analytics is to inform decision-making rather than execute it. The guidance does not perform remediation on its own, but it provides a clear direction for what should happen next. It ensures that actions taken during investigation and response are based on an informed understanding of the threat, rather than reactive judgment.

Distinction from hunting and alerts

Threat analytics sits alongside other capabilities in Microsoft Defender XDR, but it serves a different purpose. Hunting focuses on searching raw data to uncover suspicious activity, while alerts represent detections that have already been triggered. Threat analytics does neither. Instead, it provides structured insight into known threats, explaining how they operate and why they matter.

This distinction defines how each capability is used. Hunting is exploratory, driven by questions about what might be happening in the environment. Alerts are reactive, signaling that something has already been detected. Threat analytics, by contrast, is interpretive. It does not search for activity or generate detections but helps make sense of threats that have already been identified.

Keeping these roles separate avoids confusion during investigation. When threat analytics is treated as a source of context rather than a detection mechanism, it becomes easier to understand how it complements the rest of the workflow. It informs decisions without replacing the need for hunting or alert-driven investigation, ensuring that each capability contributes its intended value.

Creating hunting graphs, including blast radius

Not all investigations are driven by queries. Once an alert or suspicious activity is identified, the focus shifts to understanding how that activity connects across the environment. In Microsoft Defender XDR, this is where graph-based investigation becomes valuable, providing a visual way to explore how entities involved in an incident are connected.

Instead of examining events one at a time, the graph presents activity as a set of connected elements that can be explored from a single starting point. *Figure 6.1* shows how graph-based investigation links related entities to reveal how activity is connected across an incident.

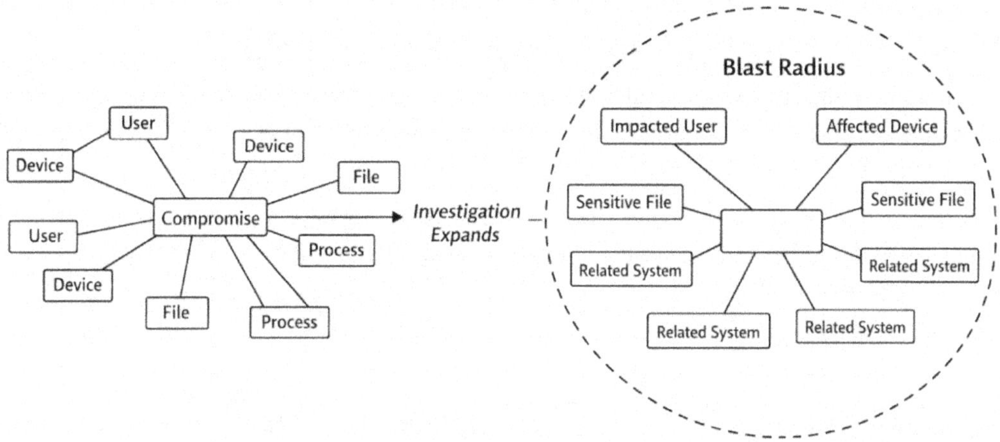

Figure 6.1 - Graph-based investigation showing relationships between entities involved in an incident

The graph expands outward from an initial entity to reveal related users, devices, processes, and network activity. By following these connections, the investigation moves from isolated events to a connected view of how the activity unfolded.

At this stage, the focus shifts to understanding scope. The blast radius represents how far the activity extends beyond the initial point of compromise, highlighting both directly affected and potentially affected entities. This allows the investigation to move beyond what happened and assess how far the impact reaches, providing the context needed to guide response and prioritization.

Graph-based investigation in Defender XDR

Graph-based investigation presents incident data in a way that reflects how activity is connected rather than how it was recorded. Instead of reviewing individual alerts or events in isolation, the investigation brings related entities together into a single view. This allows the analyst to see how users, devices, files, and processes relate to each other within the context of an incident.

The approach changes how information is interpreted. When entities are connected visually, relationships that would otherwise require manual tracing become immediately visible. An action on one system can be seen alongside the account that initiated it, or a file can be viewed in relation to the device where it appeared. The structure of the graph makes these connections explicit, reducing the effort required to understand how activity is linked.

The result is a more cohesive view of the incident. Rather than piecing together separate records, the investigation unfolds as a set of connected elements that can be explored in context. This allows the analyst to move through the activity with a clearer understanding of how each part contributes to the overall behavior being examined.

Expanding investigations from an alert or entity

Graph-based investigation is not static. It begins from a specific point such as an alert, a user, or a device, and then expands outward to reveal related activity. This starting point anchors the investigation, providing a reference from which connections can be explored.

From there, the investigation moves by following those connections. Each linked entity introduces additional context, showing how activity spreads within the same incident. A user account can lead to a device, that device to a process, and that process to further actions. That progression allows the analyst to move through the activity without losing sight of how each element is related to the original event.

The value of this expansion lies in maintaining context. As the investigation grows, it remains tied to the initial alert or entity, ensuring that the analysis stays focused on the incident being examined. This prevents unrelated activity from being introduced and keeps the investigation aligned with the behavior that triggered it.

Understanding blast radius

As an investigation expands, it becomes necessary to understand not just what is connected, but how far the activity may have spread. Blast radius provides that view by showing the extent of impact from the original point of compromise. It highlights which entities are directly involved and which may be affected as the activity continues to propagate.

This perspective shifts the investigation from connections to scope. Instead of focusing only on relationships, the emphasis shifts to reach and impact. A single compromised account, for example, may lead to multiple devices or additional actions that extend beyond the initial event. Blast radius makes that expansion visible, helping to identify how wide the activity extends within the environment.

A common scenario is when a compromised user account accesses multiple devices; the blast radius view will show all affected systems. It helps determine whether the incident is limited to a single device or has spread across the environment.

The purpose of this view is to support decision-making. By understanding how far the activity reaches, it becomes possible to assess the severity of the incident and determine where attention should be focused. Without this context, it is easy to underestimate the impact or overlook affected systems. With it, the investigation can account for both the initial compromise and its broader consequences.

Investigation context of Defender graphs

Graph views in Microsoft Defender XDR are designed to support investigation within the boundaries of a single incident. The relationships they display are built around the alert or activity that initiated the investigation, keeping all connected entities tied to that context. This ensures that what is being analyzed remains relevant to the case at hand.

This context acts as both a constraint and a guide. While the graph can expand to include multiple related entities, those connections remain limited to activity associated with the incident, allowing the investigation to stay focused without introducing unrelated data from elsewhere in the environment. Understanding this boundary is important when interpreting results. The graph provides a detailed view of relationships within an incident, but it is not intended to represent all possible connections across the entire environment. Its value lies in maintaining clarity and relevance, ensuring that the investigation stays aligned with the activity being examined.

Within this investigation context, additional views and tools provide different perspectives on the same incident:

- The **device timeline** shows activity on a specific endpoint in chronological order, allowing process execution, network connections, and file activity to be traced over time. The **user timeline** provides a similar view focused on account activity, showing sign-ins and actions associated with a user.
- The **evidence list** aggregates all entities linked to the alert, including users, devices, files, and IP addresses, providing a structured view of what is involved. The **alert story** presents a summarized narrative of the incident, highlighting how the activity progressed and which entities were affected.
- An **investigation package** allows the collected evidence and context to be exported, supporting further analysis or sharing with other teams.
- **Live response** enables direct interaction with an affected device, allowing actions such as collecting forensic data or running commands as part of the investigation.

These capabilities complement the graph view by providing additional ways to explore, validate, and act on the relationships identified within the incident.

Analyzing relationships between entities using Sentinel Graph

Some investigations extend beyond the boundaries of a single incident. Activity may span multiple systems, timeframes, or data sources, making it difficult to understand using isolated views. In Microsoft Sentinel, this is addressed through Sentinel Graph, which focuses on analyzing how entities relate across the broader environment.

Instead of being tied to a single alert or case, Sentinel Graph connects data from different sources into a unified structure. This allows relationships between users, devices, and other entities to be examined at a wider scope. The focus shifts from incident-level understanding to how activity is linked across datasets, providing a more complete picture of how behavior unfolds over time.

At this level, the goal is to understand relationships at scale. Rather than following activity within one investigation, Sentinel Graph enables analysis of how entities interact across the environment. It helps reveal patterns and connections that are not visible when data is viewed in isolation, supporting a deeper understanding of how activity is related. Consider a case where Sentinel Graph can show how a user account is linked to multiple devices and IP addresses over time, allowing the analyst to trace activity across datasets without manually correlating each event.

Figure 6.2 shows how Sentinel Graph expands an investigation beyond a single data source into a broader view of related entities across the environment.

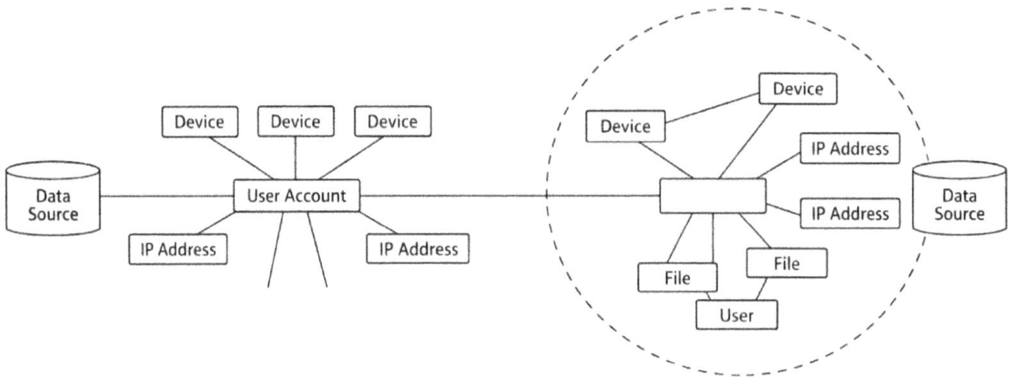

Figure 6.2 - Sentinel Graph showing relationships across users, devices, and IP addresses

On the left, activity is viewed from a single data source, where a user account is linked to a limited set of devices and IP addresses. This represents an isolated view of the data, constrained to one context. On the right, Sentinel Graph expands this view by connecting additional entities across datasets, bringing together devices, files, users, and network activity into a unified structure. This broader perspective makes it possible to trace how activity spans systems and evolves over time, revealing patterns that are not visible when events are examined in isolation.

Sentinel Graph data model and scope

Sentinel Graph represents security data by focusing on entities and the relationships between them, rather than individual events. Users, devices, and other elements are connected based on their interactions, allowing activity to be understood as a set of related behaviors rather than isolated records.

This approach expands the scope of analysis beyond a single incident, bringing together data from multiple sources so connections can be explored across the environment. Activity that appears unrelated in isolation can be linked through this model, revealing how different elements interact over time.

Relationship and attack chain modeling across datasets

When data is connected across multiple sources, individual events begin to form sequences rather than isolated points. Sentinel Graph makes this possible by linking entities in a way that reveals how activity progresses from one stage to another.

This is where attack chains become visible. A single action may appear insignificant on its own, but when connected to other activity, it forms part of a larger sequence. By modeling these relationships, it becomes possible to trace how an initial event leads to subsequent behavior across different parts of the environment. This provides a structured way to understand how activity unfolds beyond a single dataset. This allows investigations to move beyond isolated events and follow how activity unfolds as a connected sequence across the environment.

Cross-dataset investigation using Sentinel Graph

When investigations extend beyond a single source of data, Sentinel Graph provides a way to analyze relationships across datasets in a single connected view. Unlike Defender graphs, which are limited to the context of one incident, Sentinel Graph connects activity across the environment, allowing analysts to pivot between users, devices, and related activity without switching between separate queries or tools.

For example, a user sign-in can be connected to multiple devices, those devices to network activity, and that activity to further actions elsewhere in the environment, forming a continuous chain of related activity. In the exam, Sentinel Graph is used when the scenario requires correlating activity across multiple data sources or understanding relationships beyond a single incident. Tools such as Graph Explorer enable these relationships to be explored interactively within the graph.

Summary

This chapter focused on how to move from an alert to the underlying data by selecting the correct starting point and applying the appropriate query approach. Identifying the correct table in Advanced Hunting is critical, as it determines whether the data reflects the activity being investigated or produces misleading results.

You saw how filtering and time scoping reduce data to a relevant subset, while aggregation and correlation expose patterns and relationships that are not visible in isolated events. These techniques allow activity to be interpreted as behavior rather than raw data.

The chapter also emphasized how threat analytics provides context and prioritization, and how graph-based investigation in Defender XDR and Sentinel helps visualize relationships and assess the blast radius of an incident. Together, these concepts ensure that investigations remain aligned to the scenario, produce meaningful results, and avoid incorrect conclusions.

In the next chapter, you will build on these concepts by focusing on how detections are created and tuned in Microsoft Sentinel, exploring how analytics rules are used to identify suspicious activity and generate alerts that feed into the investigation process.

Exam Readiness Drill – Chapter Review Questions

Apart from mastering key concepts, strong test-taking skills under time pressure are essential for acing your certification exam. That's why developing these abilities early in your learning journey is critical.

Exam readiness drills, using the free online practice resources provided with this book, help you progressively improve your time management and test-taking skills while reinforcing the key concepts you've learned.

HOW TO GET STARTED

- Open the link or scan the QR code at the bottom of this page
- If you have unlocked the practice resources already, log in to your registered account. If you haven't, follow the instructions in *Free Benefits with Your Book* section in this book's *Preface* and come back to this page.
- Once you log in, click the START button to start this chapter's quiz

- We recommend attempting a quiz multiple times till you're able to answer most of the questions correctly and well within the time limit.
- You can use the following practice template to help you plan your attempts:

Working On Accuracy		
Attempt	**Target**	**Time Limit**
Attempt 1	40% or more	Till the timer runs out
Attempt 2	60% or more	Till the timer runs out
Attempt 3	75% or more	Till the timer runs out
Working On Timing		
Attempt 4	75% or more	1 minute before time limit
Attempt 5	75% or more	2 minutes before time limit
Attempt 6	75% or more	3 minutes before time limit

The above drill is just an example. Design your drills based on your own goals and make the most out of the online quizzes accompanying this book.

Link to this Chapter's Quiz

You need to unlock the online practice resources to access the link below. Check the *Free Benefits with Your Book* section in the *Preface* for detailed instructions on how to do this. You only need to unlock the resources once.

Open Quiz `https://packt.link/sc200js-ch6` or scan the QR code

7

Detect Threats by Using the Microsoft Sentinel Platform

At this stage, you are already working with detections and investigations. This chapter moves into how analysts actively search through Microsoft Sentinel data, work with larger or older datasets, and use advanced analysis methods when standard queries are not enough.

This chapter focuses on detecting threats by using Microsoft Sentinel. It aligns with the SC-200 exam objectives and addresses the following Skills Measured:

- Create and monitor hunting queries.
- Create and manage KQL jobs in data lake.
- Create and manage Summary rule tables for querying.
- Hunt for threats using Notebooks, including connection to Microsoft Sentinel MCP Server.

By the end of this chapter, you will be able to explain how Microsoft Sentinel hunting queries support manual threat exploration, how Search Jobs are used to query larger or older datasets in the data lake, and how summary rules improve performance when repeated analysis is required. You will also be able to distinguish when to use notebooks for multi-step investigation, enrichment, visualization, and deeper analysis that cannot be completed with a single query.

Create and monitor hunting queries

A hunting query is a KQL query that an analyst runs manually in Microsoft Sentinel to search collected data for suspicious behavior that has not necessarily generated an alert. Unlike an analytics rule, a hunting query does not run continuously or create alerts by itself. It is used to explore data, test a suspicion, and decide whether the returned activity needs further investigation.

This approach is most useful when a threat is subtle, emerging, or not yet covered by an existing detection rule. A subtle threat might involve repeated failed sign-ins followed by a successful sign-in from an unusual location. An emerging threat might involve a newly reported command line, domain, IP address, or file hash that analysts want to search for across recent telemetry before a formal analytic rule has been created.

For example, an analyst may suspect credential misuse but see no alerts. A hunting query can then be used to search for sign-ins from unusual locations, impossible travel indicators, repeated failures, or successful access from unfamiliar IP addresses.

> **Tip**
>
> The exam distinction is important: use a hunting query when the requirement is manual investigation or hypothesis testing; use an analytics rule when the requirement is continuous detection and alert generation.

Hunting queries and the Sentinel hunting workflow

The Sentinel Hunting blade uses KQL in the same way as the Logs blade, but the workflow is different. A Logs query is often used to retrieve or troubleshoot known data, such as checking sign-in events for a specific user during a defined time range. A hunting query uses similar query logic for a different purpose, which is to investigate whether the data contains suspicious behavior that has not already generated an alert.

For example, an analyst may use the Logs blade to confirm whether a user signed in yesterday. The same analyst may use a hunting query to look for a wider pattern, such as repeated failed sign-ins followed by successful access from an unfamiliar location across multiple users. The first task retrieves known activity; the second tests whether the activity suggests a threat.

This workflow remains analyst-led. The analyst runs the query, reviews the results, bookmarks important findings where needed, and decides whether the activity should be investigated further, converted into an analytics rule, or linked to an incident.

Data sources for hunting queries (Log Analytics tables)

Hunting queries can only return results from data that has been ingested into the Microsoft Sentinel workspace. The query must target the correct Log Analytics table for the type of evidence being investigated. If the required connector is not enabled, the table is empty, or the data has aged beyond the configured retention period, the query may return no results even when suspicious activity has occurred.

This is important because a failed or empty hunting query does not always mean the threat is absent. It may mean the required data was never collected, the wrong table was queried, or the relevant events are no longer retained. For example, a query looking for process execution cannot return useful results if endpoint telemetry has not been onboarded. In that case, the problem is a data coverage gap, not a query logic problem.

The same rule applies when selecting tables. A sign-in investigation should target identity-related tables, while a process execution investigation should target endpoint-related tables. Choosing the wrong table can produce incomplete or misleading results because the query is searching the wrong evidence source.

> **Tip**
>
> For exam purposes, treat hunting queries as dependent on three things:
>
> - The data connector must be enabled,
> - The data must still be retained,
> - The query must target the correct table.
>
> If any of these are missing, the hunting query may not return the evidence needed for the investigation, even if suspicious activity occurred.

Hunting queries vs analytics rules vs log queries

The key distinction is between querying data, manually investigating suspicious behavior, and automating detection. Analytics rules run automatically based on their execution model and generate alerts when defined conditions are met. Hunting queries do not run automatically or generate alerts by themselves. They rely on the analyst to execute the query, interpret the results, and decide whether the activity is significant.

A typical exam scenario may describe a requirement to investigate suspicious activity that is not generating alerts. In this case, a hunting query is the correct choice because the task is exploratory. If the requirement is to continuously monitor for the same condition and generate alerts, an analytics rule is required. Use the Logs blade when the requirement is simply to query or troubleshoot data without a threat-hunting workflow. Use a hunting query when the requirement is manual investigation or hypothesis testing. Use an analytics rule when the requirement is automated detection and alert generation.

Saving and reusing hunting queries

Hunting queries do not always need to be written from a blank query window. Microsoft Sentinel includes built-in hunting queries and templates that provide starting logic for common threat behaviors. Using the template you can review existing query logic, modify the KQL for the environment, and adjust filters such as time range, user, IP address, device, or event type.

Once a query is useful, it can be saved and reused during later investigations. Saving the query preserves the hunting logic so the analyst can run it again as new data is ingested, compare results over time, and apply the same investigation method consistently across similar incidents.

The following figure shows the Microsoft Sentinel Hunting queries page in the Microsoft Defender portal. You can go to **Microsoft Sentinel |Hunting | Queries** and review built-in hunting queries, inspect query logic, and reuse query patterns during investigations.

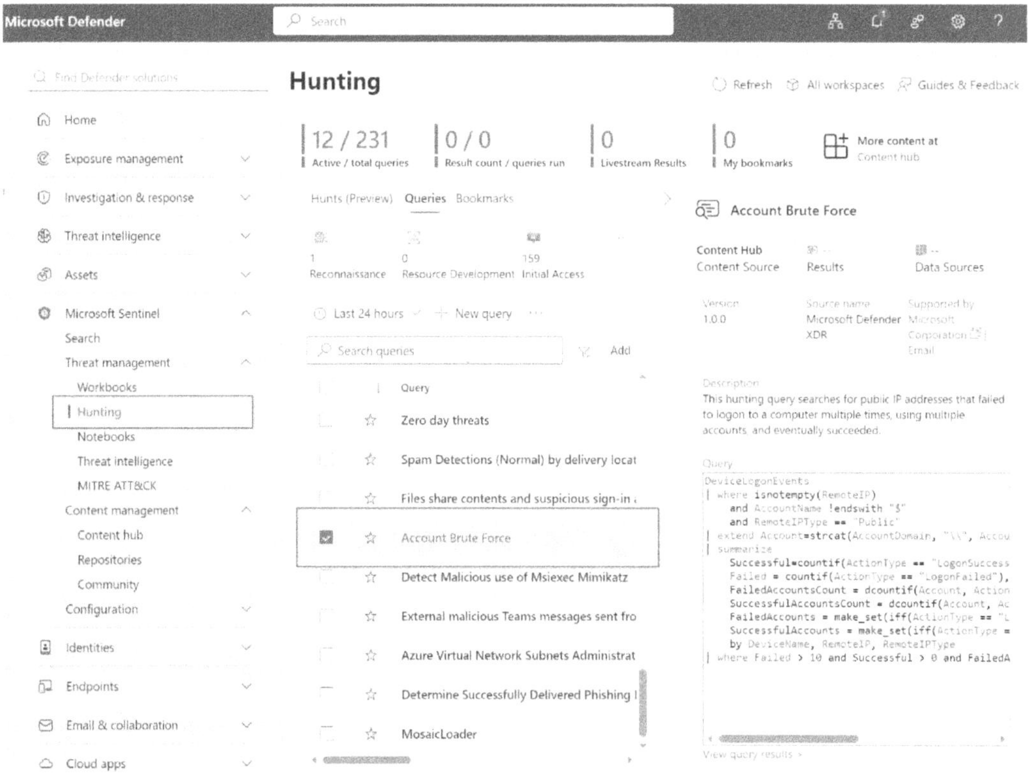

Figure 7.1 – Reviewing and reusing Microsoft Sentinel hunting queries in the Microsoft Defender portal

A saved hunting query remains analyst-led; it does not automatically generate alerts. If the same logic needs to run continuously and create alerts when matches are found, the query logic should be reused in an analytics rule.

Tip

Key exam distinction: save a hunting query when the requirement is reusable manual investigation; use an analytics rule when the requirement is automated detection and alert generation.

This workflow supports reusable manual investigation. If the same logic must run continuously and generate alerts, it should be implemented through an analytics rule instead.

Using bookmarks in hunting investigations

Not every hunting result needs to be retained, but some findings are significant enough to become part of the investigation record. You can create bookmarks from hunting query results in Microsoft Sentinel, to save selected results so that important evidence can be preserved without rerunning the query and locating the same result again.

A bookmark can capture the query result, relevant entities, notes, and investigation context. When the finding is related to an active incident, the bookmark can be associated with that incident so the evidence remains connected to the wider investigation. This is useful when a hunting query identifies activity that was not part of the original alert but still helps explain the incident.

Bookmarks also support visual investigation. When entity mappings are included, bookmarked results can appear as separate nodes in the investigation graph, helping you see how users, devices, IP addresses, or other entities relate to the incident. This turns a query result into linked investigation evidence rather than leaving it as an isolated row in a result set.

From a case management perspective, bookmarks help analysts retain evidence, document why a result matters, and keep investigation context available for later review. They do not generate alerts or perform detection by themselves. Their role is to preserve important findings, link those findings to incidents where appropriate, and support a more complete investigation record.

Create and manage KQL jobs in data lake

Not all investigations can be completed using recent or readily accessible data. In Microsoft Sentinel, older or high-volume data is moved into the data lake tier. This tier is not designed for interactive querying and must be accessed using search jobs.

Search jobs are submitted to process large volumes of archived data rather than running queries directly against the analytics tier. They prioritize scale and historical reach over immediate, interactive results and are used when the investigation needs to retrieve data across extended time ranges or large datasets that are not practical to query directly in the analytics tier.

For instance, if an investigation requires reviewing activity from six months ago, the data will likely reside in the data lake tier. In this case, a search job must be used, as standard log queries cannot access that data interactively.

Here, the goal is access rather than speed. Search jobs provide a way to reach data that would be impractical to query interactively, especially when the time range is large or the dataset is substantial. For the exam, you can determine the correct answer by whether the requirement is fast investigation of current data or deeper analysis across retained historical data.

Data lake tier and archived data in Sentinel

Data in the analytics tier is kept in a hot, interactive state for high-performance queries, hunting, analytics rules, workbooks, and near-real-time investigation. Data in the Data lake tier is kept in a colder, lower-cost state for long-term retention and larger historical analysis, but it is not queried in the same interactive way.

Table 7.1 compares the analytics tier and data lake in Microsoft Sentinel:

Area	Analytics tier	Data lake tier
Access model	Hot, interactive access	Cold, non-interactive access
Main purpose	Fast investigation, hunting, analytics rules, and workbooks	Long-term retention, large-scale analysis, and historical retrieval
Query experience	Standard KQL queries return results interactively	KQL/Search Jobs process data in the background
Result speed	Immediate or near-immediate	Delayed until the job is complete
Cost model	Higher-cost tier for active analytics and faster access	Lower-cost tier for longer retention and larger data volumes
Retention role	Used for recent operational security data	Used when data must be retained beyond active analytics needs
Archived/historical data	Not the primary target for long-term historical retrieval	Used to retain and retrieve older or high-volume data for investigations

Table 7.1: Analytics tier and data lake tier comparison in Microsoft Sentinel

Data movement between the analytics tier and data lake tier is controlled by retention and tier configuration; you cannot do this by manually copying records between locations.

KQL jobs can process data lake data and promote the job results into the analytics tier so analysts can continue working with the returned dataset using standard KQL. Operational data is queried interactively while it remains in the analytics tier, retained historical data is accessed through the data lake tier, and job results can be promoted back into the analytics tier for further analysis.

Search jobs vs. standard log queries

Search jobs and standard log queries both use KQL, but they are used for different investigation needs. Standard log queries are used when analysts need immediate, interactive results from data in the analytics tier. Search jobs are used when the investigation needs to retrieve large or historical datasets from the data lake tier, where results are processed in the background. *Table 7.2* compares standard log queries and search jobs in Sentinel:

Area	Standard log query	Search Job
Query mode	Interactive	Background processing
Result timing	Immediate or near-immediate	Delayed until the job completes
Data location	Analytics tier	data lake tier
Best used for	Fast investigation of recent data	Large-scale or historical retrieval
Analyst workflow	Adjust query and review results in real time	Submit job, wait for completion, then query the results table
Exam decision point	Choose when the scenario needs fast, interactive analysis	Choose when the scenario needs older, larger, or retained historical data

Table 7.2: Standard log queries and Search Jobs comparison in Microsoft Sentinel

The table shows that the difference is not the query language, but the execution model and data location. A standard log query supports fast, iterative investigation, while a Search Job supports delayed retrieval from the data lake when the dataset is too large, older, or retained for historical analysis.

Tip

Use a standard log query when the analyst needs immediate results from recent data. Use a Search Job when the requirement is large-scale or historical analysis from the data lake.

Execution model of search jobs (asynchronous processing)

Search Jobs do not execute in the same way as standard log queries. Standard queries are designed for interactive investigation, where results are returned quickly and you can refine the query in real time. Search Jobs are used for larger or historical datasets in the data lake tier, so the query is submitted as a background job rather than executed as an immediate interactive query.

This asynchronous model changes how the investigation is handled. You define the query, set the time range, submit the job, and then track its status until processing completes. Only after the job has finished can the output be reviewed reliably. If you attempt to use the results too early, the output may be missing, incomplete, or unavailable. *Table 7.3* presents some common search job properties and what they are used for:

Properties	Description
Start time and end time	The time range searched by the job
Search query	The KQL or search logic submitted for processing
Search Job ID	The identifier used to track the submitted job
Search job status	The current state of the job, such as running, completed, or failed
Search job results	Results returned by the completed search job for later review and analysis
Search job errors	Any issue that prevents the job from completing or returning usable results

Table 7.3 – Common Search Job properties in Microsoft Sentinel

The reason for this model is scale. Large time ranges and high data volumes are not suited to immediate query execution in the analytics tier. By processing the request in the background,

Microsoft Sentinel can retrieve data that would otherwise be impractical to query interactively. The trade-off is that Search Jobs provide reach and scale, but not instant results.

> **Note**
>
> For exam purposes, the key point is that a Search Job is a managed background process. The analyst must define the query and time range, monitor the job status, and review the results only after completion. Use a Search Job when the requirement is historical or large-scale retrieval from the data lake, not when the requirement is immediate interactive investigation.

Search job results and results tables

When a search job completes, the results are not returned directly to the query interface. Instead, the output is written to a new table within the workspace. This separates the execution of the query from the analysis of the results, creating a two-step process where data is first retrieved and then queried again.

A typical situation involves analysts repeatedly querying failed sign-in counts per user. A summary rule can pre-calculate these values and store them in a table, allowing future queries to return results instantly instead of recalculating the same aggregation each time.

This behavior is different from standard queries, where results are immediately visible and can be refined interactively. With search jobs, the initial operation focuses on extracting the data from the data lake tier. Once complete, the resulting table becomes the dataset that can be queried using standard KQL. This allows the analyst to work with the results in a more familiar and responsive way after the heavy processing has finished.

The result table, therefore, acts as a bridge between large-scale data retrieval and interactive analysis. It allows historical data to be brought into a form that can be explored without repeating the original search job. This separation is essential when working with large datasets, ensuring that complex retrieval operations are performed once, while analysis can be performed multiple times on the resulting data.

Managing the search job lifecycle

Search jobs are not single-step operations. Because they run asynchronously and operate on large datasets, they follow a defined lifecycle that must be managed from submission through to completion. Once a job is created, it enters a processing state where the data is scanned, and the results are prepared in the background.

Search jobs depend on job status before results can be used. Unlike standard queries, where results are immediately available, a search job must finish processing before its output can be queried reliably. Attempting to query the output before the job has completed may return no data or incomplete results, which can lead to incorrect conclusions during an investigation.

Managing the lifecycle ensures that the results are reliable and ready for analysis. It also involves tracking the job until completion and then working with the generated results table. This separation between execution and validation is necessary when dealing with large-scale data retrieval, where the timing of the results is as important as the query itself.

Create and manage summary rule tables for querying

As data volumes grow, repeatedly querying raw datasets becomes inefficient. In Microsoft Sentinel, summary rules help you optimize this process by transforming large volumes of raw data into smaller, pre-aggregated datasets that are easier to query. Instead of processing the same data repeatedly, the work is performed in advance and stored for reuse. Instead of scanning raw datasets each time, you query the pre-aggregated summary table. Since the required aggregations are calculated in advance and stored in a separate table, queries operate on a dataset that has been reduced by volume and already contains the necessary results. Therefore, queries that would otherwise require significant compute and time can return results quicker because the heavy processing has already been completed. This improves performance, particularly in environments where the same patterns are analyzed frequently, and where reprocessing raw data each time would be inefficient.

For instance, instead of you repeatedly querying failed sign-in counts per user, a summary rule can help you pre-calculate these values and store them in a table, allowing future queries to return results instantly instead of recalculating the same aggregation each time.

At this level, the focus is not on accessing more data, but on making existing data more efficient to use. Summary rules move processing effort away from query time and into scheduled preparation by providing an optimized layer that supports faster querying. This separates performance optimization from data retrieval, ensuring that the correct approach is used depending on the requirement.

Summary rules vs. search jobs vs. standard queries

Summary rules, search Jobs, standard log queries, hunting queries, analytics rules, and notebooks all use or interact with Sentinel data, but they serve different purposes. The key exam skill is selecting the correct capability based on the requirement. Remember the following:

- Standard log queries run directly against data in the analytics tier, providing immediate results and supporting interactive investigation.

- Search Jobs retrieve larger or historical datasets from the data lake tier when interactive querying is not practical.
- Summary rules improve performance for repeated analysis by pre-aggregating results into summary tables.
- Hunting queries support analyst-led investigation when suspicious activity has not generated an alert. Analytics rules are used when the same logic must run continuously and generate alerts.
- Notebooks extend investigation when analysis requires multiple steps, enrichment, visualization, or dataframe-based work.

Table 7.4 summarizes common requirements and the Sentinel feature best suited to each scenario:

Requirement	**Choose**	**Why**
Query recent data interactively	Standard log query	Used for direct KQL investigation and troubleshooting in the analytics tier
Manually investigate suspicious activity that has not generated an alert	Hunting query	Used for analyst-led threat hunting and hypothesis testing
Continuously detect a condition and generate alerts	Analytics rule	Used for automated detection and alert generation
Retrieve older, larger, or retained historical data	Search Job	Used to query data Lake data through background processing
Improve performance for repeated analyses	Summary rule	Used to pre-aggregate data into summary tables
Perform multi-step analysis, enrichment, or visualization	Notebook	Used when an investigation requires more than a single query

Table 7.4 – Choosing the correct Microsoft Sentinel query and investigation capability

This comparison is commonly tested in the exam as tool selection. Use standard log queries for immediate interactive investigation, hunting queries for manual threat hunting, analytics rules for automated alerting, Search Jobs for historical or large-scale data lake retrieval, summary rules for repeated-query optimization, and notebooks for deeper analytical workflows.

Summary tables and preprocessed data

When a summary rule runs, it writes aggregated results to a summary table rather than returning raw events. The summary table contains pre-processed data based on the rule logic, such as counts, groupings, distinct counts, sums, averages, or time-based summaries. This allows repeated queries to use prepared results instead of scanning the original source tables each time. *Table 7.5* compares summary tables with raw data tables:

Area	Summary table	Raw data table
Data type	Aggregated and preprocessed results	Full event-level records
Main purpose	Faster repeated analysis	Detailed investigation
Performance	Faster because the aggregation has already been calculated	Slower when large volumes of raw data must be scanned
Detail level	Lower detail because events are summarized	Full detail because individual events remain available
Best used when	The same calculation or pattern is queried repeatedly	The analyst needs to inspect the original events
Investigation trade-off	Improves speed but may hide event-level details	Provides detail but may require more processing

Table 7.5 – Summary tables and raw data comparison in Microsoft Sentinel

Summary tables and raw tables work together. The summary table supports faster analysis when the same pattern is queried repeatedly, while the raw table remains available when the analyst needs full event-level detail. Moving between summary tables and raw tables allows investigations to balance performance with depth, depending on what the situation requires.

Tip

Key exam point: use summary tables for repeated-query efficiency, and use raw data when the investigation requires the original events.

Scheduling and data freshness in summary rules

Summary rules operate on a defined schedule, which determines how often the aggregated data is refreshed. Each execution processes new data from the source tables and updates the summary table with the latest results. This means the data in the summary table reflects the most recent run of the rule, not the current state of the raw data in real time.

A summary rule is created by defining the source query, choosing the aggregation logic, setting the schedule, and specifying the summary table that will store the output. The query can use aggregation functions such as **count**, **dcount**, **sum**, or **avg** to reduce raw events into calculated results. The summary table should be named clearly enough to show what it contains, such as failed sign-in counts by user or high-volume network activity by source IP. This naming matters because analysts query the summary table later, often without returning to the original rule definition.

This creates a trade-off between performance and freshness. Running the rule more frequently keeps the summary data closer to real time but increases processing overhead. Running it less frequently improves efficiency but creates a gap between the latest raw data and what is available in the summary table. The schedule, therefore, defines how current the summarized data will be when queried.

> **Note**
>
> Understanding this timing is important when interpreting results. Queries against summary tables return the most recently processed data, which may not include the latest events if they occurred after the last execution. This means the summary table is optimized for efficiency, but not for real-time visibility, and the timing of updates must be considered during analysis.

Hunt for threats using notebooks, including connection to Microsoft Sentinel MCP Server

Some investigations require more than structured queries and tabular results. When analysis becomes more complex—spanning multiple datasets, requiring transformation, or involving deeper exploration—Microsoft Sentinel provides notebooks as an advanced investigation environment. Notebooks extend beyond the capabilities of standard KQL queries by allowing data to be processed, enriched, and analyzed more flexibly.

Instead of running a single query and interpreting the results, notebooks allow multiple steps to be combined into a single workflow, building a chain of analysis that can incorporate additional data sources and techniques. This is particularly useful when relationships between datasets need to be explored or when patterns are not immediately visible through standard queries. For example, an analyst investigating a complex incident may use a notebook to combine sign-in data, device activity, and external threat intelligence, applying multiple steps of analysis to understand how the activity evolved across the environment.

At this level, the goal is not just to retrieve data, but to work with it. Notebooks enable a deeper form of analysis that supports complex investigations, where queries alone are not sufficient. Additionally, by connecting to the Sentinel MCP Server, notebooks also allow Sentinel data to be accessed within this environment, extending analysis beyond the limits of the Sentinel interface.

Notebooks vs KQL queries and hunting queries

Notebooks, KQL queries, and hunting queries all operate on the same underlying data, but they differ in how that data is accessed and used during an investigation. KQL queries return a defined result set from a specific dataset, and hunting queries use that same query capability but place it within an investigation workflow, where the analyst manually explores activity and interprets the results. Notebooks allow analysis to be built as a sequence of steps, where data is retrieved, transformed, and re-used across multiple stages of investigation.

With KQL alone, each query produces an output that must be redefined if further analysis is needed. In notebooks, the same dataset can be refined repeatedly, allowing multiple operations to be applied without starting from the original query each time. This enables more complex workflows where intermediate results are used to drive further analysis. Use cases include scenarios where data must be combined, enriched, or analyzed in stages. Instead of returning a single result, notebooks support a structured analytical process that allows investigations to evolve step by step.

Choosing between them depends on whether the task requires a single query result, iterative exploration, or multi-stage analysis. A simple investigation that can be completed with a single query should use KQL, while a more complex scenario requiring multiple stages of analysis or data enrichment should use notebooks.

Data enrichment and visualization in notebooks

Notebooks extend analysis beyond querying by allowing data to be enriched and visualized as part of the investigation process. While KQL queries return structured results, they do not modify or expand the data beyond what is already stored. Notebooks allow additional context to be introduced, enabling data from different sources to be combined and analyzed together.

This changes how patterns are identified. In tabular query results, relationships between data points may not be immediately visible. By applying transformations and visual representations, notebooks make it possible to highlight trends, group related activity, and expose connections that would be difficult to detect through raw query output alone.

Enrichment also allows investigations to incorporate external or derived data, providing additional context that is not present in the original dataset. This enables a broader analysis, where activity can be examined alongside supplementary information. For instance, a notebook can retrieve data from Microsoft Sentinel, enrich IP addresses with geolocation information, compare file hashes against threat intelligence feeds, or correlate user activity across multiple datasets. The result is a more complete view of the data, supporting deeper investigation when standard query results are not sufficient.

Sentinel MCP Server integration

Notebooks are useful when a Sentinel investigation requires more than a single query result. In MCP-enabled workflows, the Microsoft Sentinel MCP Server provides controlled access to Sentinel data through MCP-compatible clients and AI-assisted tools. Access is permission-aware, so the signed-in identity or client must have the required roles to list and invoke the relevant Sentinel MCP tools and access the underlying Sentinel data.

After access is established, the workflow can retrieve Sentinel data for investigation by using available MCP tools or KQL-based query logic, depending on the notebook and client environment. The query defines what data is needed, such as sign-in activity, device events, or alert-related records. The retrieved result can then become part of a broader notebook workflow rather than being manually exported from Sentinel and handled separately.

Returned results can also be loaded into dataframes for further analysis. A dataframe allows the analyst to filter, transform, enrich, group, and visualize data across multiple steps. This is where notebooks differ from a single KQL query: the query or tool call retrieves the data, while the notebook lets the analyst reuse and reshape that data through a longer investigation workflow.

For example, an analyst could retrieve sign-in activity, load the results into a dataframe, enrich the data with device or threat intelligence context, and compare the output with other investigation evidence. This supports investigations where one query is not enough and where the analyst needs to combine, transform, and visualize data over several steps.

The key point is that MCP Server integration provides controlled access to Sentinel data for supported AI-assisted workflows; KQL or MCP tools retrieve the investigation data; and dataframes allow the returned results to be analyzed inside the notebook.

When to use notebooks for threat hunting

KQL and hunting queries are still the right choice for direct querying, but notebooks become more useful when the investigation depends on working with the same dataset repeatedly.

This typically occurs when data must be combined, transformed, or examined from different perspectives within the same investigation. Instead of running separate queries and manually stitching results together, use notebooks to build a continuous workflow. Each stage can build on the previous one, using intermediate results to guide further investigation without restarting from the original data source.

The decision to use notebooks is therefore based on complexity. If the requirement can be satisfied with a single query or a small number of queries, KQL is sufficient. When the investigation requires iterative analysis, enrichment, or multi-step processing, notebooks provide the structure needed to carry out that work effectively.

Summary

In this chapter we covered how Microsoft Sentinel supports threat detection beyond automated alerts. Hunting queries are used when analysts need to manually investigate suspicious activity or test a hypothesis. Analytics rules are used when the same logic needs to run continuously and generate alerts. Standard log queries are used when the task is simply to retrieve, validate, or troubleshoot data.

Search Jobs and summary rules solve different problems. Search Jobs are used when an investigation needs to query large or historical data from the data lake. Summary rules improve performance by pre-aggregating data for repeated analysis. A useful way to separate them is access versus optimization: Search Jobs retrieve data that is not practical to query interactively, while summary rules make repeated queries faster.

Notebooks extend hunting when a single query is not enough. They are most useful when the investigation requires multi-step analysis, enrichment, visualization, or working with dataframes through the Sentinel MCP Server. Choose notebooks when the scenario describes deeper analytical work rather than simple querying, alerting, or repeated aggregation.

The next chapter moves from Sentinel threat hunting into Microsoft 365 investigation techniques. It focuses on how analysts use Microsoft Purview Audit, Content Search, and Microsoft Graph activity logs to reconstruct activity, locate evidence, and understand user-driven and application-driven actions across Microsoft 365.

Exam Readiness Drill – Chapter Review Questions

Apart from mastering key concepts, strong test-taking skills under time pressure are essential for acing your certification exam. That's why developing these abilities early in your learning journey is critical.

Exam readiness drills, using the free online practice resources provided with this book, help you progressively improve your time management and test-taking skills while reinforcing the key concepts you've learned.

HOW TO GET STARTED

- Open the link or scan the QR code at the bottom of this page
- If you have unlocked the practice resources already, log in to your registered account. If you haven't, follow the instructions in *Free Benefits with Your Book* section in this book's *Preface* and come back to this page.
- Once you log in, click the START button to start this chapter's quiz
- We recommend attempting a quiz multiple times till you're able to answer most of the questions correctly and well within the time limit.
- You can use the following practice template to help you plan your attempts:

Working On Accuracy		
Attempt	**Target**	**Time Limit**
Attempt 1	40% or more	Till the timer runs out
Attempt 2	60% or more	Till the timer runs out
Attempt 3	75% or more	Till the timer runs out
Working On Timing		
Attempt 4	75% or more	1 minute before time limit
Attempt 5	75% or more	2 minutes before time limit
Attempt 6	75% or more	3 minutes before time limit

The above drill is just an example. Design your drills based on your own goals and make the most out of the online quizzes accompanying this book.

Link to this Chapter's Quiz

You need to unlock the online practice resources to access the link below. Check the *Free Benefits with Your Book* section in the *Preface* for detailed instructions on how to do this. You only need to unlock the resources once.

Open Quiz `https://packt.link/sc200js-ch7` or scan the QR code

Part 4

Investigate and Respond to Incidents

In this part of the book, you will move from detection into incident investigation and response. You will learn how Microsoft 365 audit data, Content Search, Microsoft Graph activity logs, Microsoft Defender XDR incidents, and Microsoft Defender for Endpoint evidence help analysts reconstruct activity, validate suspicious behavior, and respond to threats across identities, endpoints, email, cloud apps, data, and workloads.

This part of the book includes the following chapters:

8

Investigate Microsoft 365 Activities to Identify Threats

At this stage, you are already working through investigations using alerts and platform data. This chapter focuses on Microsoft 365 activity, where investigations rely on audit records, content, and application-driven operations to reconstruct user and application actions.

In this chapter, you will learn how to investigate Microsoft 365 activities to identify threats. It aligns with the SC-200 exam objectives and addresses the following Skills Measured:

- Investigate threats by using Audit from Microsoft Purview
- Investigate threats by using Content Search in Microsoft Purview
- Investigate threats by using Microsoft Graph activity logs

By the end of this chapter, you will be able to work through Microsoft 365 investigations using audit data, Content Search, and Microsoft Graph activity logs. Audit data helps confirm actions and reconstruct activity across workloads. Content Search helps locate and examine relevant messages and files, while Microsoft Graph activity logs show application-driven behavior, including permissions, consent, and API activity.

Investigate threats by using Audit from Microsoft Purview

Audit in Microsoft Purview provides the centralized record of activity across Microsoft 365, capturing operations performed by users, administrators, and system processes. Each recorded event includes the action performed, the identity involved, the affected resource, and the time at which the activity occurred. Together, these records provide a centralized audit log of operations that investigators can rely on to confirm what actions took place across services.

For example, if an alert indicates that a file may have been accessed, modified, or shared, audit records can confirm whether the action actually occurred, which user or process performed it, which resource was affected, and when it took place. This moves the investigation from suspicion to confirmed activity, giving analysts evidence they can use to validate the alert and attribute the action to the correct identity.

Audit also helps reconstruct activity as a sequence of events rather than isolated records. By aligning operations using timestamps and shared identifiers, investigators can reconstruct how activity progressed across workloads. This allows relationships between actions to be identified, including preceding and subsequent operations that form part of the same activity pattern.

Because the audit spans multiple Microsoft 365 services, it provides a unified view of activity that would otherwise remain fragmented. This makes it possible to correlate actions across workloads and understand how behavior moves between services. As a result, the audit becomes the foundation for verifying activity, reconstructing timelines, and establishing the factual basis of an investigation. This directly affects investigation decisions by determining whether an action can be confirmed, who performed it, and whether the activity sequence can be relied on as evidence.

Initiation and scoping of audit investigations

Audit investigations begin with a defined starting point, such as a user account named in an alert, a suspicious IP address, an alert ID, or a specific file activity. This anchor gives investigators a clear place to begin and keeps the search focused on activity that may be connected to the incident. Without that starting point, audit searches can quickly return large volumes of unrelated records.

From this starting point, the investigation is scoped by applying filters that define the boundaries of the search. These filters include the identity being investigated, the type of operation performed, the workload in which the activity occurred, and the relevant time range. Scoping determines whether the resulting data is usable or overwhelming.

In exam scenarios, this often appears as selecting the correct filters, such as the user account, the operation being investigated, and the time range around the alert. For instance, narrowing results to a specific user, operation, and timeframe ensures that only relevant activity is returned, rather than reviewing large volumes of unrelated audit data.

Additionally, targeting specific workloads is a key part of this process. Activity in Microsoft 365 is distributed across services such as Exchange, SharePoint, Teams, and identity-related components, and each workload records different types of operations. Narrowing the investigation to the relevant workload reduces irrelevant results and aligns the search with the type of activity being analyzed.

Effective scoping ensures that audit data reflects only the evidence relevant to the investigation. By combining a clear starting indicator with precise filtering and workload targeting, the investigation is constrained to a manageable dataset that can be analyzed accurately in subsequent steps.

Audit Standard and Audit Premium investigation impact

Audit scoping also depends on which Microsoft Purview Audit capability is available. *Audit Premium* includes all *Audit Standard* functionality, but adds longer retention, audit log retention policies, and intelligent insights that can affect whether evidence is available during an investigation. The following table presents the capabilities and investigation impacts for both:

Capability	**Audit Standard**	**Audit Premium**	**Investigation meaning**
Enabled by default	Yes	Yes	Audit capability is available by default when the tenant and licensing support it.
Thousands of searchable audit events	Yes	Yes	Analysts can search broad user and admin activity across Microsoft 365.
Audit search tool in the Microsoft Purview portal	Yes	Yes	Analysts can search audit records directly from the Purview portal.
Audit Search Graph API	Yes	Yes	Audit search can be accessed programmatically through Microsoft Graph.
Search-UnifiedAuditLog cmdlet	Yes	Yes	Audit records can be searched through Exchange Online PowerShell.
Export audit records to a CSV file	Yes	Yes	Results can be exported for filtering, review, reporting, or escalation.

Capability	Audit Standard	Audit Premium	Investigation meaning
Access to audit logs via Office 365 Management Activity API	Yes	Yes	Audit records can be retrieved through the management activity API.
180-day audit log retention	Yes	Yes	Investigators can search audit records within the default retention period.
Up to 1-year audit log retention	No	Yes	Older evidence may require Audit Premium.
10-year audit log retention	No	Yes	Long-term retention requires the appropriate add-on licensing.
Audit log retention policies	No	Yes	Premium allows retention to be controlled beyond the default behavior.
Intelligent insights	No	Yes	Premium adds deeper investigation signals for high-value audit events.

Table 8.1 – Audit Standard and Audit Premium capabilities in Microsoft Purview investigations

For SC-200, the key point is whether the evidence exists and is still retained. If the activity falls outside the available retention period or requires an Audit Premium capability that is not available, the absence of a record does not automatically prove that the activity never occurred. Investigators should also account for audit ingestion delay, because recent audit records may not appear immediately during an active investigation.

Interpretation of audit record data

Once relevant audit data has been scoped and retrieved, you must now interpret the records themselves. Each audit entry represents a specific operation and is structured using consistent fields, including the user identity, the operation performed, the workload, the affected object, and the timestamp.

Audit records are useful because their fields turn a raw event into a structured investigation fact. The exact fields available vary by workload and operation, but analysts commonly use the following values to understand who acted, what happened, where it happened, and which object was affected:

Audit field	What it shows	Investigation meaning
Operation	The action recorded in the audit log, such as FileAccessed, FileModified, or Send	Shows what happened and helps distinguish viewing, changing, sending, deleting, or configuring activity
UserId	The user or identity associated with the operation	Helps attribute the action to the account or identity involved
Workload	The Microsoft 365 service that produced the event, such as SharePoint, Exchange, Teams, or Microsoft Entra	Shows where the event occurred and helps analysts interpret the action in the correct service context
ObjectId	The affected object, such as a file path, mailbox item, message, site, or configuration object	Identifies what resource was accessed, modified, shared, or affected
Parameters	Additional operation details, often stored as structured or JSON-style values	Provides extra detail that can clarify how the action was performed or which settings were involved

Table 8.2 – Common Microsoft Purview audit fields used during investigations

For example, an audit record showing UserId as user@domain.com, Operation as FileAccessed, Workload as SharePoint, ObjectId as /Finance/Salary.xlsx, and a timestamp within the alert window tells the investigator that this user opened that file in SharePoint at that time. Reading these fields together turns a raw audit entry into an investigation fact: who acted, what action occurred, where it happened, which object was affected, and when it took place.

The operation field is the primary indicator of action. FileAccessed shows that a file was opened, while FileModified shows that the file was changed. Both fields are important because viewing data and altering data lead to different investigation conclusions.

The remaining fields complete the record. UserId shows who performed the action, Workload shows where it occurred, ObjectId identifies the affected resource, and Parameters can provide additional detail about how the action was performed. Read together, these fields allow investigators to confirm the action without relying on assumptions.

The timestamp anchors the event in time and enables it to be placed within the broader sequence of activity. This is critical when multiple operations are involved, as it allows investigators to understand order and progression.

Activity analysis across Microsoft 365 workloads

After individual audit records are understood, the investigation expands to analyzing activity within the context of specific Microsoft 365 workloads. Each service records different types of operations. Understanding these differences is necessary to correctly interpret what the activity represents.

The same audit fields mean different things depending on the workload that produced the record. *Table 8.1* shows how common Microsoft 365 workload activity maps to the operations analysts review and the investigation questions those operations help answer:

Workload area	Common operations	What analysts can determine
SharePoint and OneDrive	File access, download, modification, deletion, and sharing	Whether data was accessed, changed, removed, or shared, and whether the activity matches expected use
Exchange	Message sending, reading, deletion, access, forwarding, and mailbox rule activity	How messages were handled and whether forwarding, deletion, or rule changes form part of a broader pattern
Administrative and configuration activity	Changes to settings, roles, permissions, and policies	Whether elevated activity occurred or whether controls were modified during the incident

Table 8.3 – Interpreting audit activity across Microsoft 365 workloads

This comparison prevents audit records from being read in isolation. For instance, a FileAccessed operation in SharePoint, a forwarding rule in Exchange, and a permissions change in an administrative workload each point to a different investigation question. Analysts need that workload context before deciding whether the activity is expected, suspicious, or part of the wider incident pattern.

Timeline reconstruction and event sequencing

With activity understood at the record and workload level, the investigation can move to reconstructing the sequence of events. Individual audit records provide discrete points of activity, but it is their sequence that reveals how behavior progressed.

Timeline reconstruction is based on ordering events using their timestamps. By arranging operations chronologically, investigators can identify the sequence in which actions occurred and gain context. For instance, an investigation may show a user signing in, accessing a file, and then sharing it externally. When ordered chronologically, these events form a sequence that contextualizes how an attacker may have gained access, moved through the environment, and achieved their objective.

Earlier operations may establish context for later ones or may also establish cause and effect by linking preceding and subsequent actions such as access preceding modification, or configuration changes occurring before data interaction. These relationships help determine whether actions are connected and whether they form part of a single pattern of behavior.

Further, sequencing the events allows gaps, overlaps, or unexpected ordering to be identified. Missing activity, out-of-sequence operations, or unusually rapid sequences can indicate incomplete data, automated behavior, or abnormal activity patterns. These observations become important signals for further investigation.

Correlation and pivoting across audit records

Once a timeline has been established, the investigation shifts to connecting related activity across audit records. Individual events and their sequence provide structure, but correlation is what links those events into a broader pattern of behavior.

Correlation uses shared attributes across audit records to identify related activity. Fields such as user identity, object identifiers, operation types, and workloads are used to connect related events. By following these shared values, investigators can move from one record to another and expand the scope of the investigation beyond the initial dataset.

Pivoting is used to expand the investigation using a known piece of information as a starting point for further investigation. Starting from a known record, investigators use one of its attributes—such as the user or object—to locate additional related activity or records with the same attributes. This process is then repeated, with each new discovery as the pivot, to build out a chain of events, allowing the investigation to follow activity across multiple actions and services. For instance, when starting from a file access event, an investigator can pivot on the user account to identify additional actions performed by that user, such as downloading other files or sending emails, expanding the scope of the investigation.

Thus through correlation and pivoting, activity that initially appears isolated can be linked into a single investigative thread. This makes it possible to identify patterns such as repeated actions, related operations across workloads, or sequences that involve multiple resources. It also helps surface activity that was not part of the original scope but is connected through shared identifiers.

Thus correlation and pivoting turns the timeline into a connected investigation thread, helping investigators build a more complete picture of behavior across the environment.

Validation of activity and investigation findings

The final step in an audit-based investigation is confirming that the identified activity is accurate and can be relied on as evidence. By this stage, events have been scoped, interpreted, sequenced, and correlated, but the findings still need to be checked against the audit records that support them.

Essentially, validation means checking that each investigation finding is backed by a matching audit record. If the analysis says a user accessed a file, changed a setting, or created a forwarding rule, the audit data must show the operation, the identity involved, the affected resource, and the timestamp. This prevents investigators from treating only an alert, pattern, or assumption as a confirmed fact.

Analysts also check whether related records agree with each other. The sequence, identity, workload, and timing should support the same story. If records are missing, timestamps conflict, or the sequence does not make sense, the finding needs more review before it can be treated as evidence.

Once activity has been confirmed and reconstructed, the investigation moves to understanding the data involved and how it was accessed, shared, or modified.

Investigate threats by using Content Search in Microsoft Purview

Not all investigations are resolved by understanding activity alone. For example, audit records may show that a file was shared externally, but those records do not show whether the file contained sensitive data. Once actions have been identified, the next question is often what data was involved. Content Search addresses the gap between activity logs and actual data by allowing investigators to locate and review the content affected by the activity; it does this by showing what content was accessed, shared, or modified.

Content Search in Microsoft Purview provides the ability to search across Microsoft 365 for stored data, including emails, documents, and files. Rather than focusing on operations, it focuses on the content that exists within services such as Exchange, SharePoint, OneDrive, and Teams.

Investigations using Content Search are driven by known indicators. These indicators may include a user account, an email address, a file name, or specific keywords associated with the incident. By using these inputs, searches are targeted toward relevant data rather than broad discovery, ensuring that results remain focused on the investigation context.

Since Content Search complements Audit data, it allows investigators to connect actions with the content involved, providing a more complete view of the incident because behavior and data can be examined together. It also directly affects whether investigators can confirm data exposure, identify sensitive information, and validate the impact of the activity identified in audit logs.

Content search scope and limitations

Content Search is useful when the investigation needs to locate Microsoft 365 content, but it should not be treated as a search tool for every file, application, or real-time interaction in the environment. It searches supported Microsoft 365 locations, so you must understand what is in scope before relying on the results. *Table 8.4* presents the limitations of Content Search and how they impact the investigation:

Limitation	What it means	Investigation impact
Teams content must be stored and searchable in Microsoft 365	Teams content can be searched in Microsoft Purview, but Content Search should not be treated as a real-time Teams chat monitoring tool	Recent Teams messages may not appear immediately, so timing must be considered before concluding that no message exists
Local-only files are outside Content Search scope	Files that remain only on a local endpoint are not searched by Content Search	Use endpoint investigation or device evidence when the file has not been stored in SharePoint, OneDrive, Exchange, Teams, or another supported Microsoft 365 location

Limitation	What it means	Investigation impact
Third-party app content is outside scope unless stored in Microsoft 365	Content Search does not search arbitrary third-party SaaS apps directly	Use the relevant app logs, Defender for Cloud Apps, Microsoft Sentinel, or the third-party platform when the content is not stored in a supported Microsoft 365 location
Encrypted or protected content may require additional handling	Some protected content may be searchable, decryptable, partially indexed, or harder to review depending on encryption type, permissions, and export/review workflow	Do not assume that a search hit means the content can be fully reviewed without the correct permissions and handling process

Table 8.4 – Content Search scope limitations in Microsoft Purview investigations

Tip

For SC-200, the decision point is the evidence location. Use Content Search when the evidence is stored in supported Microsoft 365 content locations. Use audit records to confirm actions, endpoint investigation for local files, and Defender for Cloud Apps, Microsoft Sentinel, or third-party logs when the evidence is outside Microsoft 365 content stores.

Content search scope and location targeting

Content Search investigations begin by defining where the search will be performed. Microsoft 365 stores data across multiple services, and selecting the correct locations ensures that the search targets only the environments relevant to the investigation.

Search locations include Exchange mailboxes, SharePoint sites, OneDrive accounts, and Teams data. Each of these locations contains different types of content, and selecting the appropriate combination depends on the nature of the activity being investigated. For example, email-related investigations focus on mailboxes, while file-related investigations require targeting SharePoint and OneDrive.

In addition to selecting workloads, searches are scoped to specific users, mailboxes, or sites. This narrows the investigation to the entities associated with the known indicators and prevents unrelated data from being included in the results. Defining this scope before executing the search is critical to maintaining relevance and reducing unnecessary data. For instance, when investigating a specific user, limiting the search to that user's mailbox or OneDrive ensures that results are relevant, rather than returning data from across the entire organization.

> **Note**
>
> Effective location targeting ensures that Content Search operates within clearly defined boundaries. By selecting the correct services and scoping the search to the appropriate users or resources, investigators establish a focused dataset that supports accurate and efficient content discovery.

Query construction and condition-based filtering

Once the search scope has been defined, the next step of the investigation is to construct queries that identify relevant content within that scope. This step determines how effectively the search isolates data associated with the investigation.

Queries are built using keywords and conditions that reflect known indicators. Keywords may include specific terms, phrases, or identifiers related to the incident, while conditions define how those terms are applied. These conditions can include attributes such as sender, recipient, file properties, or other metadata that describe the content being searched. For example, an investigator may search for the keyword "confidential," limit the sender to user@domain.com, and set the date range to the last seven days.

Further, filtering is applied to refine the results returned by the query. Rather than returning all possible matches, filters narrow the dataset based on attributes such as date ranges, communication participants, or content characteristics. This reduces the volume of results and ensures that the search focuses on the most relevant data.

Query construction and filtering work together to control both the breadth and precision of the search. Well-defined queries identify the correct content, while filters remove irrelevant data. This combination ensures that the resulting dataset is targeted, manageable, and aligned with the investigation requirements. Queries that are too broad introduce noise, while overly restrictive queries risk excluding relevant evidence, making precision critical to maintaining investigation accuracy. The correct approach is to balance keywords and filters so that results remain targeted and manageable.

Content identification and evidence discovery

With queries executed and results returned, the investigation focuses on identifying the specific items that are relevant to the incident. Search results often contain a mixture of relevant and unrelated data, so the task at this stage is to isolate the content that directly aligns with the investigation context.

Relevant content is identified by matching returned items against the known indicators and conditions used in the search. This may include emails associated with specific users or subjects, files that match identified names or properties, or messages that contain keywords linked to the activity being investigated. The goal is to move from a broad result set to a defined set of items that represent potential evidence. Selection is based on alignment with the timeframe, participants, and content characteristics established earlier in the investigation.

Investigators then review the returned items by matching them against known users, checking that timestamps fall within the investigation window, and confirming that keywords appear in a relevant context. Not every returned item is meaningful, so investigators must determine which results genuinely relate to the activity under investigation. This means checking whether the content matches the participants and characteristics defined earlier in the search.

By isolating relevant items, the investigation establishes a set of content that can be examined in detail. These items represent the data associated with the activity and form the basis for understanding what information was involved.

Analysis of retrieved content for investigative context

Once relevant items have been identified, we now move to examining their contents to understand how they relate to the activity being investigated. At this stage, the goal is no longer finding data, but determining whether that data explains the incident.

Analysis at this point involves reviewing the content itself to determine its significance. For emails, this includes examining message content, participants, and intent. For files, this includes understanding the type of data stored, its sensitivity, and how it may have been used. The objective is to establish whether the content supports or contradicts the activity identified through earlier investigation steps.

Context is critical during this process. The content must be evaluated against the user, timeframe, and incident being investigated. An item may appear relevant based on keywords or attributes, but its significance is determined by how it aligns with the broader investigation context. This determination may include confirming that specific data was shared, identifying sensitive information within files or messages, or understanding how communication or data usage contributed to the activity being examined. This step transforms identified items into contextualized evidence that can support investigation findings. For example, reviewing an email may reveal whether sensitive information was shared intentionally or as part of a phishing attempt, providing context that cannot be determined from audit logs alone.

Export and handling of investigation data

After content has been identified and analyzed, the investigation may require the data to be preserved or reviewed outside the search interface. This is achieved by exporting the selected results and allowing them to be handled outside the investigation tool as part of the broader investigation process. Exported data is often used to support additional review, documentation, or escalation, whether the investigation continues within another tool or is shared with other teams.

Exporting creates a defined evidence dataset that reflects the items selected during the investigation. This dataset can include emails, documents, and associated metadata, ensuring that both the content and its context are retained. Only the relevant items should be exported to maintain a controlled and focused set of evidence. Further, The relationship between the content, the users involved, and the timeframe must remain clear because evidence becomes significantly less valuable if the circumstances surrounding it are lost. This also ensures that exported results continue to accurately represent the findings established *during* the investigation.

> **Note**
>
> Exporting enables findings to be examined independently while preserving the connection to the original investigation.

The exported data can then be accurately interpreted and correlated back to the originating activity.

Correlation of content with audit activities

Once content or evidence has been identified, analyzed, and preserved, it must be connected back to the activity that led to its discovery. Content on its own shows what data exists, but it does not explain how or why that data was accessed, shared, or modified. Correlation with audit activity provides that missing link.

This process involves aligning content findings with the corresponding audit records that describe user or administrative actions. Attributes such as user identity, timestamps, and affected resources are used to connect content with the operations that involved it. By matching these elements, investigators can determine how specific data relates to recorded activity.

Content correlation further allows the investigation to progress from isolated evidence to a connected view of behavior. For example, a file identified through Content Search can be linked to audit records showing its access, download, or sharing operations. Similarly, an email located in search results can be associated with send or read actions recorded in the audit log.

By combining content and audit activity, investigators can confirm what happened, what data was involved, and whether exposure occurred. This strengthens the finding because it is supported by both the content evidence and the recorded operation.

> **Note**
>
> Unlike event correlation, which connects related actions across multiple audit records, content correlation links discovered content to the actions performed on that content.

This completes the link between discovered content and the recorded actions behind it so that investigators can ensure that conclusions are based on both the concrete evidence of the existence of data and the actions performed on it.

For investigations to examine the wider activity occurring across Microsoft 365 services, Microsoft Graph activity logs provide a broader perspective by recording interactions between users, applications, and resources. Let's go through this next.

Investigate threats using Microsoft Graph activity logs

Not all activity in Microsoft 365 is performed directly by users. Applications, scripts, and integrations interact with services through APIs, often operating without visible user interaction. These actions can access data, modify resources, or perform operations at scale, making them a critical part of an investigation when activity cannot be explained through user behavior alone.

Microsoft Graph provides the interface through which these application-driven operations occur. For example, an application may access multiple user mailboxes through Microsoft Graph without direct user interaction. This type of activity would not appear as standard user behavior and must be identified through application activity analysis.

Activity associated with Microsoft Graph further reflects how applications interact with Microsoft 365 services, including access to mail, files, and directory data. This activity is not captured as a single standalone log, but is reconstructed from audit logs, Entra ID sign-in logs, and service principal activity records that together expose API-driven operations.

Therefore, Investigations in this area are driven by *application context*. This includes examining service principals, application permissions, and authorization events to determine what level of access an application has and how that access is being used. Understanding whether activity is performed through delegated permissions or application permissions is also central to determining how the action was executed.

> **Note**
>
> Microsoft Graph activity analysis focuses on identifying what actions applications performed, how frequently they occurred, and whether that behavior aligns with expected patterns.

By combining application activity with audit and identity data, investigations can distinguish between user-driven and application-driven behavior. This provides a complete view of how activity is occurring within Microsoft 365, ensuring that automated or background operations are fully understood and included in the investigation. This directly affects attribution by distinguishing between user-driven actions and application-driven operations.

Microsoft Graph audit fields used in application investigations

Microsoft Graph activity investigations rely on fields that identify the application, the service principal, and the authorization path used to perform the action. These fields help investigators determine whether an action came from a user session, delegated access, or app-only permissions. The following table shows the different audit fields and how they work for investigations:

Graph audit field	What it shows	Investigation meaning
AppId	The application ID associated with the activity	Identifies which application is linked to the operation
ServicePrincipalId	The service principal object used by the application in the tenant	Helps attribute the action to the tenant-specific application identity
Delegated permissions	Permissions used when an application acts on behalf of a signed-in user	Shows that the action depends on both the user session and the application permission
Application permissions	Permissions used when an application acts without a signed-in user	Shows app-only access, where the application can act directly based on granted permissions

Graph audit field	What it shows	Investigation meaning
Consent events	Records showing when permissions were granted and by whom	Helps determine whether access was expected, newly introduced, or suspicious
OAuth flows	Authorization flow used to obtain access	Helps investigators understand how access was granted and whether the flow matches expected application behavior

Table 8.5 – Microsoft Graph audit fields used in application investigations

For SC-200, the decision point is attribution. If the action depends on a signed-in user, investigate the user session and delegated permission path. If the action is app-only, investigate the service principal, application permissions, consent history, and whether the application's behavior matches its expected function.

Identification of application and service principal activities

Investigating Microsoft Graph activity begins by identifying which applications are responsible for the observed behavior. Unlike user-driven activity, these actions are performed by applications operating under service principal identities, which represent the application within Microsoft 365.

Each service principal is associated with a specific application and is used to authenticate and perform operations across services. Identifying the correct service principal allows the investigation to attribute activity to a specific application rather than a user account. This distinction is critical when activity cannot be explained through normal user behavior. For instance, repeated access to data without corresponding user sign-in activity may indicate that an application, rather than a user, is performing the operations.

To determine which application initiated the action and where that action occurred, investigators need to examine records that include information about the application, the service principal, and the resources accessed. Note that application activity may not align with interactive user patterns. Applications may perform repeated operations, access multiple resources in quick succession, or operate without direct user input. Identifying these patterns helps distinguish application-driven behavior from user activity.

Analysis of API-driven operations across Microsoft 365

After identifying the application or service principal responsible for the activity, the investigation focuses on the operations performed through Microsoft Graph. These operations represent how the application is interacting with Microsoft 365 services and what actions it is executing.

API-driven operations are reflected in records that describe the action taken, the resource accessed, and the service involved. This includes interactions with workloads such as mail, files, and directory data. By analyzing API-driven operations, investigators can see whether the application is reading, modifying, or administering Microsoft 365 resources in a way that matches its expected purpose. When that behavior changes, the next step is to check whether the service principal, permissions, or token use indicate misuse.

API-driven activity implies risk when the application identity or token is misused. The following table presents some common risk scenarios and their investigation impacts:

API risk scenario	**What it means**	**Investigation impact**
Compromised service principal	An attacker gains control of an application identity or credential used by a service principal	The application may access Microsoft 365 data without normal user interaction, so investigators must review AppId, ServicePrincipalId, permissions, consent history, and affected resources
Token replay	A stolen or captured token is reused to access Microsoft 365 services without re-authenticating	Activity may appear authorized even though the token is being used by an attacker, so investigators must correlate sign-in, token use, location, timing, and application activity

Table 8.6 – API risk scenarios in Microsoft Graph investigations

For SC-200, the key decision point is whether the API activity reflects expected application behavior or misuse of an application identity or token. If the service principal is compromised, investigate permissions and affected resources. If token replay is suspected, correlate the activity with identity signals, sign-in behavior, and unusual timing or location.

Permission and access analysis

After understanding what actions an application is performing, the next step is to check whether those actions are authorized. Application behavior is defined by the permissions it has been granted, and analyzing these permissions determines the scope of access available to the application.

Permissions are assigned either as delegated permissions or application permissions. *Table 8.7* shows how the two models affect investigation context and attribution:

Permission model	How it works	Investigation meaning
Delegated permissions	The application acts on behalf of a signed-in user.	Activity should be reviewed in the user context because the action depends on both the application and the user session.
Application permissions	The application operates independently without a signed-in user.	Activity should be reviewed as app-only behavior because the application can act directly based on its granted permissions.

Table 8.7 – Delegated and application permissions in Microsoft 365 investigations

Analyzing permissions also involves identifying whether the application has read-only access, modification capabilities, or broader administrative control. Investigators then check whether the permissions match the application's expected function. Applications should only have access required for their intended purpose, and excessive or unrelated permissions may indicate misconfiguration or risk. Identifying over-permissioned applications is critical, as over-permissioned applications are key indicators of risk.

Investigation of OAuth consent and permission grants

After understanding the permissions assigned to an application, next we examine how those permissions were granted. OAuth consent and permission grants define when and how an application obtained access, making them critical for determining whether that access was expected or introduced as part of suspicious activity.

Consent events represent the point at which an application is authorized to access Microsoft 365 resources. This may occur through user consent or administrative approval, depending on the permissions requested. Investigating these events involves identifying who granted the consent, when it occurred, and what permissions were approved.

Permission grants must be analyzed to understand the extent of access provided at the time of authorization. This includes determining whether the granted permissions align with the application's intended purpose or whether they introduce unnecessary or excessive access. Unexpected or high-privilege permissions can indicate risk, particularly if they were granted without clear justification.

This step also involves identifying newly introduced or recently modified consent. Changes in application authorization—such as new permissions or updated access—can signal the introduction of a new application, a change in behavior, or potential misuse. Tracking these changes helps establish whether application access has evolved in a way that requires further investigation. Recent or unexpected consent events are strong indicators of newly introduced or unauthorized access. For example, if a user grants consent to an application that requests broad access to mail or files, this may indicate a malicious or unauthorized application gaining access to organizational data.

By examining consent and permission grants, investigators can determine how application access was established and whether it was appropriate. This provides visibility into the origin of access, ensuring that application activity is evaluated not only by what it does, but by how it was authorized.

Detection of abnormal application behavior

After establishing what an application is doing and how it was authorized, the investigation focuses on whether its behavior matches its expected function. Applications usually follow consistent patterns, so sudden changes in volume, resource access, workload use, or timing can indicate misuse, misconfiguration, or compromise.

Analysts look for activity that falls outside the application's normal operating pattern. For example, an application that usually accesses a small set of SharePoint files may suddenly begin reading large volumes of data across multiple users or workloads. This change indicates that the application may be using its permissions in a way that does not match its intended purpose.

The goal is not just to label behavior as normal or abnormal. It is to identify which activity needs closer review and why. When application activity exceeds expected use, reaches unrelated resources, or appears at an unusual frequency, investigators can treat it as a signal for deeper analysis.

Correlation with audit and identity data

The final step in investigating Microsoft Graph activity is to connect application behavior with audit and identity records. Application activity on its own shows what actions were performed, but it does not fully explain how those actions relate to user context or broader activity across Microsoft 365. Correlation links those actions back to the identity and audit evidence.

To do this, investigators align application-driven operations with audit and identity records. Audit logs provide visibility into the operations performed on resources, while identity logs provide context about authentication, sign-ins, and service principal activity. By combining these sources, investigators can understand both the action and the identity context in which it occurred.

Correlation is performed using shared attributes such as application identity, user context (where applicable), timestamps, and affected resources. These attributes allow investigators to link application activity with related events, such as sign-in activity, permission changes, or resource access operations recorded in audit logs.

This step is critical for distinguishing how activity was initiated and executed. For example, application activity can be linked to identity events to determine whether it was triggered through delegated access or performed independently using application permissions. It also allows investigators to trace how application actions align with other activity occurring at the same time.

By correlating application, audit, and identity data, investigators can see whether application-driven behavior is connected to user activity, authorization changes, or recorded operations. They can then confirm whether the action came from a user session, delegated access, or direct application permissions, making attribution reliable.

For the exam, remember that the correct investigation choice depends on correlating application activity with audit and identity data.

Summary

This chapter focused on how you investigate Microsoft 365 activity using audit data, content, and application-driven operations. We covered how audit records are used to confirm actions, interpret activity, and reconstruct timelines across workloads.

You learned how Content Search is used to locate and examine the data involved, allowing you to move from recorded activity to the actual content affected and use that as part of the investigation. You also examined how Microsoft Graph activity is analyzed to understand application behavior, including identifying service principals, reviewing permissions and consent, and correlating that activity with audit and identity data.

For the SC-200 exam, the key points are the investigation boundaries between audit data, Content Search, and Microsoft Graph activity logs. Audit records help confirm who performed an action, what operation occurred, which resource was affected, and when it happened. Content Search helps identify the actual data involved, while Microsoft Graph activity logs help investigate application-driven behavior, permissions, consent, and API activity.

The next chapter builds on this investigation workflow by moving from evidence review into response. After analysts understand what happened, which data was involved, and whether user or application activity contributed to the incident, the next step is deciding what action to take to contain, remediate, and reduce further risk.

Exam Readiness Drill – Chapter Review Questions

Apart from mastering key concepts, strong test-taking skills under time pressure are essential for acing your certification exam. That's why developing these abilities early in your learning journey is critical.

Exam readiness drills, using the free online practice resources provided with this book, help you progressively improve your time management and test-taking skills while reinforcing the key concepts you've learned.

HOW TO GET STARTED

- Open the link or scan the QR code at the bottom of this page
- If you have unlocked the practice resources already, log in to your registered account. If you haven't, follow the instructions in *Free Benefits with Your Book* section in this book's *Preface* and come back to this page.
- Once you log in, click the START button to start this chapter's quiz
- We recommend attempting a quiz multiple times till you're able to answer most of the questions correctly and well within the time limit.
- You can use the following practice template to help you plan your attempts:

Working On Accuracy		
Attempt	**Target**	**Time Limit**
Attempt 1	40% or more	Till the timer runs out
Attempt 2	60% or more	Till the timer runs out
Attempt 3	75% or more	Till the timer runs out
Working On Timing		
Attempt 4	75% or more	1 minute before time limit
Attempt 5	75% or more	2 minutes before time limit
Attempt 6	75% or more	3 minutes before time limit

The above drill is just an example. Design your drills based on your own goals and make the most out of the online quizzes accompanying this book.

Link to this Chapter's Quiz

You need to unlock the online practice resources to access the link below. Check the *Free Benefits with Your Book* section in the *Preface* for detailed instructions on how to do this. You only need to unlock the resources once.

Open Quiz `https://packt.link/sc200js-ch8` or scan the QR code

9

Respond to Alerts and Incidents in Microsoft Defender XDR

At this point, you are already investigating alerts and interpreting activity across the environment. This chapter moves into response: containment, remediation, and coordinated incident handling across Microsoft security platforms. The chapter focuses on responding to alerts and incidents across Microsoft Defender XDR, Microsoft Sentinel, Microsoft Purview, Microsoft Defender for Cloud, and identity protection tools.

It addresses the following exam objectives of SC-200:

- Investigating and remediating threats using Microsoft Defender for Office 365
- Investigating and remediating threats or compromised entities identified by Microsoft Purview
- Investigating and remediating alerts and incidents identified by Microsoft Defender for Cloud workload protections
- Investigating and remediating security risks identified by Microsoft Defender for Cloud Apps
- Investigating and remediating compromised identities identified by Microsoft Entra ID
- Investigating and remediating security alerts from Microsoft Defender for Identity
- Investigating and remediating alerts and incidents identified by Microsoft Sentinel
- Investigating incidents using agentic AI, including embedded Copilot for Security
- Investigating complex attacks, such as multi-stage, multi-domain, and lateral movement
- Managing security incidents by using case management

By the end of this chapter, you will understand how investigation leads to response across Microsoft security platforms. You will learn how incidents are interpreted and acted on in Defender XDR, how data and user activity are handled in Purview, how workload and cloud app risks are contained, and how identity-based threats are investigated and remediated. You will also explore how incidents are managed in Microsoft Sentinel, how automation and AI-assisted analysis support response, and how complex attacks are assessed across multiple stages and domains.

Investigating and remediating threats using Microsoft Defender for Office 365

Email threats are rarely the full story. A malicious message is often just the starting point. Its real impact is determined by what happens after delivery—whether a user interacts with it, credentials are exposed, or the activity leads to further compromise across devices or services.

In Microsoft Defender for Office 365, investigation therefore looks beyond the message itself and examines how that message fits into a broader incident. Email threats are handled within the wider Microsoft Defender XDR experience for this reason. Alerts generated from email activity are automatically correlated with identity, endpoint, and cloud signals, forming a single incident that reflects the progression of the attack. The investigation moves from asking whether the email was malicious to determining what it enabled and how far the attack progressed.

A common scenario is when a user clicks a phishing link and enters credentials, and the investigation must extend beyond the email to include sign-in activity, device access, and any subsequent actions performed using those credentials. This perspective is critical because the same message can result in very different outcomes depending on user interaction and subsequent activity.

Your role as the analyst changes at this point. Instead of performing every action manually, you validate automated decisions, confirm that the scope of the attack has been fully identified, and ensure that remediation aligns with the actual behavior observed. If the investigation is incomplete or the response is applied too narrowly, parts of the attack can remain active, allowing it to continue beyond the initial containment.

Email entity investigation within Defender XDR incidents

Within Microsoft Defender XDR, an email is investigated as one entity in a broader incident. Its significance comes from the relationships around it: the recipient, sender, embedded URLs, attachments, affected devices, and any follow-on activity after delivery.

Before you reach the email entity itself, the investigation normally starts in the Microsoft Defender XDR **incident queue**. This gives you the first triage view: incident name, severity, status, assigned analyst, affected assets, related alerts, and the time the activity was detected or last updated. This is where you decide whether the incident requires immediate attention, whether it belongs to an existing investigation, and whether the alert activity suggests a broader attack rather than an isolated message.

Figure 9.1 shows the Microsoft Defender XDR incident queue, where incidents are reviewed, prioritized, assigned, and opened for deeper investigation.

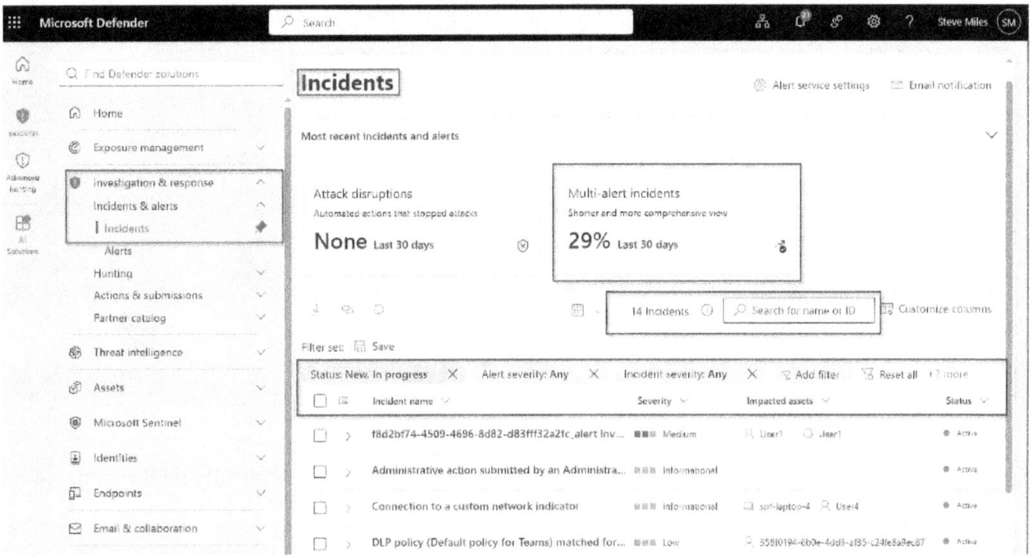

Figure 9.1 – Incident queue in Microsoft Defender XDR

After the incident is opened, the incident page provides the working view for the investigation. The **incident summary** explains what Defender XDR has correlated, while the **Entities** tab exposes the users, devices, mailboxes, URLs, files, and other objects connected to the activity. The **Evidence** tab shows the specific items Defender XDR has collected, the **Timeline** places activity in sequence, the **Investigation graph** shows relationships between entities, and the alert story explains how the alert was raised and how the activity developed.

For an email-based incident, these views matter because the message is rarely the whole investigation. You can use the incident page to move from the original email alert into the recipient, sender, URLs, attachments, devices, and follow-on activity that show whether the attack stopped at delivery or expanded into user interaction, credential use, or endpoint activity.

Figure 9.2 shows the Microsoft Defender XDR incident page used to move from alert triage into entity, evidence, timeline, graph, and alert story analysis.

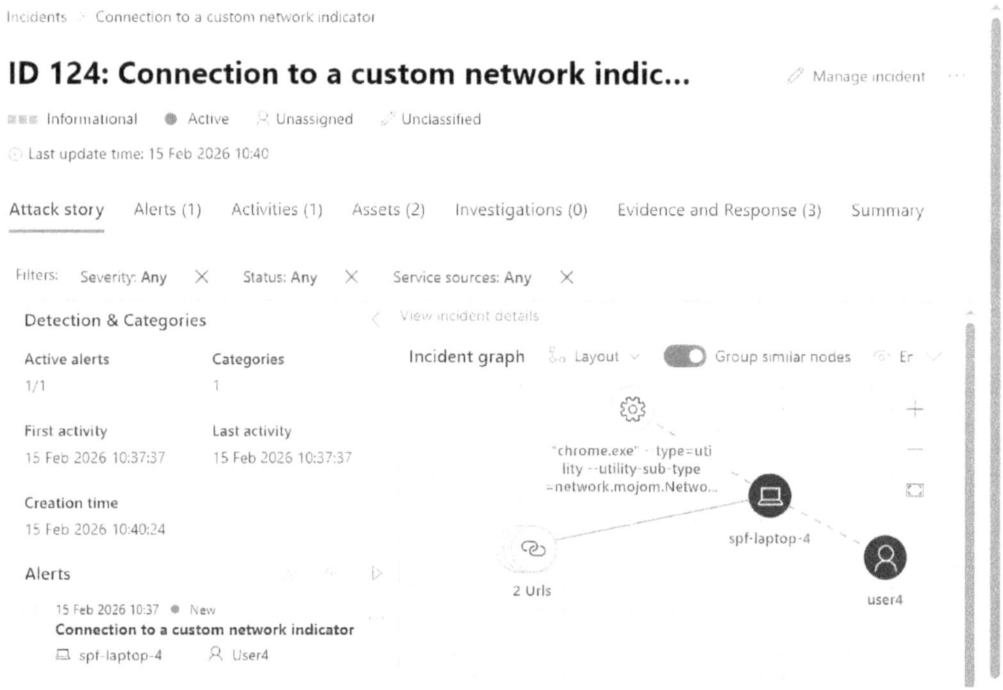

Figure 9.2 – Incident investigation page in Microsoft Defender XDR

The core of this process is entity expansion. A single incident can expose several connected investigation paths, such as the affected user, device, process activity, embedded URLs, files, and related indicators. Each entity becomes a pivot point into more telemetry, allowing the analyst to follow how one signal connects to another across the incident graph. This becomes clear when a clicked link becomes a pivot into web activity, potential credential use, and downstream access attempts. Similarly, an attachment is not just analyzed statically; it is traced into execution behavior on a device.

This changes how evidence is interpreted. The email itself provides initial context including delivery time, sender reputation, and detection verdict. But the investigation quickly moves into verifying impact. You must determine whether the message was ignored, interacted with, or triggered further activity. The difference between these outcomes defines whether the incident remains contained in the email layer or expands into a broader compromise.

Entity relationships are what make this possible. Defender XDR links email artifacts to identities and devices automatically, allowing the analyst to move between them without rebuilding context. This enables rapid correlation between user actions and system behavior, which is essential when determining whether an attack has progressed beyond initial access. If these relationships are misunderstood or not followed through, the investigation can stop too early, leaving secondary activity undetected.

Automated investigation and response (AIR) execution and outcomes

Automated investigation and response (AIR) operate as an automated decision process within Microsoft Defender XDR. AIR analyzes incident evidence across emails, users, devices, and related artifacts to determine whether malicious activity is confirmed, whether it is isolated or part of a broader compromise, and what response is appropriate.

From this evaluation, AIR produces outcomes in the form of remediation actions. These can include removing emails from mailboxes, blocking malicious URLs or files, or taking containment actions against affected entities. Each action is tied to the evidence that triggered it, creating a traceable link between what was observed and what response was applied. This is critical because the investigation does not end when automation runs—you must interpret whether those actions fully address the threat.

Response actions vary depending on the affected entity and the evidence found during the investigation. Device isolation is used when an endpoint may still be able to communicate with other systems or attacker infrastructure; it limits that communication while preserving access for investigation. An antivirus scan checks the device for known malicious files or active threats. File quarantine removes a suspicious or malicious file from normal use so it cannot continue executing or spreading.

Identity-focused actions address the attacker's ability to keep using compromised access. A user password reset reduces the value of stolen credentials, while session revocation ends active sessions that may still allow access without another sign-in. Indicator-based actions block known malicious infrastructure or artifacts. Blocking a URL or domain prevents users or devices from reaching a malicious destination, while blocking a file hash stops a known malicious file from running or being trusted elsewhere. Where the investigation involves a risky OAuth application, blocking app consent prevents the application from continuing to gain or use permissions that expose Microsoft 365 data.

The key question is whether automated actions such as message removal or account restriction are sufficient, or whether additional steps are required to fully contain the threat.

AIR behavior also depends on the automation level configured for the affected device group or workload. In some environments, AIR can investigate and apply remediation automatically. In others, it can complete the investigation but wait for analyst approval before certain actions are taken. This distinction matters because the same detection can lead to different operational outcomes depending on whether automation is fully enabled, partially enabled, or approval-based.

Approval workflow is important because not every automated action should be treated as final without analyst review. Some remediation actions may be pending approval, especially where the action could affect users, devices, or legitimate business activity. The analyst must review the recommended action, confirm that the evidence supports it, approve it where appropriate, or reject it if the action could create unnecessary disruption.

AIR also has limitations. It can only act on the evidence and response actions available to Microsoft Defender XDR and the configured workload protections. If the investigation context is incomplete, if a related activity occurred outside the connected telemetry, or if an action requires manual business judgment, AIR may not fully contain the threat by itself. This is why analysts still need to validate the outcome, check whether related entities were missed, and confirm that the incident has been contained across email, identity, endpoint, and cloud activity.

The effectiveness of AIR depends on how accurately the incident context is understood. If the evaluation is based on incomplete or misleading signals, remediation may be partial, leaving parts of the attack active. Conversely, overly aggressive action can impact legitimate activity. As an analyst, your role is therefore to review AIR outcomes, validate that the correct entities were targeted, and determine whether additional investigation or remediation is required to fully contain the incident.

Automatic attack disruption and containment actions

Automatic attack disruption operates beyond investigation, focusing on actively interrupting an attack while it is still in progress. Within Microsoft Defender XDR, this capability targets the entities involved in the incident and applies containment actions designed to break the attack chain, rather than simply responding to individual detections.

This approach differs from standard remediation because it is driven by attack progression rather than isolated evidence. Instead of evaluating a single artifact, disruption identifies critical points in the attack path (such as compromised user accounts, active sessions, or malicious infrastructure) and applies actions that prevent further movement. This may include restricting account activity, blocking communication with malicious endpoints, or limiting the ability of an attacker to continue operating within the environment. For instance, containing a **compromised user account** can immediately limit attacker access, even if malicious files or emails still exist, preventing further progression while remediation continues.

In a compromised user scenario, attack disruption focuses on cutting off the identity paths the attacker is using. If Defender XDR identifies that a user account is being used as part of an active attack, containment can restrict the account's ability to continue suspicious activity while the investigation continues. This reduces the attacker's ability to use the account for lateral movement, mailbox access, data access, or further authentication attempts.

Session interruption and token revocation are important because attackers often rely on active sessions rather than only passwords. If a session or token remains valid after compromise, the attacker may continue operating even after the initial alert has been raised. **Revoking tokens** forces reauthentication and helps break access that was already established, while session interruption limits the attacker's ability to continue using an active authenticated connection.

Device containment applies the same principle to endpoints. If a device is involved in the attack path, containment can limit communication from that device while preserving investigation access for security teams. This helps stop the device from being used to reach other systems, communicate with malicious infrastructure, or continue execution while evidence is reviewed.

These actions create **attack chain breakpoints**. A breakpoint is the point where Defender XDR interrupts the attacker's ability to continue the next stage of the attack. In practice, this may mean stopping account use, ending a session, revoking a token, isolating a device, or blocking communication with malicious infrastructure. The value of attack disruption is not that it fixes every affected artifact immediately, but that it prevents the attack from continuing while remediation catches up.

However, disruption depends on correctly identifying the attack path. If the disruption targets only part of the activity, the attacker may still retain access through other vectors. Similarly, if legitimate entities are incorrectly identified as compromised, disruption can impact normal operations. The analyst must therefore verify that the containment aligns with the observed behavior and confirm that all relevant entities have been addressed before considering the incident contained.

Analyst-driven validation and remediation decisions

Automation can accelerate containment, but it does not conclude the investigation. Once automated investigation, remediation, or disruption actions have been applied, the incident still requires your judgment as an analyst to determine whether those actions matched the actual attack path and whether the threat has been fully contained. At this point, you move from reviewing system-led action to confirming whether the incident is actually contained.

The analyst validates two things: scope and correctness. **Scope** means that all affected entities have been accounted for, including the user, message artifacts, resulting device activity, and follow-on access or session behavior. **Correctness** means that the automated actions targeted the right entities, went far enough to contain the threat, and did not act too broadly. A message may have been removed and a user session interrupted, but if related access attempts or downstream activity remain unaddressed, the incident is not resolved.

Remediation becomes a decision process, where the analyst decides whether containment is sufficient or whether more action is needed. You must determine whether to maintain containment, extend it to additional entities, reverse actions that proved unnecessary, or escalate the investigation if the observed behavior suggests a broader compromise. In other words, automation performs the first response, but the analyst decides whether that response was sufficient.

This is commonly tested when identifying whether additional investigation or remediation is required after automated actions have completed. That distinction matters because email threats often act as the opening move rather than the full attack. If analyst validation is weak, remediation becomes too narrow, and the incident appears closed while parts of the compromise remain active. If validation is too aggressive or poorly reasoned, legitimate activity can be disrupted unnecessarily. The analyst, therefore, acts as the final control point between automated response and confirmed incident resolution.

Investigating and remediating threats or compromised entities identified by Microsoft Purview

Not all threats begin with malware or external compromise. In many cases, risk originates from how data is accessed, shared, or handled within the organization itself. Activities such as unusual data access, policy violations, or insider-driven behavior can signal security issues that are not immediately visible through traditional detection mechanisms. In Microsoft Purview, these signals are surfaced through audit logs, data protection alerts, and insider risk detections, forming a different type of investigation surface focused on data and user behavior.

Purview investigations move away from malicious artifacts and toward data handling: who accessed data, how it was used, and whether that use matches expected activity. The investigation is centered on reconstructing actions over time, using audit records and alert context to determine whether the behavior represents normal activity, a policy violation, or a potential security threat. For example, repeated access to sensitive files outside normal working hours may indicate potential data exfiltration, even if no malware or external attack is detected.

Remediation in this context is also different. Rather than isolating devices or blocking infrastructure, actions are typically focused on controlling access, enforcing policy, or mitigating risk associated with user behavior. Actions may involve restricting access to sensitive data, escalating the case for further review, or applying controls that prevent similar activity from continuing. The objective is not just to stop a single event, but to reduce the risk of ongoing or repeated exposure.

The analyst must determine whether the activity represents normal usage, a policy violation, user error, or malicious behavior. Data-related alerts can be ambiguous, and the same activity may be legitimate in one context and risky in another. The analyst must correlate the signals, understand the user context, and decide whether the activity reflects misuse, error, or malicious intent. If this interpretation is incorrect, remediation can either fail to address a real risk or unnecessarily disrupt legitimate business activity.

Audit log search and activity timeline reconstruction

Investigation in Microsoft Purview often starts with audit records, where user and administrator actions are captured as discrete events across Microsoft 365 services. These records provide visibility into operations such as file access, sharing activity, permission changes, and administrative actions, but on their own, they represent isolated points in time rather than a complete picture. The investigation relies on querying audit logs and correlating related events into a timeline. Analysts use that timeline to see how actions unfolded, how often they occurred, and which users, workloads, or objects were involved.

Timeline reconstruction is what transforms audit data into investigative insight. By aligning events across services such as Exchange, SharePoint, and OneDrive, as analysts, you can detect patterns that are not visible in single records. Repeated access, unusual sharing behavior, or administrative changes occurring in close succession may indicate risk, even when each action appears legitimate in isolation. For instance, a timeline showing a user accessing multiple sensitive files and then sharing them externally can indicate potential data exposure.

The same timeline may represent normal business activity or potential misuse depending on the user's role, access patterns, and timing. You must compare the timeline with expected usage before treating it as risky. Without that comparison, normal work can be escalated unnecessarily or genuine misuse can be missed.

The limitation of this approach is completeness. Audit logs only reflect recorded activity, so missing events or incomplete correlation can result in gaps in the timeline. If key actions are not included or relationships are not followed through, the investigation may stop short of identifying the full scope of activity, leaving potential issues unresolved.

Content search and review using eDiscovery

Content investigation in Microsoft Purview moves beyond activity logs and into the actual data involved in an incident. Where audit logs show what actions occurred, Microsoft Purview content investigation helps analysts locate, preserve, review, and export the content those actions affected, including emails, files, and other stored information across Microsoft 365 services.

The process is driven by search-based evidence collection. Analysts define search criteria based on users, locations, keywords, or conditions, then retrieve relevant content from sources such as Exchange mailboxes, SharePoint sites, and OneDrive accounts. The investigation shifts from behavioral signals to tangible evidence, allowing analysts to determine what data was accessed, shared, or modified.

The tool choice depends on the requirement. If the task is only to find content across Microsoft 365 locations, Content Search is the direct choice. If the requirement is to preserve content for investigation or legal review, eDiscovery Hold is used. If the requirement is to review collected content in a managed review workflow, eDiscovery Review Set is the correct choice. Export can appear in both workflows, but the exam distinction is based on whether the scenario asks only to find content or to preserve and review it as part of an eDiscovery process.

Once located, content must be reviewed against the incident. The presence of a file or email alone is not sufficient; the analyst must determine whether it is relevant to the suspected activity. This includes examining the content itself, understanding how it was used, and identifying whether it contains sensitive or inappropriate information tied to the suspected activity. The goal is to establish whether the content supports or contradicts the suspected behavior identified through other signals.

eDiscovery also plays a role in scoping the investigation. By identifying all instances of relevant content, analysts can determine whether the activity is isolated or part of a broader pattern. For instance, a single email may not represent significant risk, but multiple related items across different locations can indicate wider exposure.

The effectiveness of this process depends on how precisely the search is defined and how thoroughly the results are reviewed. Narrow searches can miss critical evidence, while overly broad searches can introduce noise that obscures relevant findings. If relevant content is overlooked or misinterpreted, the investigation may fail to accurately assess the impact of the activity or the extent of data exposure.

Insider risk case investigation and activity correlation

Insider risk investigation in Microsoft Purview focuses on patterns of user behavior rather than isolated actions. Unlike audit logs or single alerts, insider risk cases aggregate multiple signals over time, allowing analysts to evaluate whether a sequence of activities indicates potential misuse, negligence, or malicious intent.

A typical situation involves a user downloading large volumes of sensitive data before leaving the organization, which may indicate potential insider risk when viewed as a pattern of behavior over time. Investigation relies on case-based correlation. Activities such as unusual file access, data movement, policy triggers, or behavioral anomalies are grouped into a case tied to a specific user. The approach allows analysts to determine how actions relate across time, building a behavioral profile rather than reviewing disconnected records.

Correlation is what gives meaning to these signals. A single action such as downloading files or accessing sensitive content may be normal, but when combined with other indicators like access outside typical patterns, repeated policy triggers, or changes in activity volume, it can signal elevated risk. The investigation, therefore, depends on identifying how these indicators align and whether they represent a deviation from expected behavior.

Time is a critical factor in this analysis. Insider risk cases are not evaluated at a single point but across a sequence of events, allowing trends and escalation patterns to emerge. Analysts must determine whether behavior is increasing in risk, remaining consistent, or returning to normal, as this influences how the case is interpreted and handled.

The challenge lies in distinguishing intent. Behavioral indicators do not inherently confirm malicious activity; they require interpretation. If correlation is incomplete or context is misunderstood, normal user activity may be escalated unnecessarily, or genuine risk may be underestimated. As an analyst, you need to link the indicators to the user's normal pattern before deciding whether the case reflects misuse, error, or malicious intent.

Data loss prevention alert investigation and context analysis

Data loss prevention (DLP) investigation in Microsoft Purview centers on understanding how sensitive information is being handled at the moment a policy is triggered. Unlike behavioral or timeline-based investigations, DLP focuses on specific events where content has matched defined conditions, making context the most critical factor in determining risk.

The process begins with the alert itself. Each DLP alert is generated when content meets policy criteria such as sensitive information types, classification labels, or pattern matches. However, the alert alone does not determine severity. Analysts must examine what data was involved, where it was located, how it was accessed or shared, and who performed the action. They examine the sensitive data involved, the action taken, and the destination or recipient. They then compare those details with expected business use. The same DLP alert can mean different things depending on whether the data was sent to an approved partner, copied to a personal email account, or shared with an unknown external recipient.

The investigation also depends on policy interpretation. DLP policies define what constitutes a violation, but they can generate alerts for both malicious and legitimate activity. Analysts must determine whether the alert reflects intentional data exfiltration, accidental exposure, or acceptable use that triggered policy conditions. This requires evaluating both the data and the user's intent against normal business use. For example, sending a sensitive file to an approved external legal adviser may be acceptable business activity, while sending the same file to a personal email account may indicate accidental exposure or deliberate exfiltration. The correct response depends on whether the action was malicious, accidental, or acceptable business use, not on the alert alone.

A key challenge is noise versus signal. Overly broad or poorly tuned policies can generate large volumes of alerts, making it difficult to identify genuine risk. If context is not properly analyzed, critical incidents may be overlooked while low-risk activity is escalated unnecessarily. Analysts assess the alert by combining the policy match with the data involved, the action taken, the user, and the destination.

Purview-based remediation and response handling

Remediation in Microsoft Purview moves the investigation from understanding risk to controlling its impact. Once activity has been validated through audit, Insider Risk, or DLP analysis, response actions are applied to contain exposure, enforce policy, and manage the outcome of the case.

Response actions are applied based on investigation outcomes, so remediation reflects the full scope of the activity, including access restriction, data control, escalation, and documentation. Remediation operates across multiple Purview domains. In audit-based investigations, actions focus on tracking and documenting activity. In insider risk scenarios, responses may involve escalating the case, applying user-level controls, or initiating review processes. In DLP scenarios, actions are applied directly to data handling, such as blocking sharing, enforcing encryption, or triggering user notifications. Remediation aligns with the type of risk identified.

Consistency of response is critical. Similar types of incidents should lead to comparable actions, ensuring that policies are enforced predictably across the environment. This reduces ambiguity in decision-making and supports governance requirements, particularly where regulatory or legal considerations apply. Risk arises when there is a disconnect between investigation and response. If remediation is applied without fully understanding the context, it can disrupt legitimate business activity or fail to contain actual data exposure. Response handling works when the action matches the finding: access restriction for exposure, escalation for user risk, and policy enforcement for repeated misuse.

Investigating and remediating alerts and incidents identified by Microsoft Defender for Cloud workload protections

Investigation and remediation of alerts and incidents in Microsoft Defender for Cloud focuses on understanding threat activity across workloads and determining how that activity affects cloud resources. The emphasis is on interpreting alerts in context, understanding how activity unfolds within workloads, and ensuring that response actions address the full scope of the threat. If alert details are not fully interpreted or resource activity is not traced thoroughly, remediation may be insufficient, leaving workloads vulnerable or misconfigured.

The following sections follow that response path from alert interpretation, through resource activity tracing and threat behavior identification, to containment and Sentinel correlation.

Workload alert interpretation and threat context analysis

The process in Microsoft Defender for Cloud begins with the alert, but the alert itself is only the starting point. What matters first is understanding what type of threat has been detected, how serious it appears to be, and which workload resource has been affected. Without that interpretation, the investigation has no reliable direction.

Interpretation determines whether the alert represents expected workload behavior or a real security risk. Analysts must evaluate the detected threat type, the severity assigned to it, and the specific workload resource named in the alert. These elements work together. Severity on its own does not explain the incident, and the threat label on its own does not show business impact. The meaning of the alert depends on how those details fit the role and importance of the affected workload.

Workload context matters immediately. A high-severity alert on a sensitive production workload carries a different level of urgency than the same alert on a low-value or noncritical resource. In the same way, a suspicious action against a database workload must be interpreted differently from similar activity against a virtual machine or container. Analysts must understand not only what the alert says, but what that alert means in the environment where it appeared.

Threat context analysis also determines the next step in the investigation. If the alert indicates a likely active compromise, the investigation moves quickly toward tracing related activity and preparing containment. If the context suggests suspicious but unconfirmed behavior, the analyst may need to validate the signal before escalating. In both cases, correct interpretation at the alert stage prevents the investigation from moving in the wrong direction.

If analysts treat severity or threat type as self-explanatory, they may overreact to noise or underestimate real compromise. As an analyst, you should first decide what the alert means for that specific workload before choosing the next response step.

Resource activity investigation and event tracing

Once the alert has been interpreted, the investigation moves to the affected resource itself. At this stage, the analyst is no longer asking what the alert claims, but what actions actually took place on the workload. That shift is what turns detection into evidence.

In practice, an alert indicating suspicious execution on a virtual machine must be validated by examining the actual processes and commands executed on that resource. Activity is examined, and events are traced across the workload. Analysts review the actions performed on the affected resource and follow the sequence of execution or interaction within the workload. The investigation determines what ran, what connected, what changed, and how those actions relate to the time and context of the alert. The goal is to move from a high-level signal to a concrete sequence of resource activity.

Alerts rarely tell the whole story on their own. A workload alert may indicate suspicious execution, unusual access, or potentially malicious interaction, but only resource activity reveals how that behavior unfolded. Tracing events allow you to see whether the activity was isolated, whether it triggered additional behavior, and whether it spread beyond the initial point of concern.

The workload itself shapes how those events are interpreted. Execution on a virtual machine, interaction inside a containerized service, or activity against a managed resource each carries different investigative meaning. Analysts must understand what normal execution and interaction look like for that workload so they can separate expected operations from suspicious behavior.

If relevant actions on the resource are missed, or if the sequence of events is only partially reconstructed, the investigation can stop before the real scope is known. The analyst needs to follow the activity trail far enough to understand what the workload actually did after the alert condition appeared.

Workload-specific threat behavior identification

Threat behavior identification in Microsoft Defender for Cloud focuses on determining whether the activity observed on a workload represents malicious or abnormal behavior. The investigation moves beyond individual events into understanding how those events reflect attacker techniques within the workload.

The investigation now turns to behavior. After tracing activity at the resource level, analysts must assess whether the observed actions align with expected workload operations or indicate compromise.

Analysts do this by looking for behavior patterns that do not match the workload's expected role. *Table 9.1* shows common workload behavior patterns and what each one may indicate during investigation:

Pattern type	What it may indicate
Unusual process execution	Unexpected code execution, suspicious scripts, or processes that do not match the workload's normal behavior.

Pattern type	What it may indicate
Unexpected network communication	Connections to unusual destinations, command-and-control behavior, or traffic that does not match expected workload communication.
Privilege escalation attempts	Attempts to gain higher permissions or perform actions beyond the normal role of the workload.
Abnormal access patterns	Access from unusual users, locations, or paths that suggest misuse or compromise.

Table 9.1 – Workload behavior patterns and investigation meaning

These patterns do not confirm compromise on their own. Their meaning depends on the workload, its normal activity, and the surrounding alert context. A process that is suspicious on an application server may be expected on an administration system, so the analyst must interpret each pattern against the resource being investigated. That context is what prevents misclassification. The same administrative action may be expected on a management system but suspicious on an application workload.

Behavior identification also involves mapping activity to known attack patterns. Rather than viewing events in isolation, analysts interpret sequences of actions to determine whether they reflect techniques such as persistence, lateral movement, or execution of malicious code. This helps confirm whether an alert represents an actual threat or benign activity.

The primary risk is misclassification. If normal workload behavior is incorrectly identified as malicious, it can lead to unnecessary escalation. If malicious behavior is missed due to lack of context or pattern recognition, the compromise may continue undetected. Accurate threat behavior identification depends on correctly interpreting activity within the workload's operational context.

Workload remediation and containment actions

Once malicious or abnormal behavior has been identified, the investigation transitions into action. In Microsoft Defender for Cloud, remediation focuses on directly controlling the affected workload to stop the threat and prevent further impact.

Response actions are executed on the resource itself. These actions are applied to the affected workload based on what was observed during investigation. Rather than analyzing signals, the system now enforces control, changing the state of the resource to limit or remove the threat. Containment is the immediate priority. This involves securing or isolating compromised workloads to prevent further interaction with other resources. Isolation may restrict network communication, limit access, or stop execution paths that could allow the threat to spread. The goal is not to fully resolve the incident at this stage, but to stabilize the environment and prevent further escalation.

Remediation actions must align with the type of workload and the nature of the threat. Actions applied to a virtual machine differ from those applied to containers or managed services. Analysts must ensure that the response matches both the workload architecture and the behavior identified during the investigation.

If containment is applied too late, the threat may expand across workloads. If actions are too aggressive or misapplied, they can disrupt legitimate operations. Remediation works when the right action is applied to the right workload at the right time, based on validated investigation findings.

Sentinel integration for workload alert correlation

Integration between Microsoft Defender for Cloud and Microsoft Sentinel extends workload investigations beyond a single resource by bringing alerts into a broader incident context. This allows workload signals to be analyzed alongside identity, endpoint, and application data.

Alerts are forwarded into Sentinel and correlated within incidents. Alerts generated from workload protections are sent into Sentinel, where they are grouped into incidents and combined with signals from other sources. The result is a single workload alert becoming part of a larger investigative picture, enabling analysts to understand how the activity relates to events elsewhere in the environment.

Correlation is the key outcome of this integration. Once workload alerts are inside Sentinel, they can be linked with other alerts based on shared entities such as users, IP addresses, devices, or resources. This allows analysts to identify whether the workload activity is isolated or part of a broader attack that spans multiple domains.

The scope of investigation changes. Instead of focusing only on the affected workload, analysts can trace activity across services, identities, and endpoints. A workload compromise may be connected to credential misuse, lateral movement, or external access patterns that are only visible when data is combined across platforms.

If workload alerts are not integrated into Sentinel, investigations remain siloed and may miss connections between related activities. Workload signals need to be included in the wider security data set so multi-domain attacks can be identified and understood.

Investigating and remediating security risks identified by Microsoft Defender for Cloud Apps

Security risks in Microsoft Defender for Cloud Apps arise from how users interact with cloud applications, how applications are connected to the environment, and how data is accessed and shared across those services. Unlike workload or endpoint security, the focus here is not on infrastructure but on SaaS activity, identity-driven access, and application-level behavior.

The investigation model is built around visibility into cloud activity. Defender for Cloud Apps collects signals from connected applications, user sessions, and access patterns, allowing analysts to observe how cloud services are being used. These signals form the basis for identifying abnormal behavior, risky application integrations, and suspicious access to sensitive data.

Risk is determined through context rather than single events. A user accessing a cloud application, granting permissions to an app, or interacting with data may all be legitimate actions in isolation. The risk emerges when those actions deviate from expected patterns, involve excessive permissions, or expose sensitive information in ways that do not align with normal usage.

App governance adds another layer to this investigation because many cloud risks are created through applications rather than direct user activity. Analysts review connected apps, permission grants, publisher information, consent activity, and usage behavior to determine whether an application is expected, overprivileged, or behaves in a way that creates risk. This is especially important when an app has access to mail, files, users, or other Microsoft 365 data because the application may continue operating even when no user is actively signed in.

OAuth app investigation focuses on how an application was authorized and what access it received. A suspicious OAuth app may request broad permissions, receive consent from a user or administrator, and then use that access to read data, send messages, or interact with resources through APIs. The analyst needs to determine who granted consent, which permissions were approved, what resources the app accessed, and whether the activity matches a legitimate business purpose.

These investigations connect application access back to user behavior and data interaction. A risky app is not judged only by its name or permission list; it is judged by how it was authorized, what it accessed, which users or data were affected, and whether its behavior fits the organization's expected SaaS activity. For instance, a user accessing a cloud application from an unusual location while downloading sensitive data may indicate account compromise when those signals are combined.

Investigation evaluates three dimensions together: user behavior, application access, and data interaction. *Table 9.2* shows how each dimension shapes cloud app investigation:

Dimension	**What to analyze**
User	Behavior patterns, access locations, session activity, and deviations from normal usage.
Application	Permissions, OAuth grants, integrations, publisher trust, and whether the app has more access than expected.
Data	Access, downloads, sharing activity, sensitivity, and whether data movement creates exposure.

Table 9.2 – Cloud app investigation dimensions

These dimensions need to be reviewed together because risk often appears in the relationship between them. A user action may look normal until it is linked to an unusual session, an overly permissive app, or sensitive data movement.

Remediation follows directly from this analysis. Once risky behavior, applications, or data access patterns are identified, actions are applied to control sessions, restrict access, or remove unsafe integrations. The effectiveness of the response depends on how accurately the initial risk was interpreted across these dimensions.

The challenge is that risky SaaS access can look normal until user behavior, app permissions, and data movement are reviewed together. Cloud environments introduce indirect access paths, delegated permissions, and session-based interactions that are not always obvious. If these signals are not correctly interpreted, risks can remain hidden within normal-looking activity. Effective investigation depends on recognizing how these signals combine to create security exposure.

Cloud app activity analysis and user behavior investigation

In Microsoft Defender for Cloud Apps, analysts examine user activity across cloud applications to identify behavior that does not match expected usage. Actions such as accessing applications, interacting with files, sharing data, or switching between services are grouped into patterns so the analyst can distinguish normal variation from suspicious behavior.

Behavior is interpreted against expected usage. Each user has a baseline of normal activity based on role, location, application usage, and access patterns. Analysts must determine whether observed actions deviate from this baseline, including unusual access times, unfamiliar application use, or unexpected changes in activity volume. This deviation is what signals potential risk.

Pattern recognition is critical. A single abnormal action may not indicate compromise, but repeated or combined anomalies can reveal suspicious behavior. For example, changes in access patterns combined with unusual application usage can indicate account misuse or unauthorized activity. The investigation depends on identifying these patterns rather than relying on isolated indicators.

If baseline activity is not understood, normal usage may appear suspicious or genuine anomalies may be dismissed. Analysts need to separate normal variation from behavior that suggests account misuse or unauthorized cloud access.

Risky application and OAuth permissions investigation

The scope in Microsoft Defender for Cloud Apps extends beyond user activity to include applications that have been granted access to cloud services. These applications, often connected through OAuth permissions, can operate on behalf of users and access data without direct user interaction, making them a critical area of risk.

The investigation examines application permissions and access levels. Analysts review connected applications and the permissions they have been granted to determine what level of access exists within the environment. This includes identifying which applications can read data, modify content, or act on behalf of users, and understanding how those permissions align with expected usage.

Risk emerges from excessive or inappropriate permissions. An application with broad access rights, especially if it is not trusted or well understood, can introduce significant exposure. Analysts must identify applications that request more permissions than necessary, have an unclear purpose, or originate from unverified sources. These characteristics can indicate potentially malicious or risky applications.

OAuth access introduces indirect control paths. Once permissions are granted, applications can maintain access independently of user activity, meaning that risk persists even if the user is not actively using the application. Investigation must therefore consider both the application itself and the scope of its permissions, not just the initial consent event. Identify and remove overly permissive or untrusted applications as a key remediation step to eliminate unauthorized access.

If application access is not evaluated, hidden access paths may remain active. If investigation focuses only on user actions, malicious or overly permissive applications may remain undetected while continuing to access data. The analyst must identify both the application and the permissions it holds before deciding whether the access path is acceptable.

Data access and session activity investigation

The investigation then moves into how users interact with data during cloud application sessions. Analysts review actions such as viewing, downloading, sharing, or modifying content, while also checking where access came from, how long the session lasted, and what happened during that session.

The risk depends on both the sensitivity of the data and the action performed. Viewing a low-risk document may be expected, while downloading or sharing sensitive data from an unusual session can indicate exposure. Analysts need to evaluate the data and the session together before deciding whether the activity is acceptable or risky.

Session behavior provides additional indicators. Abnormal session patterns such as unusual locations, atypical access sequences, or unexpected activity during a session can signal compromised accounts or unauthorized access. These behaviors often appear subtle when viewed individually but become significant when evaluated as part of a session pattern. As an analyst, you must examine data access and session behavior together to decide whether the interaction deviates from expected behavior.

User, session, and application remediation actions

Remediation in Microsoft Defender for Cloud Apps focuses on applying control over users, sessions, and connected applications once risk has been identified. This stage translates investigation findings into actions that limit exposure and prevent further misuse of cloud services.

Response is applied through **governance and control actions**. Based on the investigation outcome, actions are applied to the affected user account, active sessions, or connected applications. These actions are not generic; they are targeted to the specific source of risk, whether that risk originates from user behavior, session activity, or application permissions.

Session control is a primary response capability. Active sessions can be restricted or terminated to immediately stop ongoing activity. This is critical when abnormal behavior or unauthorized access is detected, as it prevents further interaction with cloud resources while the investigation continues.

User and application control extends beyond sessions. Actions may involve restricting user access, removing or limiting application permissions, or enforcing governance policies to prevent recurrence. These controls ensure that both direct and indirect access paths are addressed, reducing the likelihood of continued exposure.

If only one aspect (such as the user or the session) is addressed, other access paths may remain active, allowing the threat to persist. Containment must cover the affected user, active session, and connected application so another access path does not remain open.

Cross-signal correlation with identity and endpoint data

The investigation does not end at cloud activity. To understand the full scope of risk, cloud signals must be correlated with identity and endpoint data, allowing analysts to determine whether observed behavior is part of a broader attack.

Correlation links cloud activity with identity and endpoint signals. Cloud app activities such as abnormal access, risky applications, or suspicious data interaction are linked with signals from identity systems and endpoint telemetry. This allows analysts to trace whether the same user, device, or session appears across multiple security domains.

Identity correlation is a key component. User activity observed in cloud applications can be matched with sign-in behavior, authentication patterns, and risk signals from identity systems. This helps determine whether suspicious cloud activity aligns with compromised credentials, unusual sign-ins, or elevated identity risk.

Endpoint correlation extends this further. If a user's device shows signs of compromise, that context changes how cloud activity is interpreted. Actions that might appear normal in isolation can indicate threat activity when linked to a compromised endpoint. This connection allows analysts to move from isolated cloud signals to a confirmed multi-domain incident.

This correlation determines whether cloud activity is part of lateral movement, credential misuse, or a broader multi-domain attack path. If cloud, identity, and endpoint signals are investigated separately, relationships between them may be missed. Accurate investigations depend on linking these signals to build a complete view of the incident.

Investigating and remediating compromised identities identified by Microsoft Entra ID

Compromised identity investigation in Microsoft Entra ID focuses on detecting and responding to risks associated with user accounts. Unlike workload or cloud app investigations, the core concern here is whether an identity has been exposed, misused, or taken over.

The investigation model is risk-driven. Entra ID evaluates risk signals such as sign-in behavior, credential exposure, and anomalous activity to identify potentially compromised identities and determine the level of risk associated with each user. Identity risk is built from multiple signals, not one event. For example, a user with leaked credentials and multiple risky sign-ins presents a higher likelihood of compromise than a single isolated signal. Analysts must interpret these signals collectively rather than relying on one event to determine whether the identity is likely compromised.

This creates a dependency on both user-level and sign-in-level analysis working together. User risk reflects the overall likelihood that an identity is compromised, while sign-in risk reflects the likelihood that a specific authentication attempt is suspicious. Understanding how these two perspectives relate is essential for accurate investigation.

Remediation depends on correctly interpreting risk. Actions such as forcing password reset, requiring reauthentication, or enforcing access controls are applied based on the level and type of risk detected. If risk is misinterpreted, remediation may be ineffective or unnecessarily disruptive. The key challenge is distinguishing real compromise from false positives. Identity systems generate risk signals based on patterns and heuristics, which require validation. Analysts should confirm whether risk detections represent actual compromise before applying remediation actions.

Risky user investigation and compromise assessment

The process in Microsoft Entra ID begins with evaluating users flagged as risky. This focus is on determining whether the identity itself is likely compromised based on accumulated risk detections and behavioral indicators.

Evaluation focuses on overall user risk based on aggregated signals. Entra ID assigns risk levels to users based on detected indicators such as leaked credentials, abnormal behavior patterns, or suspicious activity across services. These detections are aggregated to represent the overall likelihood that the identity has been compromised.

Assessment requires interpreting multiple signals together. A single detection may not confirm compromise, but a combination of indicators increases confidence in the risk. Analysts must evaluate the type of detections, their frequency, and their severity to determine whether the user account is genuinely at risk.

This analysis also considers persistence of risk. User risk is not tied to a single event but reflects ongoing exposure. If risk detections continue to appear or remain unresolved, the likelihood of compromise increases. Analysts must determine whether the risk is transient or sustained.

If risk is underestimated or overstated, response actions may be ineffective or disruptive. If user risk is underestimated, a compromised identity may continue to be used undetected. If overestimated, legitimate users may be unnecessarily disrupted. Effective investigation depends on accurately assessing whether the identity is truly compromised based on those indicators.

Risky sign-in investigation and authentication analysis

The investigation extends to analyzing individual authentication attempts that are flagged as risky. This stage focuses on evaluating individual authentication events within the broader investigation. Each authentication attempt is evaluated using signals such as location, device,

IP address, and behavioral patterns. These signals are used to determine whether the sign-in deviates from expected patterns and therefore represents a potential risk.

Location, device, and session context shape how the sign-in is assessed. A sign-in from an unusual location, unfamiliar device, unexpected IP address, or abnormal access time may indicate unauthorized access when it does not match the user's normal authentication pattern. This stage is event-specific. Unlike user risk, which reflects overall identity compromise likelihood, sign-in risk focuses on a single authentication attempt. Analysts must determine whether that specific event should be trusted, blocked, or investigated further.

Incorrect interpretation of authentication signals can either allow unauthorized access or disrupt legitimate users. Analysts must evaluate each sign-in against the user's normal location, device, IP address, and access pattern before deciding whether to trust, block, or investigate it.

Differentiation and validation of identity risk signals

Effective analysis in Microsoft Entra ID determines whether risk is associated with the user or the sign-in by distinguishing between different identity risk signals. This stage focuses on understanding the difference between user risk and sign-in risk and validating whether detected conditions represent a real threat.

User risk represents the likelihood that an identity is compromised based on aggregated detections over time, while sign-in risk reflects the risk associated with a specific authentication event. These signals operate independently but must be interpreted together during investigation.

Validation requires contextual analysis. A high sign-in risk does not always mean the user is compromised, and a high user risk does not always indicate an active attack in progress. Analysts must correlate detections, timelines, and activity patterns to determine whether the signals reinforce each other or represent isolated events. This also involves confirming detection accuracy. Risk signals are generated based on machine learning and behavioral analysis, which means false positives can occur. Analysts must validate whether the detected condition aligns with known user behavior or expected activity.

Correlation between signals is critical. When user risk and sign-in risk align such as a risky user combined with a high-risk sign-in, the likelihood of compromise increases significantly. When they do not align, further investigation is required before taking action.

If relationships between signals are misunderstood, the investigation may follow the wrong path. Treating all risk detections equally can lead to unnecessary remediation or missed compromise. Analysts should distinguish and validate identity risk signals before taking remediation action.

Identity remediation and risk reduction actions

Once identity risk has been validated, response actions in Microsoft Entra ID are used to reduce or eliminate that risk. This stage focuses on executing remediation actions that directly affect the compromised identity and enforcing outcomes that restore a secure state.

Remediation is applied directly to the identity. Actions are applied to the user account to interrupt potential compromise and prevent further unauthorized access. These actions are tied to risk signals and are designed to reduce the likelihood that the identity can continue to be misused. Remediation typically targets authentication and access. This can include requiring the user to reauthenticate, enforcing additional verification, or resetting credentials. These actions ensure that any potentially compromised session or credential is no longer valid.

Risk reduction also involves enforcing policy outcomes. Identity Protection policies can automatically trigger remediation actions when defined risk thresholds are met. This ensures that risk is addressed consistently and does not rely solely on manual intervention.

The effectiveness of remediation depends on alignment with the detected risk. Actions must match the severity and type of risk identified. Overly weak remediation may allow compromise to persist, while overly aggressive actions may unnecessarily disrupt legitimate users. If actions do not fully address the underlying risk, the identity may remain vulnerable or continue to be exploited. Effective response ensures that risk is both reduced and validated as resolved.

Correlation of identity risk with security incidents

Identity risk signals in Microsoft Entra ID do not exist in isolation. This stage focuses on linking identity-related events with broader incidents across platforms such as Microsoft Defender XDR and Microsoft Sentinel to build a complete attack picture.

Correlation connects identity events with broader security activity. Identity events such as risky users or sign-ins are connected with signals from endpoints, email, cloud applications, and workloads. This allows analysts to understand how identity compromise fits into a wider attack chain. Correlation provides context. A risky sign-in on its own may appear isolated, but when linked with endpoint activity or cloud access patterns, it can reveal lateral movement or multi-stage attacks. Identity often acts as an entry or pivot point in broader incidents.

This stage enables incident-level visibility. In unified incident views, identity signals are combined with alerts from multiple sources, allowing analysts to track activity across domains without switching contexts. This improves both investigation speed and accuracy.

Effective correlation depends on recognizing relationships between signals. Analysts must determine whether identity events are related to other alerts or represent separate activity. This requires understanding timelines, entities, and behavior across systems. If identity signals are not linked to broader activity, critical parts of the attack may be missed. Identity risk should be reviewed in the broader incident context, not treated as a separate signal.

Investigating and remediating security alerts from Microsoft Defender for Identity

Identity attacks are different from other security events because the attacker is often trying to use the environment as it was designed to work. Instead of dropping obvious malware or triggering a clearly isolated exploit, they move through authentication paths, directory relationships, privileges, and trust between systems. That makes identity compromise especially dangerous: the activity can look legitimate on the surface while still representing reconnaissance, credential theft, privilege abuse, or lateral movement in progress. Microsoft Defender for Identity exposes attacker behavior against the identity layer. The value comes from identifying the technique being used, the users or assets involved, and how that activity connects to the wider incident.

Lateral movement paths are central to identity investigation because attackers rarely stop at the first compromised account. Defender for Identity helps analysts understand how an attacker may move between users, devices, and resources by abusing credentials, directory relationships, privileged access, or trusted authentication paths. The analyst uses these relationships to determine whether the activity is limited to one account or whether the attacker has a route toward more sensitive systems.

Honeytoken accounts provide a high-confidence signal. These are decoy accounts that should not be used in normal activity. If a honeytoken account is queried, authenticated against, or used in suspicious activity, it can indicate reconnaissance or attempted credential misuse. Because legitimate users should not interact with these accounts, activity involving them carries stronger investigative weight than ordinary account activity.

Suspicious activities must be interpreted in context. An alert may involve reconnaissance, abnormal authentication, credential misuse, privilege escalation, or attempts to access resources through trusted identity paths. The analyst reviews what happened, which account or device was involved, and whether the activity fits a known attack technique or normal administrative behavior.

The **identity timeline** helps place these signals in sequence. Instead of reviewing each alert as an isolated event, the analyst can see how authentication attempts, directory queries, account activity, and related alerts developed over time. This timeline view is important because identity attacks often look harmless when viewed one event at a time, but become clear when the sequence shows reconnaissance, access attempts, and movement toward higher-value accounts or systems.

Investigation starts by identifying the identity attack technique represented by the alert, not by assessing general account risk. Some alerts indicate early-stage probing, where the attacker is learning the environment and testing access paths. Others indicate direct credential misuse or attempts to operate across multiple systems using trusted identity relationships. The investigation must distinguish between those stages, because the meaning of the alert depends on what the attacker is trying to achieve through identity.

It also means the investigation cannot stop at the alert label. Identity alerts must be interpreted in relation to the affected user, the associated device, the surrounding authentication activity, and any evidence that the same behavior is appearing elsewhere in the incident. What matters is the attack path around the identity. An alert about suspicious identity activity becomes far more significant if it connects to unusual endpoint behavior, compromised credentials, or repeated movement across systems. That is why Defender for Identity investigation sits so naturally inside the broader Defender XDR incident context, even though its investigative lens remains identity-specific.

Remediation follows the same logic. The purpose is not only to acknowledge that identity risk exists, but to limit the attacker's ability to continue using that identity path. Once the alert has been understood and the affected entities have been investigated, the response must contain the misuse, reduce the value of the compromised identity, and prevent further unauthorized access. If that containment is delayed or too narrow, the attacker can continue to move through the environment using valid-looking identity activity.

The main challenge is that identity attacks are easy to underestimate when the investigation is too shallow. If analysts treat the alert as just another suspicious event instead of reading it as evidence of attacker technique and identity-path abuse, they can miss the real significance of what is happening. In Defender for Identity, analysts should treat identity alerts as signals of attacker behavior, not merely account warnings. They show how an attacker may be using trust, credentials, and access relationships to advance the attack. This pattern is most visible when the same credentials are used repeatedly across multiple systems, because that behavior can indicate lateral movement through the environment.

Identity alert analysis and attack technique identification

The investigation in Microsoft Defender for Identity determines which identity attack technique the alert represents. These alerts are not generic signals; they are detections mapped to specific identity attack techniques occurring within Active Directory and hybrid identity environments.

Observed activity is mapped to known identity attack techniques. Each alert is generated based on patterns that indicate known identity attack methods, such as reconnaissance of directory structure, credential harvesting, or misuse of privileged access. The alert is therefore a representation of attacker intent rather than just anomalous activity.

Analysis requires identifying the attack stage. Some alerts indicate early reconnaissance, where the attacker is attempting to discover accounts, permissions, or relationships. Others indicate credential access or misuse, where valid identities are already being used or tested. The meaning of the alert depends on where it sits in this progression.

It also involves interpreting how the activity was detected. Identity alerts are often based on authentication behavior, directory queries, or abnormal use of protocols and credentials. Analysts must understand what triggered the detection to determine whether the behavior reflects real attacker activity or benign variation.

Technique identification provides direction for the rest of the investigation. Reconnaissance alerts lead the analyst to assess what the attacker may have learned, while credential misuse alerts require containment and a review of where those credentials have been used.

Without identifying the underlying attack technique, analysts may misjudge the severity or stage of the threat. Effective investigation depends on translating each alert into a clear understanding of attacker behavior.

Entity-based investigation of users and related assets

After identifying the attack technique, investigation in Microsoft Defender for Identity shifts to the entities involved. This stage focuses on analyzing the affected identity and its related assets to understand how the activity occurs and what scope the compromise may have.

The investigation expands from the identity to related entities and assets. Alerts are anchored to identities, but those identities are connected to devices, services, and other accounts through authentication and access relationships. Investigation, therefore, expands from the alert to everything associated with that entity.

This requires examining the user account in context. Analysts review authentication patterns, recent activity, and interactions with other systems to determine whether the behavior is consistent or indicative of misuse. The identity is treated as a pivot point for the investigation rather than an isolated object. Associated assets must also be analyzed. Identities do not act alone; they authenticate devices, access services, and interact with other entities. Investigating related devices and systems helps determine whether the activity is confined to a single point or part of a broader compromise.

Relationship analysis is critical. Connections between identities, devices, and services can reveal how activity propagates. For example, repeated access between systems or unusual authentication paths may indicate that the identity is being used to move through the environment. Without examining related assets and interactions, the investigation can miss the broader scope of the compromise. Investigation must expand from the identity to all associated entities and their activity.

Identity-focused detection of lateral movement activities

As investigation progresses in Microsoft Defender for Identity, attention shifts to how identities are used across systems, with a focus on detecting lateral movement where compromised credentials are used to access additional devices and expand control. This involves tracking identity usage across authentication patterns to identify abnormal access and expansion beyond expected scope. Defender for Identity highlights patterns that indicate movement rather than normal access behavior. This includes identifying credential reuse across systems. When the same identity authenticates to multiple hosts in a short timeframe or accesses systems outside its normal scope, it may indicate lateral movement. In these cases, the pattern of access is more significant than any single event.

Authentication pathways are central to this analysis. Lateral movement typically follows trust relationships within the environment, such as domain authentication or delegated access. Analysts evaluate whether the authentication flow aligns with expected behavior or represents abnormal traversal across systems. Sequence and progression also provide context. Movement follows a path, often showing repeated access attempts, escalation in system sensitivity, or expansion of access scope. Because valid credentials are used, the activity may not trigger traditional endpoint detections, making recognition of identity usage patterns essential.

Correlation within Defender XDR incident context

Identity alerts from Microsoft Defender for Identity gain full meaning when viewed within the broader incident context provided by Microsoft Defender XDR. This stage focuses on linking identity-based detections with signals from endpoints, email, and cloud applications to understand how identity activity fits into the overall attack.

Alerts are correlated within a unified incident context. Alerts generated by Defender for Identity are not investigated in isolation. They are grouped and connected within a unified incident that aggregates related signals across domains. This allows analysts to move from a single identity alert to a complete view of attacker activity.

Correlation provides timeline continuity. Identity events can be aligned with other detections to show how an attack evolves. For example, a credential-related alert may align with endpoint execution or suspicious access to cloud resources, revealing the sequence of actions taken by the attacker. This stage also enables multi-entity visibility. Incidents bring together users, devices, IP addresses, and applications into a single investigative context. Identity alerts become one component of a larger set of relationships that define the attack path.

Effective correlation requires identifying meaningful relationships. Not all alerts within an incident are equally relevant. Analysts must determine which signals are connected and how identity activity contributes to the progression of the attack. If identity activity is not correlated with other signals, the attack path may be incomplete. Accurate investigation depends on understanding how identity signals integrate into the full attack narrative.

Containment and remediation of identity-based threats

Once identity-based threat activity has been confirmed, response in Microsoft Defender for Identity focuses on limiting the attacker's ability to continue using compromised credentials or identity paths. This stage is about containing identity misuse and enforcing actions that prevent further unauthorized access.

Containment focuses on restricting identity-based access. Unlike endpoint containment, where a device can be isolated, identity-based threats require controlling how the identity can authenticate and what it can access. This shifts the response to the authentication and authorization layer. Containment targets active misuse. If an identity is being used across systems, immediate action is required to interrupt that activity. This may involve restricting access, forcing reauthentication, or removing the conditions that allow continued use of the compromised identity.

Remediation must also address persistence. Attackers often attempt to maintain access through credential reuse, delegated permissions, or privilege escalation. Simply stopping one session is not sufficient if the identity can be reused elsewhere. Actions must ensure that the identity can no longer be leveraged across the environment.

This stage depends on aligning response to the attack behavior. If lateral movement has been detected, containment must prevent further movement. If credential misuse is confirmed, remediation must ensure those credentials are no longer valid in any context. Effective remediation ensures that identity-based access is fully controlled and that unauthorized use cannot continue.

Investigating and remediating alerts and incidents identified by Microsoft Sentinel

In Microsoft Sentinel, investigation operates at the point where detection has already been aggregated across multiple systems. Instead of working from isolated alerts, analysts begin with incidents that represent correlated activity drawn from different data sources, including identity, endpoint, cloud, and network signals.

The investigation is centered on how related alerts, entities, timelines, and behavior patterns connect, what they collectively indicate, and how the activity has progressed across the environment. Sentinel functions as the aggregation and correlation layer. It ingests and normalizes data from multiple sources so analysts can see activity across the broader attack surface rather than within the boundary of a single product or workload.

Investigation depends on interpreting relationships between entities. Users, devices, IP addresses, and resources are linked within the incident, forming the structure of the attack path. Analysts must determine which entities are central, how they interact, and which actions represent meaningful attacker activity. The scale of data introduces complexity. Incidents may contain multiple alerts and large volumes of related activity. Effective investigation requires filtering, prioritization, and the ability to focus on signals that define the attack rather than surrounding noise.

Response actions are applied at the incident level. Remediation is based on the full context of the attack rather than individual alerts, ensuring that actions address the complete activity chain and not just isolated events. If alerts are investigated individually, the overall attack path may be missed.

Sentinel incident investigation using aggregated alerts

In Microsoft Sentinel, investigation begins with incidents that already contain related alerts, entities, and activity over time. The analyst uses that grouped context to determine how events are connected. This reduces fragmentation and gives analysts a unified starting point for assessing activity across domains.

Analysis requires examining how alerts relate to each other. Not all alerts within an incident carry equal weight. You must determine which alerts represent core attacker actions and which are secondary or contextual signals. This involves reviewing alert types, severity, and how they align within the incident timeline.

Entity analysis is central to this stage. Incidents include entities such as users, devices, IP addresses, and resources. These entities provide the structure of the investigation, allowing analysts to trace how activity moves across the environment and identify the components involved in the attack.

Timeline reconstruction shows how the incident evolved, including initial access, progression, and potential escalation. This timing is critical for determining both impact and next steps.

If the relationships between alerts, entities, and timelines are not analyzed, the investigation may miss how the activity connects into a coherent attack. The incident should be understood as one set of correlated signals, not as separate alerts.

Incident workflow management and tracking

Once an incident is being investigated in Microsoft Sentinel, it must be managed as a structured workflow rather than an informal analysis. This stage focuses on maintaining control over the investigation process through status, ownership, and documented progress.

The investigation is managed through defined incident lifecycle states. Each incident moves through defined states such as new, active, or closed, reflecting its current stage in the investigation. These states provide visibility into progress and ensure that incidents are not left unresolved or overlooked.

Ownership defines accountability. Assigning an incident to a specific analyst ensures that investigation responsibility is clear. Without ownership, incidents can remain unaddressed or be duplicated across analysts, leading to inconsistent handling. Tracking requires continuous updates. As investigation progresses, analysts record findings, actions taken, and observations within the incident. These notes provide context, support collaboration, and create a record of how conclusions were reached. Structured workflow enables coordination. In environments where multiple analysts may interact with the same incident, consistent updates and status management ensure that investigation efforts are aligned and not duplicated.

This stage also supports audit and review. Maintaining a clear record of actions and decisions allows incidents to be reviewed after closure, supporting lessons learned and improving future response.

Without proper tracking, incidents may stall or lack sufficient documentation. A structured incident record keeps ownership, findings, actions, and closure decisions traceable throughout the lifecycle.

Automated responses using automation rules and playbooks

Response in Microsoft Sentinel can be applied automatically once incident conditions are met. This stage focuses on how automation rules and playbooks are used to trigger and execute response actions without requiring manual intervention for every step.

Automation rules evaluate incidents as they are created or updated and apply logic based on conditions such as severity, alert type, or involved entities. When those conditions are met, predefined actions are triggered. Automation rules act as the decision layer. They determine when automation should occur, such as assigning incidents, updating status, or initiating a response workflow. This ensures consistent handling of incidents that meet known patterns or criteria.

Playbooks act as the execution layer. Built on workflow automation, they perform actions such as collecting additional data, notifying stakeholders, or initiating remediation steps. Playbooks extend response beyond simple updates and allow integration with other systems and services. This separation is critical because automation rules decide when response should occur, while playbooks define what actions are executed.

Table 9.3 shows the practical distinction:

Capability	Role in response
Automation rules	Evaluate incident conditions and decide when predefined handling should occur, such as assignment, status updates, or triggering a playbook.
Playbooks	Execute the response workflow, such as collecting more data, notifying stakeholders, or initiating remediation actions.

Table 9.3 – Automation rules and playbooks in Microsoft Sentinel response

Together, automation rules and playbooks give Sentinel a repeatable way to handle known incident patterns without waiting for every step to be performed manually.

Automation improves speed and consistency. Repetitive or time-sensitive actions can be executed immediately, reducing response time and ensuring that similar incidents are handled in a standardized way. If automation conditions are incorrect, actions may trigger inappropriately or fail to execute when required. If it is too restrictive, automation may fail to activate when needed. Automation works best when the trigger conditions match real incident patterns.

SIEM-based investigation using multisource data

The investigation in Microsoft Sentinel extends beyond predefined alerts by allowing analysts to query and analyze data directly across all connected sources. This stage focuses on expanding the investigation using raw and normalized data from multiple systems to validate findings and uncover additional activity.

Investigation analyzes data across multiple sources. Sentinel ingests data from a wide range of connectors, including identity, endpoint, cloud, and network sources. This data is stored in a centralized workspace, enabling analysts to investigate across domains without being limited to a single product's perspective.

Query-based investigation enables deeper analysis. Using search and query capabilities, analysts can examine specific events, filter activity, and correlate data across tables. This allows investigation to move beyond alerts and into the underlying telemetry that produced them. This stage is critical for expanding scope. Alerts may only represent part of the activity. By querying additional data, analysts can identify related events, confirm whether suspicious behavior occurred elsewhere, and determine the full extent of the incident.

Cross-source correlation is key. Activity from different systems can be combined to reveal patterns that are not visible within a single data source. For example, identity activity may align with endpoint behavior or network access, providing a more complete understanding of the attack. This approach also supports validation. Analysts can confirm whether alerts are accurate, identify false positives, and verify whether detected behavior represents actual compromise or benign activity.

If investigation does not expand into underlying data, important context may be missed, and the true scope of the incident may remain unclear. Analysts use multi-source data to validate the alert, find related activity, and confirm the true scope of the incident.

Investigating incidents using agentic AI, including embedded Copilot for Security

Microsoft Security Copilot supports investigations across Microsoft Defender XDR, Microsoft Sentinel, and Microsoft Purview by helping analysts interpret large volumes of security data, identify relationships, and summarize activity within existing investigation workflows. Copilot does not change the investigation process. It helps analysts get from raw alerts, queries, and telemetry to an initial understanding faster.

The role of Copilot is to act as an interpretation and acceleration layer. It consumes available telemetry, incident data, and alert context, and produces outputs such as summaries, correlations, and explanations. These outputs help analysts understand what is happening without needing to manually reconstruct every detail from underlying data sources.

This matters most in complex incidents, where identity, endpoint, cloud, and data signals can quickly overwhelm the analyst if they are reviewed one by one. Manually correlating these signals is time-consuming and error-prone. Copilot surfaces relationships and highlights relevant activity, allowing analysts to focus on validation and response.

Copilot can also assist with KQL generation when an investigation needs to move from summarized context into direct query-based validation. Instead of writing every query from scratch, the analyst can use Copilot to draft KQL that searches for related activity, affected entities, suspicious sign-ins, device events, or matching indicators. The generated query still needs analyst review, because the analyst must confirm that the table, fields, filters, and time range match the investigation question.

Copilot may also provide remediation suggestions based on the incident context and observed activity. These suggestions can help the analyst identify possible next steps, such as isolating a device, restricting a compromised account, removing malicious messages, blocking indicators, or collecting more evidence. These recommendations should not be treated as automatic approval. The analyst still needs to validate the evidence, confirm the affected scope, and choose the response that fits the actual incident.

Embedded Copilot usage within investigation workflows

Embedded use of Microsoft Security Copilot occurs directly within investigation surfaces across Microsoft Defender XDR, Microsoft Sentinel, and Microsoft Purview. Analysts can use it while reviewing incidents, alerts, and investigation workspaces instead of leaving the workflow to analyze data elsewhere.

Copilot is used directly within investigation workflows. Copilot is available within incident views, alert panels, and investigation workspaces, allowing analysts to request analysis while actively working on an incident. This removes the need to switch tools or manually reconstruct context elsewhere.

Integration ensures continuity of investigation. Analysts remain within the same workflow while using Copilot to interpret alerts, summarize activity, or explore relationships. This keeps investigation aligned with the current incident state and avoids fragmentation of analysis across different tools.

Copilot operates consistently across domains. Whether the investigation involves identity activity, endpoint behavior, cloud application usage, or data access, the same AI capability is embedded within each platform. This creates a unified investigation experience across different security domains. This embedded model supports faster triage and analysis. Routine interpretation tasks, such as understanding alert context or identifying related activity, can be performed directly within the workflow, reducing the time required to move from detection to understanding.

However, Copilot does not change the investigation structure. It supports the workflow but does not define it. Analysts must still follow investigation steps, validate findings, and determine appropriate actions based on the context of the incident. If analysts rely on Copilot outputs without understanding how those outputs were derived, they may misinterpret findings or miss important context. Analysts still need to understand the underlying data and investigation logic before relying on the output.

AI-assisted incident summarization and data interpretation

AI-assisted summarization using Microsoft Security Copilot focuses on converting large volumes of investigation data into structured, understandable outputs. This stage is centered on how Copilot generates summaries and extracts key findings from alerts, incidents, and related telemetry.

Copilot interprets large volumes of investigation data. During an investigation, incidents often contain multiple alerts, entities, and activity records. Copilot processes this data and produces summaries that highlight what occurred, which entities are involved, and how events are related. This reduces the need for analysts to manually review each component in detail.

Summarization operates across different data types. Alerts, incident timelines, user activity, device behavior, and data access events can all be interpreted and condensed into a single narrative. This allows analysts to quickly understand the situation without needing to manually correlate every signal. Extraction of key findings is a critical part of this stage. Copilot identifies relevant indicators such as suspicious actions, affected users, or anomalous behavior patterns, and presents them as part of the summarized output. This helps prioritize investigation focus and identify areas that require deeper analysis. This capability supports faster triage. Analysts can move from raw data to an initial understanding of the incident more quickly, allowing them to decide whether further investigation or response is required.

However, summarization introduces abstraction. Important details may be condensed or omitted depending on how the AI interprets the data. Analysts must ensure that summarized outputs accurately reflect the underlying activity and do not overlook critical indicators. If summaries are accepted without reviewing underlying data, subtle but important signals may be missed. Summaries should be treated as a starting point, then checked against the underlying alerts, timelines, and entity data.

Context-aware analysis based on security telemetry

Context-aware analysis using Microsoft Security Copilot focuses on how AI interprets investigation data by using the full context of available security telemetry. The analysis goes beyond summarization and involves analyzing relationships between signals across different data sources.

Copilot interprets activity using combined security context. Copilot evaluates telemetry from multiple domains, including identity, endpoint, cloud applications, and data activity, and uses that combined context to interpret what the activity represents. Rather than analyzing signals in isolation, it considers how events relate to each other. This enables cross-domain understanding. For example, identity activity may be correlated with endpoint behavior or cloud access patterns. By combining these signals, Copilot can identify patterns that indicate coordinated or multi-stage activity, which would be difficult to detect when reviewing each signal separately.

Context is derived from available data. Copilot relies on the telemetry ingested into platforms such as Microsoft Defender XDR, Microsoft Sentinel, and Microsoft Purview. The accuracy and completeness of analysis depend on the quality and scope of this data. This supports interpretation of complex activity. Copilot can highlight relationships, suggest possible attack paths, and provide explanations of how different events are connected within an incident. This helps analysts understand not just what happened, but how and why it happened.

However, context-aware analysis is dependent on data completeness. If relevant telemetry is missing, incomplete, or incorrectly ingested, the analysis may be inaccurate or incomplete.

Copilot can only interpret what is available. If relationships between events are inferred incorrectly, analysts may follow the wrong investigation path or misidentify the nature of the threat. Validation against underlying data remains essential.

Analyst validation and decision-making based on AI output

AI-generated insights from Microsoft Security Copilot must be validated before they influence investigation outcomes or response actions. The focus is on the analyst's role in reviewing, verifying, and acting on Copilot-generated outputs.

Analysts validate AI-generated interpretations. Copilot provides summaries, correlations, and contextual analysis, but these outputs are derived from available data and inferred relationships. Analysts must confirm that these interpretations accurately reflect the underlying telemetry and incident context.

Validation requires comparison with source data. Analysts review alerts, logs, timelines, and entity activity to ensure that Copilot's conclusions align with observable evidence. This step ensures that no assumptions or inferred relationships are accepted without verification.

Decision-making is directly affected. Actions such as containment, remediation, or escalation are based on the analyst's confirmed understanding of the incident. Copilot may suggest insights, but the analyst determines whether those insights justify action. Decision-making remains a human responsibility. Analysts apply experience, contextual awareness, and organizational knowledge to determine appropriate responses. This includes identifying false positives, recognizing incomplete analysis, and deciding when further investigation is required. This stage also reinforces accountability. All investigation outcomes and response actions are ultimately owned by the analyst, regardless of whether AI-assisted insights were used during the process.

If Copilot output is accepted without verification, incorrect conclusions may lead to inappropriate remediation, missed threats, or disruption of legitimate activity. AI output should be treated as advisory; the analyst still owns the final interpretation and response decision.

Investigating complex attacks, such as multi-stage, multi-domain, and lateral movements

Complex attacks rarely occur as isolated events. Instead, they unfold across multiple systems, identities, and services, often progressing through several stages before detection. Investigation in platforms such as Microsoft Defender XDR and Microsoft Sentinel requires correlating activity across domains to understand how an attack develops and spreads.

You should focus on connecting signals rather than analyzing them individually. Identity activity, endpoint behavior, email events, cloud interactions, and workload activity must be considered together to reveal patterns that indicate coordinated or evolving threats. Multi-stage attacks introduce temporal complexity. For instance, an attack may begin with a phishing email, followed by credential use, then lateral movement across systems, requiring correlation across multiple stages to understand the full scope.

Activity must be analyzed across time to understand how an attacker progresses from initial access through persistence, privilege escalation, and lateral movement. Individual alerts may appear unrelated unless they are placed within a broader sequence. Lateral movement adds another dimension. Attackers often move between systems using compromised credentials, expanding access and increasing impact. Identifying this movement requires tracking how identities interact with multiple resources over time.

Entity correlation becomes central to investigation. Users, devices, applications, and resources must be linked together to determine how activity is connected. This allows analysts to move from isolated events to a full understanding of the attack. The goal of this investigation is scope determination. Analysts must identify not only what happened, but how far the attack has spread, which systems are affected, and what actions have been taken by the attacker.

When signals are analyzed separately, relationships between them may be missed. If activity is reviewed in isolation, the attack may appear incomplete or benign. Analysts reconstruct the attack path by linking signals across domains, timelines, and affected entities.

Multi-domain correlation across security data sources

Multi-domain correlation involves combining data from multiple security domains to understand how activity is connected across the environment. In platforms such as Microsoft Defender XDR and Microsoft Sentinel, this means linking signals from identity, endpoint, email, cloud applications, and workload sources into a unified investigation.

Signals are integrated across multiple security domains. *Table 9.4* maps each domain to the primary telemetry analysts use during multi-domain correlation.

Security domain	**Primary telemetry**
Identity	Sign-ins, authentication events, risky users, and credential-related signals.
Endpoint	Process execution, device alerts, file activity, and network connections.
Email	Message activity, sender, and recipient data, URLs, attachments, and delivery events.

Security domain	Primary telemetry
Cloud applications	User activity, session behavior, app permissions, and data access events.
Workloads	Resource alerts, workload activity, configuration changes, and runtime behavior.

Table 9.4 – Security domains and primary telemetry for multi-domain correlation

Individually, these signals may appear isolated, but when correlated, they reveal relationships that indicate coordinated activity. Correlation enables visibility across attack surfaces. An attacker may move between domains, such as using a compromised identity to access an endpoint, then interacting with cloud resources or email systems. By integrating signals across these domains, analysts can trace how activity spans different parts of the environment.

Correlation relies on normalized and connected data. Data connectors and integration between platforms ensure that signals from different sources can be aligned and analyzed together. Without this integration, correlation is limited and investigation becomes fragmented.

Multi-domain correlation supports detection of complex behavior. Patterns that are not visible within a single data source can be identified when signals are combined. This includes coordinated activity, unusual sequences, or interactions between entities across domains. If domains are analyzed separately, connections between them can be missed, leading to incomplete understanding of the attack.

Multi-stage attack sequence reconstruction

Multi-stage attack reconstruction focuses on identifying how an attack progresses over time by linking related activities into a coherent sequence. Within platforms such as Microsoft Defender XDR and Microsoft Sentinel, this involves organizing events, alerts, and entity activity into a timeline that reflects the attacker's progression.

Events are correlated across time to reconstruct attack progression. Each event or alert represents a point in time, but on its own does not explain how the attack evolved. By aligning these events chronologically, analysts can reconstruct the sequence of actions taken by the attacker. This enables identification of attack phases. Activities can be grouped into stages such as initial access, execution, persistence, privilege escalation, and movement. Recognizing these phases helps analysts understand where the attack started, how it developed, and what objectives the attacker may have had.

Reconstruction requires linking related activity. Events across different systems or domains must be connected to determine how one action led to another. This may involve correlating identity activity with endpoint behavior or cloud access over time. This stage supports understanding of progression. Analysts can determine whether activity is ongoing, whether escalation has occurred, and whether additional stages of the attack are likely. This directly influences investigation depth and response urgency.

If events are not correctly aligned or linked, the attack sequence may appear incomplete or misleading. This can result in missed stages of the attack or incorrect assumptions about its progression. Accurate reconstruction depends on correlating events across time and context.

Lateral movement detection across identities and systems

Lateral movement detection focuses on identifying how an attacker expands access across systems by using compromised identities. Within platforms such as Microsoft Defender XDR and Microsoft Sentinel, this involves tracking how credentials and access are used beyond the initial point of compromise.

Identity usage is tracked across systems. Once an identity is compromised, attackers often use it to access additional systems, escalate privileges, or move between resources. This movement is reflected in authentication events, resource access, and system interactions tied to that identity.

Detection requires observing access expansion. Analysts track where an identity is used over time, identifying patterns such as access to new systems, unusual login locations, or interactions with resources not previously associated with that user. These patterns indicate potential lateral movement. This stage also involves system-to-system linkage. Activity is not limited to a single device or service. Movement may occur between endpoints, servers, cloud resources, and applications. Detecting this requires correlating identity activity with the systems being accessed.

Credential usage is central. Repeated authentication attempts, use of elevated privileges, or access across multiple systems can indicate that credentials are being leveraged to expand control within the environment. The goal is to identify movement paths. Analysts determine how the attacker is progressing through the environment, which systems have been accessed, and whether additional compromise is likely.

If lateral movement is not identified, the attacker may continue expanding access without detection, increasing the impact of the compromise. Effective detection depends on tracking identity usage across systems and identifying abnormal access patterns.

Full attack scope determination through entity correlation

Full attack scope determination focuses on identifying the complete impact of an attack by correlating all related entities, alerts, and incidents. Within platforms such as Microsoft Defender XDR and Microsoft Sentinel, this involves linking users, devices, applications, and resources to understand how widely the attack has spread.

Entities are correlated across alerts and incidents. Each alert or event is associated with entities such as users, endpoints, IP addresses, or cloud resources. By linking these entities across alerts and incidents, analysts can identify how activity is connected and which components of the environment are involved. This stage builds on earlier investigation steps. Multi-domain correlation, timeline reconstruction, and lateral movement detection provide the relationships needed to connect entities. Entity correlation consolidates these findings into a unified view of the attack.

Scope determination requires identifying all affected entities. Analysts determine which users are compromised, which devices are impacted, which applications or resources are involved, and whether additional entities may be at risk. This defines the breadth of the compromise. This stage also supports impact assessment. Understanding which systems and identities are affected allows analysts to determine the severity of the attack, prioritize response actions, and ensure that all compromised components are addressed.

The goal is completeness. Investigation must ensure that no affected entity is overlooked and that all related activity has been identified. This prevents partial remediation and reduces the risk of continued attacker presence.

If entities are not fully linked, parts of the attack may remain hidden, leading to incomplete remediation and potential re-compromise. Scope is confirmed by linking all relevant entities, alerts, and activity before remediation is treated as complete.

Managing security incidents using case management

Case management provides a structured way to organize investigations that involve multiple related incidents. Within Microsoft Sentinel and Microsoft Defender XDR, analysts can group related activity, coordinate ownership, track tasks, and document progress across a broader investigation scope.

Without case management, related incidents may be handled independently, leading to fragmented analysis, missed relationships, and incomplete resolution.

Case coordination, task ownership, and lifecycle tracking

Case management brings related incidents into a single investigation so analysts can work from one shared view of the activity. Related incidents may involve the same user, device, IP address, workload, or attack pattern. Grouping them into a case helps the analyst see the full investigation scope instead of treating each incident as a separate problem.

Once the case is created, the work has to be broken into clear tasks. One analyst may review identity activity, another may validate endpoint evidence, and another may check cloud or data access signals. Assigning those tasks makes ownership clear and prevents the same work from being repeated while other evidence is missed.

Collaboration matters because complex investigations rarely stay within one signal or one platform. Notes, findings, task updates, and decisions need to stay inside the case so every analyst is working from the same context. This keeps the investigation coherent when responsibility moves between analysts or when different specialists contribute to the same response.

Lifecycle tracking keeps the case moving from triage to investigation, action, and closure. A case should not be closed simply because one incident has been handled. Closure only makes sense when the related incidents have been reviewed, required tasks are complete, remediation has been applied, and the outcome has been documented.

If case management is weak, related incidents can be handled in isolation, evidence can be duplicated or missed, and the final response may not address the full attack. Case management keeps the investigation organized, traceable, and complete from initial grouping through resolution.

Summary

Responding to alerts and incidents is the point where investigation becomes action. Across Microsoft Defender XDR, Microsoft Sentinel, Microsoft Purview, Microsoft Defender for Cloud, Microsoft Defender for Cloud Apps, Microsoft Entra ID, and Microsoft Defender for Identity, the analyst's job is to move beyond the first alert and understand the full scope of the activity. A message, identity, workload, application, or incident is rarely meaningful on its own. Its real significance comes from the users, devices, sessions, permissions, data, and timelines connected to it.

This chapter showed how response depends on interpretation before action. Automated investigation and response, automatic attack disruption, Sentinel automation rules, playbooks, Purview response actions, and identity remediation can all accelerate containment, but they do not remove the need for analyst judgment. Each action still must match the attack path, target the right entities, and avoid leaving related activity unresolved. A response that is too narrow can allow the attacker to continue operating, while a response that is too broad can disrupt legitimate business activity.

The chapter also reinforced the importance of correlation. Defender XDR incidents, Sentinel incidents, Purview cases, Defender for Cloud workload alerts, Defender for Cloud Apps activity, Entra ID risk signals, and Defender for Identity alerts all provide different views of suspicious behavior. The analyst has to connect those views into a single understanding of what happened, how far it spread, and what needs to be contained. That is especially important in multi-stage and multi-domain attacks, where the visible alert may only represent one part of a larger sequence.

Case management brings that work under control. By grouping related incidents, assigning tasks, documenting findings, and tracking the lifecycle of the response, analysts reduce the chance that evidence is missed or remediation is applied inconsistently. A well-managed case gives the SOC a shared view of the investigation and a clear record of how the incident moved from detection to resolution.

The next chapter builds on this response foundation by moving deeper into investigation technique. Once analysts understand how incidents are contained and managed, they need to know how to search, validate, and reconstruct activity across the available evidence. That means using investigation data more deliberately to confirm what happened, identify related activity, and support confident response decisions.

Exam Readiness Drill – Chapter Review Questions

Apart from mastering key concepts, strong test-taking skills under time pressure are essential for acing your certification exam. That's why developing these abilities early in your learning journey is critical.

Exam readiness drills, using the free online practice resources provided with this book, help you progressively improve your time management and test-taking skills while reinforcing the key concepts you've learned.

HOW TO GET STARTED

- Open the link or scan the QR code at the bottom of this page
- If you have unlocked the practice resources already, log in to your registered account. If you haven't, follow the instructions in *Free Benefits with Your Book* section in this book's *Preface* and come back to this page.
- Once you log in, click the START button to start this chapter's quiz
- We recommend attempting a quiz multiple times till you're able to answer most of the questions correctly and well within the time limit.
- You can use the following practice template to help you plan your attempts:

Working On Accuracy		
Attempt	**Target**	**Time Limit**
Attempt 1	40% or more	Till the timer runs out
Attempt 2	60% or more	Till the timer runs out
Attempt 3	75% or more	Till the timer runs out
Working On Timing		
Attempt 4	75% or more	1 minute before time limit
Attempt 5	75% or more	2 minutes before time limit
Attempt 6	75% or more	3 minutes before time limit

The above drill is just an example. Design your drills based on your own goals and make the most out of the online quizzes accompanying this book.

Link to this Chapter's Quiz

You need to unlock the online practice resources to access the link below. Check the *Free Benefits with Your Book* section in the *Preface* for detailed instructions on how to do this. You only need to unlock the resources once.

Open Quiz `https://packt.link/sc200js-ch9` or scan the QR code

10

Respond to Alerts and Incidents in Microsoft Defender for Endpoint

By this point, you are already working through incidents and applying responses across multiple platforms. Here, the investigation moves to the endpoint, where activity is reconstructed as a sequence rather than isolated events, and response is applied directly to the device.

This chapter addresses the following exam objectives of SC-200:

- Investigating device timelines
- Performing actions on the device, including live response and collecting investigation packages
- Performing evidence and entity investigation
- Investigating and remediating incidents identified by automatic attack disruption

In this chapter, you will work through how device activity is reconstructed using timelines, how events are connected and expanded through entity-based investigation, and how response actions are applied directly to endpoints, including containment, live response, and evidence collection. You will also look at how incidents that already include automated disruption are validated and completed, so that investigation and remediation reflect the full sequence of activity on the device.

Investigating device timelines

When an alert points to a device, the immediate challenge is not identifying a single event but understanding how that activity unfolded over time. Devices do not generate isolated signals. They produce a continuous stream of actions, each one connected to what came before and what follows. The timeline brings that sequence into focus, turning scattered telemetry into a coherent chain of activity.

Instead of treating events as individual data points, the timeline frames them as part of a progression moving the investigation from "what happened" to "how it happened," allowing the analyst to see the order of execution, the relationship between actions, and the transitions between stages of activity on the device. That perspective is what separates a surface-level alert review from a structured investigation.

By working within this sequence, the analyst can anchor the investigation to a specific moment in time and then expand outward. Activity that initially appears unrelated becomes connected once placed in order, revealing how processes, user actions, and network behavior interact on the endpoint. The timeline acts as the foundation for understanding device-level activity, providing the context needed before moving into deeper analysis or response.

Timeline access and event scoping

The investigation typically begins by entering the device timeline from either an alert or the device records itself, establishing the working scope and anchoring all analysis to a specific endpoint and a defined sequence of events. Within this view, events are presented in chronological order, forming the primary working surface for the investigation and making it possible to follow how behavior unfolds across the device over time. Because this sequence contains a large volume of activity, it must be narrowed before meaningful analysis can begin.

Filtering is used to constrain the timeline to a specific time range or event category, isolating the window where suspicious behavior is likely to exist. **Search** operates differently. Instead of narrowing the dataset, it moves directly to known indicators or actions within the timeline, allowing the analyst to locate specific events and then expand outward from those points.

Controlled entry, filtering, and search keep the investigation constrained to a defined set of events, so the sequence can be examined without unrelated activity getting in the way.

Event correlation within the timeline

With the timeline narrowed to the right window, the work changes. The question is no longer where the activity is, but how the events relate to each other. Events on a device do not occur independently. Each process execution, file interaction, network connection, or logon event forms part of a sequence that reflects how the system was used or manipulated.

Correlation within the timeline brings these event types together into a single view, allowing relationships to be observed directly. A process launch can be examined alongside the file it originated from, the account that initiated it, and any subsequent network communication it generated. Events no longer need to be analyzed in isolation; they are seen as part of a connected chain. This often appears when a process spawns a child process that initiates a network connection, indicating malicious execution flow when those events are correlated.

Alerts and automated investigation actions are embedded within this same sequence. Their placement within the timeline provides immediate context, showing exactly where detections occurred relative to surrounding activity and how the system responded. This makes it possible to assess whether an alert represents the start of activity, a midpoint in an attack, or a consequence of earlier actions.

By correlating events within a single, ordered sequence, the timeline exposes relationships that are not visible when reviewing individual records. The result is a connected view of activity, where multiple actions can be understood as part of a single pattern on the device.

Pivoting from timeline events to entities

As relationships between events become clear, the investigation often needs to move beyond the device timeline to examine the objects involved in those actions. A single event in the timeline is not the endpoint of analysis; it is an entry point into a wider set of related activities tied to a process, file, user, or network indicator.

Pivoting enables this transition. From a selected event, the analyst can move directly to the associated entity and view its broader activity outside the immediate timeline context. This shifts the investigation from a device-focused sequence to an entity-focused perspective, where behavior can be examined across multiple occurrences and, where applicable, across other devices or sessions. For instance, pivoting from a suspicious process to the associated file allows analysts to determine whether that file exists on other devices or has been executed elsewhere. This becomes clear when a process execution followed by a network connection and then a file modification indicates how malware was introduced, executed, and began interacting with external infrastructure when viewed as a sequence.

That shift matters. The timeline shows activity on one endpoint. Entity-level views show how that same artifact behaves elsewhere or over time. A process can be traced back to its origin, a file can be examined for prevalence, and a user account can be assessed across authentication activity. The pivot extends the investigation from a localized sequence into a connected set of behaviors.

By moving between events and their related entities, the investigation is no longer constrained to a single timeline. Instead, it becomes a structured expansion, where each pivot introduces additional context while maintaining a clear link back to the original activity that triggered the analysis.

Exporting timeline data for analysis

Not all analysis remains within the timeline view. At certain points, the investigation requires the underlying event data to be preserved, shared, or examined outside the interactive interface. Exporting the timeline provides a way to capture a defined portion of device activity as a static dataset tied to a specific time window.

The extraction is scoped deliberately. Only the selected range of events is included, ensuring that the exported data reflects the exact portion of activity under investigation rather than the entire device history. This maintains relevance and prevents unrelated activity from obscuring the findings. Once exported, the data becomes independent of the timeline interface. It can be reviewed without relying on the live environment, retained as part of an evidence set, or used to support further analysis where direct access to the timeline is not required.

By capturing the timeline in this way, the investigation gains a fixed reference point. The sequence of events is preserved exactly as it appeared during analysis, allowing conclusions to be revisited, validated, or communicated without depending on changes in the live dataset. In practice, exported timeline data can be used to share findings with other teams or to preserve evidence for further analysis without relying on the live environment.

Performing actions on the device, including live response and collecting investigation packages

Understanding what happened on a device is only part of the investigation. At some point, the focus shifts from observation to control. The analyst is no longer just interpreting activity but is actively influencing the state of the endpoint to contain risk or extract further evidence.

These actions operate directly against the device, which introduces a different level of responsibility. Each action has an immediate effect on the system, whether that is restricting communication, limiting execution, or capturing the current state for analysis. The investigation is no longer passive; it becomes an interaction with a live system that may still be under attacker influence.

The distinction between containment and investigation becomes critical at this stage. Some actions are designed to stop activity and prevent further movement, while others are intended to reveal more detail about what has already occurred. Choosing between them is not arbitrary. It reflects whether the priority is to control the situation or to understand it more deeply before acting.

Because these actions directly alter the condition of the device, they must be treated as part of the investigation record. Each decision contributes to the overall outcome, affecting what evidence can still be observed and how the incident progresses.

Containment vs. investigation actions on a device

Once the decision is made to act on a device, the first distinction that shapes the response is whether the action is intended to contain activity or to extract more information. These two paths operate under different priorities and selecting the wrong one can either limit visibility too early or allow unwanted activity to continue longer than necessary.

Containment actions are designed to immediately reduce risk. They change the operating conditions of the device in a way that restricts what can occur next, limiting communication or execution so that attacker movement is interrupted. These actions are forward-looking, focused on preventing additional impact rather than uncovering more detail about what has already happened.

Investigation actions serve different purposes. They are used to expose the current state of the device and gather additional context that may not yet be visible through existing telemetry. Instead of restricting behavior, they preserve access to information, allowing deeper inspection of processes, configurations, and activity that may still be unfolding.

The choice between these approaches defines how the investigation progresses. Acting too quickly to contain can remove access to valuable evidence, while delaying containment can extend the window of exposure. Each action represents a trade-off between control and visibility, and that trade-off must be made deliberately based on what the investigation requires at that moment. You would isolate a device when immediate containment is required, while investigation actions are used when additional evidence must be gathered before taking disruptive action.

Device isolation and network state control

When containment is required at the device level, isolation changes how the endpoint communicates with the rest of the environment. Instead of allowing normal inbound and outbound traffic, the device is placed into a restricted state where external communication is blocked, but its connection to the management service is preserved. This ensures that the device remains accessible for investigation even as its ability to interact with other systems is limited.

This change in network state has a direct impact on how activity can continue. Any attempt by an attacker to move laterally, communicate with external infrastructure, or establish persistence through network-based methods is interrupted. The device remains active, but its ability to participate in broader activity is constrained.

At the same time, isolation does not remove visibility. The analyst retains the ability to observe and interact with the device through the platform, allowing investigation to continue without reintroducing exposure. This balance is critical. The device is effectively contained within a controlled boundary, where its behavior can still be examined without allowing it to influence or be influenced by other systems. A common scenario is when isolating a device prevents lateral movement while still allowing analysts to continue investigating the system through the management interface.

Endpoint threat control actions

Not all responses require isolating a device. In many cases, the objective is to control specific activity on the endpoint without fully restricting its communication. Endpoint threat control actions operate at this level, targeting malicious or suspicious behavior directly rather than altering the entire network state of the device.

Antivirus scanning is one such control. It evaluates the device for known threats and takes action against identified malware, addressing issues that can be resolved through detection and removal. This approach focuses on eliminating malicious components that are already present on the system without changing how the device interacts with the rest of the environment.

Application restriction works differently. Instead of removing threats that have already been identified, it prevents specific binaries or processes from being executed. This is particularly relevant when an investigation identifies a known malicious tool or script that must be blocked from running again. The control is applied at the execution level, limiting what the device is permitted to run.

These actions provide targeted intervention. Rather than applying broad containment, they focus on controlling behavior that has been identified as risky or malicious. The device remains operational, but the specific activity that triggered the investigation is restricted. For instance, blocking a malicious process may be sufficient when the threat is confined to a single artifact, whereas full device isolation is required when broader compromise is suspected.

Live response for interactive investigation

When existing telemetry does not provide enough detail, the investigation moves beyond collected data into direct interaction with the endpoint. **Live response** enables this shift by providing controlled, real-time access to the system.

Through this capability, the analyst can interact with the device while it remains in its current state. This interaction is not passive. Commands can be executed, scripts can be run, and the current condition of the system can be examined in place. This allows the investigation to uncover details that are not visible through standard event data, particularly when dealing with transient activity or artifacts that have not yet been captured by telemetry. In practice, live response can be used to inspect running processes or retrieve files that have not yet been captured in telemetry.

Because live response operates on an active system, it must be used deliberately. Each command affects the device and can influence what remains observable. That same tension applies here, but at a more immediate level; the analyst is no longer selecting predefined actions but interacting directly with the environment. The analyst is no longer selecting predefined actions; they are directly interacting with the environment under investigation.

By enabling controlled interaction with the endpoint, live response extends the investigation into areas that cannot be reached through timeline analysis alone. It provides a deeper level of inspection while maintaining the connection between the analyst and the device, allowing investigation and response to occur in real time.

Investigation package collection and forensic artifacts

There are points in an investigation where a point-in-time capture of the device is required. Unlike live interaction, which examines the system in its current state through active commands, an **investigation package** creates a fixed snapshot of the device that can be reviewed independently of the live environment.

This snapshot contains a collection of forensic artifacts that describe how the system is configured and what is currently running. Information such as active processes, startup entries, and system configuration details provide a structured view of the device at the moment the package is collected. Rather than relying on streamed telemetry, the investigation is based on a captured state that does not change as the system continues to operate. For instance, collecting an investigation package allows analysts to review system state offline, preserving evidence even if the device changes after the collection.

The value of this approach is stability. The data remains consistent, allowing it to be examined repeatedly without being affected by ongoing activity on the device. This is particularly important when investigating behavior that may be short-lived or when preserving evidence that could otherwise be altered or removed.

The captured state becomes a reliable reference point for further analysis. The device continues to operate, but the collected artifacts represent a fixed record of its condition, enabling deeper analysis without dependency on the live timeline or real-time access.

Auditing device response actions

Every action taken on a device is tracked within the same context as the activity that triggered it, creating a continuous record of both what occurred on the endpoint and how it was handled. The record shows the sequence of actions applied to the device, linking each one to the broader investigation. It establishes visibility over who initiated the action, what was performed, and how the state of the device changed as a result. The investigation is no longer limited to observed behavior; it includes the response itself as part of the overall timeline.

Maintaining this history is critical for validating outcomes. It allows the analyst to confirm that containment or investigative steps were executed as intended and provides a reference for reviewing decisions made during the investigation. If additional action is required, the existing record ensures that the current state of the device can be understood without ambiguity.

By embedding response actions within the investigation context, the platform creates a complete view of both activity and intervention. The device is not only a source of evidence but also a subject of controlled change, and those changes are fully visible as part of the investigation lifecycle.

Performing evidence and entity investigations

An investigation rarely remains confined to a single device or a single event. What begins as an isolated signal quickly expands into a set of related artifacts, each representing a different aspect of the same activity. Understanding these artifacts individually is not enough; the investigation depends on how they connect and what those connections reveal.

Evidence represents the observable elements of the activity. Files that were executed, processes that were launched, accounts that were used, and network indicators that were contacted all form part of the investigative surface. These elements provide raw material for analysis, but on their own, they do not explain how the activity unfolded.

Entities introduce structure to that material. By grouping related artifacts into identifiable objects such as users, devices, files, and network indicators, the investigation gains a way to organize and relate what has been observed. This shifts the focus from isolated data points to connected components, each with its own role in the activity being examined.

As these components are linked together, the investigation moves from observation to interpretation. Relationships between entities begin to define how actions are connected, showing how activity progresses across different parts of the environment. The result is not just a collection of findings, but a mapped sequence of behavior that reflects how the activity developed.

Evidence and entity identification in investigations

The starting point for entity-based investigation is recognizing what has been observed and how it is represented. Activity surfaces as individual artifacts, but those artifacts are not treated equally. Some are captured as direct evidence of behavior, while others are structured as entities that carry context across the investigation.

Evidence refers to the specific items involved in the activity. A file that executed, a process that spawned, an IP address that was contacted, or a user account that initiated an action are all examples of artifacts that represent what occurred. These elements are tied directly to observed behavior and form the basis of what is being investigated.

Entities organize those artifacts into recognizable objects within the investigation. The platform associates each artifact with a broader identifier, such as a user, device, file, or network indicator, so related activity can be followed consistently across the investigation. This classification provides consistency, allowing related activity to be grouped and referenced as part of a larger context. This distinction affects how the investigation is structured. One case is where a file execution event represents evidence, while the file itself is treated as an entity that can be tracked across multiple events and devices.

Evidence captures individual occurrences, while entities provide continuity across those occurrences. The same file, user, or IP can appear multiple times in different contexts, and identifying it as a consistent entity allows those instances to be linked together rather than treated as unrelated events.

By separating artifacts into evidence and entities, the investigation gains both precision and structure. Individual actions remain visible, but they are anchored to objects that can be tracked and analyzed across the broader scope of activity.

Entity pivoting across investigations

Once entities have been identified, the investigation shifts from classification to movement. A single entity is rarely confined to one event or one location. It appears across multiple points of activity, and each occurrence provides an opportunity to expand the investigation. Pivoting enables this expansion.

From a selected entity, the analyst can move to other instances where that same object appears, following its activity across different events, sessions, or devices. This creates a path through the investigation, where each step is connected by a shared entity rather than by time alone. This movement changes the structure of the analysis. Instead of progressing linearly through events, the investigation branches outward, tracing how a file, user, or network indicator behaves across the environment. A process observed on one device can be followed to other systems, a user account can be examined across authentication activity, and an IP address can be tracked across multiple connections.

Pivoting provides continuity. For instance, pivoting on a user account can reveal activity across multiple devices, indicating whether the account is being used beyond the initial point of compromise. It connects separate observations through a common element, allowing the investigation to move from isolated findings to a linked set of behaviors. Each pivot reinforces or challenges the current understanding, gradually building a more complete view of how the activity extends beyond its original point of detection.

Entity-relationship mapping

As the investigation expands across multiple entities, the number of connections between them increases. At this point, following individual pivots is no longer sufficient to understand the full structure of the activity. The investigation requires a way to represent how these entities relate to each other as a whole. Entity relationship mapping provides this view. Instead of examining connections one step at a time, the investigation surfaces the relationships between artifacts in a unified structure, showing how entities are linked through shared activity. Files, processes, users, and network indicators are positioned relative to each other based on how they interact, forming a connected model of the observed behavior.

This makes patterns easier to identify. Rather than inferring relationships from separate observations, the connections are visible directly, allowing clusters of related activity to emerge. Repeated interactions, shared dependencies, and central points of activity become easier to recognize when viewed as part of a connected structure rather than as isolated links.

The graph does not replace individual analysis, but it reframes it. Each entity remains accessible for deeper investigation, while its position within the broader structure provides context that would not be apparent when viewed alone. This allows the investigation to move from a sequence of pivots to a structured understanding of how all related activity fits together.

File and process investigation

As entities are examined more closely, files and processes become central to understanding how activity was executed on the system. These elements represent the actual execution path of behavior, showing what ran, how it was initiated, and how it progressed.

File investigation focuses on the origin and presence of an artifact. A file can be traced to where it came from, whether it has appeared elsewhere, and how frequently it is observed across the environment. This establishes whether the file represents isolated activity or something more widespread, which directly affects how it is interpreted within the investigation.

Process investigation builds on this by examining execution behavior. Processes do not operate independently; they are linked through parent-child relationships that reflect how actions are initiated and chained together. By following these relationships, it becomes possible to see how one action led to another, revealing execution flows that are not immediately visible when viewing processes individually.

Files and processes define the operational layer of the activity. They show not just what exists, but what actually ran and how those actions were connected. This allows the investigation to move beyond identifying artifacts to understanding the execution path that produced the observed behavior. This becomes clear when examining parent-child process relationships, which reveal whether a legitimate process was used to launch malicious activity.

User and network investigations

Beyond files and processes, user accounts and network indicators provide a different perspective on activity. While execution artifacts show what ran on a device, user and network investigation reveal who initiated the activity and where it communicated.

User-focused analysis examines how an account is used across the environment. Activity such as authentication patterns, device associations, and session behavior establishes whether actions align with expected usage or represent deviation. The same account appearing across multiple devices or initiating unexpected activity can indicate misuse or compromise, extending the investigation beyond a single endpoint.

Network-focused analysis examines how the device interacts with external or internal systems. IP addresses and domains associated with activity provide visibility into communication patterns, showing where connections were made and how frequently they occur. These patterns can reveal command-and-control behavior, lateral movement attempts, or repeated contact with specific infrastructure.

These perspectives connect identity and communication to execution. They show not only what happened on the device, but who was responsible for initiating it and where the activity extended beyond the endpoint. This links local behavior to activity across the environment. For instance, repeated connections to the same external IP address may indicate communication with command-and-control infrastructure.

Correlating entities in an attack chain

As individual entities are investigated and their relationships become clear, the focus shifts to assembling those findings into a single, coherent structure. At this stage, the investigation is no longer concerned with isolated artifacts or individual connections, but with how all identified elements combine to represent a complete sequence of activity.

Correlation at this level brings together entities that have been examined separately and positions them within a unified progression. A file associated with initial access, a process linked to execution, a user account involved in authentication, and a network indicator tied to communication can all be aligned to reflect how the activity developed over time. Each entity contributes a specific role within that progression.

Together, those entities show how the activity moved from one stage to the next, a structure that emerges from multiple correlated findings rather than being inferred from any single artifact. By organizing entities into this sequence, the investigation reaches a point where the activity can be interpreted as a complete chain rather than a collection of findings. This makes it possible to make decisions based on a clear view of how the activity unfolded. Consider a case where a downloaded file, executed process, and outbound connection reveal the full attack chain from initial access to external communication.

Investigating and remediating incidents identified by automatic attack disruption

Not all incidents begin with manual investigation. In some cases, activity is identified and acted upon before the analyst becomes involved. **Automatic attack disruption** changes the starting point: rather than beginning with detection, the analyst begins with what has already been contained and must determine what remains unresolved.

It operates at the incident level rather than at the level of individual events or devices. Multiple signals are correlated into a single view, where related activity is grouped and assessed as part of a broader sequence. Within this structure, affected assets and actions taken against them are already defined, establishing a baseline for the investigation.

The presence of automated containment introduces a different type of analysis. Instead of determining whether action is required, the analyst evaluates what has already been done, how it has altered the state of the environment, and whether those actions fully address the activity. This requires a shift in focus from initiating response to validating and extending it.

The correct response often involves validating automated containment and determining whether additional remediation actions are required. Remediation builds on that validation. Containment limits what can happen next, but it does not remove what has already occurred. The investigation must therefore continue beyond disruption, identifying remaining artifacts, confirming that persistence has been eliminated, and restoring affected assets to a stable state.

Incident correlation and scope definition

At the incident level, investigation begins with understanding how individual signals have been grouped and what that grouping represents. An incident is not a single alert; it is a structured aggregation of related alerts, entities, and activity that together define a broader sequence of behavior.

Correlation within the incident brings these elements together into a unified scope. Alerts that may have appeared unrelated when viewed individually are connected through shared entities, timelines, or behavioral patterns. The result is a consolidated view, allowing the investigation to focus on the full extent of activity rather than isolated detections.

Defining scope at this level is critical. The incident establishes clear boundaries for what is included in the investigation, identifying which devices, users, processes, and network indicators are involved. It also distinguishes between activity that is part of the incident and activity that remains outside of it, preventing the investigation from expanding unnecessarily.

This scope differs from a device-level investigation. Instead of focusing on activity within a single endpoint, the incident provides a cross-entity perspective, where relationships between multiple assets are already established. The investigation begins with a defined structure, allowing the analyst to work within a bounded and correlated set of activity rather than constructing that structure from the ground up.

Identifying attacker-controlled assets

Once the incident scope is established, the investigation focuses on determining which assets within that scope are actively under attacker influence. Not every entity associated with an incident represents compromise. Some reflect normal activity that has been linked through correlation, while others indicate direct control or misuse.

Identifying attacker-controlled assets isolates the elements that are driving the activity. A device may be executing unauthorized processes, an account may be used in a way that deviates from expected patterns, or a network indicator may represent active communication with external infrastructure. These assets are not simply involved in the incident; they are central to how the activity occurs.

Instead of treating all entities equally, the investigation concentrates on those that represent active control points - the assets that define where the attacker is operating and where intervention has the greatest impact. A common scenario is when a compromised user account or an infected device represents an attacker-controlled asset that must be prioritized for containment.

The process also establishes priority. Assets that are confirmed or strongly associated with attacker control become the focus for containment and remediation, while other related entities provide context but do not drive immediate response decisions. By isolating these control points, the investigation moves from broad correlation to targeted action.

Automatic containment during attack disruption

When attacker-controlled assets are identified, containment actions may already have been applied before the investigation reaches this stage. Automatic attack disruption introduces these actions directly into the incident, altering the state of affected assets without requiring initial analyst intervention. These actions operate against the identified control points, restricting their ability to continue the activity. Devices may have their communication limited, accounts may have their access constrained, and other forms of control may be applied depending on how the activity is occurring.

The objective is not to analyze but to immediately reduce the ability of the attacker to proceed. Those actions do not begin with the analyst. The platform acts on correlated signals before manual response begins. The analyst's role starts with reviewing what was restricted and why. Both exist within the same incident context, but they differ in how and when they are applied.

Because these actions change the state of assets before full analysis is complete, they become part of the investigation itself. The analyst must understand what has already been restricted, how those restrictions affect ongoing activity, and whether the applied containment aligns with the observed behavior. The investigation therefore begins from a modified environment, where control has already been partially established.

Visibility of disruption actions within incidents

Once automatic containment has been applied, the investigation depends on understanding exactly what actions were taken and where they occurred within the sequence of activity. These actions are not separate from the incident; they are embedded within it, forming part of the same structure that represents the attack.

Within the incident view, disruption actions are positioned alongside alerts and entities, making their placement in the sequence visible. This shows when containment occurred relative to the activity, allowing the analyst to determine whether the action interrupted the behavior at an early stage, during progression, or after key events had already taken place. This visibility also establishes context for the current state of the environment. By examining where actions appear in relation to other elements of the incident, the analyst can understand which assets have been affected, what restrictions are currently in place, and how those restrictions relate to the observed activity.

The placement of these actions within the incident provides more than a record of what was done. It defines how the response aligns with the attack sequence, allowing the investigation to assess the effectiveness of containment within the broader context of the activity.

Analyst validation and continued investigation

After automatic containment has been applied and its placement within the incident is understood, the investigation moves into validation. The presence of disruption actions does not conclude the response; it establishes a controlled state that must be assessed to determine whether the activity has been fully contained.

Validation focuses on confirming the effect of those actions. For instance, verifying that a device is no longer communicating externally confirms that containment actions have been effective. The analyst examines whether the identified control points are no longer active, whether related activity has stopped, and whether any additional behavior continues outside the scope of the initial containment. This step ensures that disruption has achieved its intended outcome rather than assuming it has done so.

At the same time, the investigation continues beyond the original set of actions. New evidence may emerge, previously linked entities may reveal additional connections, and activity that was not initially included in the incident may become relevant. The investigation expands beyond the initial actions to reassess the broader environment.

Automated containment is where controlled investigation begins, not where it ends. The analyst's role is to verify, extend, and complete the response, ensuring that the activity is fully understood and that no remaining elements are left unaddressed.

Remediation and recovery of affected assets

Once containment has been validated and the scope of activity is fully understood, the investigation moves into remediation. At this stage, the focus is no longer on limiting what can happen next, but on removing what has already been established within the environment.

Remediation addresses the persistence of the activity. Any artifacts, configurations, or access paths that allowed the behavior to occur must be eliminated. This ensures that the conditions required for the activity are no longer present, preventing it from reappearing once containment is lifted. A typical situation involves removing malicious files and resetting compromised credentials to ensure the attacker cannot regain access after containment is lifted.

Recovery follows this removal. Affected assets are returned to a stable and usable state, where normal operation can resume without reintroducing risk. This requires confidence that the environment has been restored to a condition where the original activity cannot continue.

This stage completes the transition from control to resolution. Containment restricts the attack, validation confirms its effectiveness, and remediation removes its presence. Together, they ensure that the incident is not only stopped but fully addressed.

Tracking actions and investigation states

Actions taken during the incident are not isolated steps; they form a continuous record that reflects how the situation has been handled and what the current state of each affected asset is. Within the incident view, this record captures the sequence and status of actions applied across entities. It shows which actions have been completed, which are still in effect, and how those actions relate to the assets involved. This creates a clear picture of the investigation's progression, where both activity and response are visible in a single context. This visibility also supports decision-making.

For instance, reviewing completed actions allows analysts to confirm which containment steps have already been applied and whether additional actions are still required. By understanding the current state of each asset, the analyst can determine whether additional action is required or whether the incident has reached a point where recovery is complete. The investigation is no longer based solely on observed behavior but also on the confirmed state of response. Tracking links each phase of the investigation into a consistent reference; without it, actions and outcomes risk becoming disconnected from the incident they were meant to address.

Summary

This chapter focused on how you investigate and respond to threats directly on the endpoint using Microsoft Defender for Endpoint. You covered how device timelines are used to reconstruct activity as a sequence, allowing you to understand how events connect rather than viewing them in isolation.

You learned how investigation expands from timeline events into entities such as files, processes, users, and network indicators, and how pivoting across those entities helps you follow activity beyond a single device. You also covered how response actions are applied at the device level, including containment, endpoint threat control, live response, and investigation package collection, and how each action affects both visibility and control during the investigation.

Finally, the chapter also discussed how incidents that include automatic attack disruption are handled, including validating containment, continuing investigation, and completing remediation so that all affected assets are fully addressed.

Exam Readiness Drill – Chapter Review Questions

Apart from mastering key concepts, strong test-taking skills under time pressure are essential for acing your certification exam. That's why developing these abilities early in your learning journey is critical.

Exam readiness drills, using the free online practice resources provided with this book, help you progressively improve your time management and test-taking skills while reinforcing the key concepts you've learned.

HOW TO GET STARTED

- Open the link or scan the QR code at the bottom of this page
- If you have unlocked the practice resources already, log in to your registered account. If you haven't, follow the instructions in *Free Benefits with Your Book* section in this book's *Preface* and come back to this page.
- Once you log in, click the START button to start this chapter's quiz
- We recommend attempting a quiz multiple times till you're able to answer most of the questions correctly and well within the time limit.
- You can use the following practice template to help you plan your attempts:

Working On Accuracy		
Attempt	**Target**	**Time Limit**
Attempt 1	40% or more	Till the timer runs out
Attempt 2	60% or more	Till the timer runs out
Attempt 3	75% or more	Till the timer runs out
Working On Timing		
Attempt 4	75% or more	1 minute before time limit
Attempt 5	75% or more	2 minutes before time limit
Attempt 6	75% or more	3 minutes before time limit

The above drill is just an example. Design your drills based on your own goals and make the most out of the online quizzes accompanying this book.

Link to this Chapter's Quiz

You need to unlock the online practice resources to access the link below. Check the *Free Benefits with Your Book* section in the *Preface* for detailed instructions on how to do this. You only need to unlock the resources once.

Open Quiz `https://packt.link/sc200js-ch10` or scan the QR code

Part 5

Automate Security Operations

In this part of the book, you will bring investigation and response together through automation. You will learn how Microsoft Defender XDR and Microsoft Sentinel use notifications, alert tuning, endpoint settings, automated investigation and response, automatic attack disruption, device groups, automation rules, and playbooks to reduce manual effort and make incident handling more consistent.

This part of the book includes the following chapters:

- *Chapter 11, Configure Automation for Microsoft Defender XDR and Microsoft Sentinel*

11

Configure Automation for Microsoft Defender XDR and Microsoft Sentinel

You are already detecting, investigating, and responding to threats across the environment. At this stage, the emphasis moves to automation, where detection, investigation, and response are applied consistently without relying entirely on manual action.

This chapter addresses the following exam objectives of SC-200:

- Configure email notifications in Microsoft Defender XDR, including incidents, actions, and threat analytics
- Configure alert notifications in Microsoft Defender XDR, including tuning, suppression, and correlation
- Configure Microsoft Defender for Endpoint advanced features
- Configure rules settings in Microsoft Defender for Endpoint
- Configure custom data collection in Microsoft Defender for Endpoint
- Configure security policies for Microsoft Defender for Endpoint, including **attack surface reduction (ASR)** rules
- Manage automated investigation and response capabilities in Microsoft Defender XDR
- Configure automatic attack disruption in Microsoft Defender XDR
- Configure and manage device groups, permissions, and automation levels in Microsoft Defender for Endpoint

- Create and configure automation rules in Microsoft Sentinel
- Create and configure Microsoft Sentinel playbooks

In this chapter, you work through the controls that shape automated communication, alert handling, endpoint protection, investigation, response, and cross-system execution. Before moving into those areas, take a look at *Table 11.1,* which establishes the main boundaries that prevent similar-sounding configuration options from being confused:

Boundary	What it controls	What it does not control
Notifications vs detection	Notifications communicate selected incidents, actions, or threat analytics updates to recipients.	They do not create alerts, change detection logic, correlate incidents, or execute response actions.
Rules vs policies	Rules define how activity is evaluated and surfaced as detections or alerts.	They do not enforce endpoint protection settings or directly control device behavior.
Automation rules vs playbooks	Automation rules manage incident workflow, such as assignment, tagging, status, classification, and invoking playbooks.	They do not perform remediation actions themselves; playbooks execute response actions through Logic Apps.

Table 11.1 – Configuration boundaries for notification, detection, enforcement, and response automation

With these boundaries established, you can now move through each automation area with a clear distinction between communication, detection, enforcement, and response execution. The first of these areas is email notification configuration, where the focus is not on changing detection behavior, but on deciding which security events should be communicated, when they should be sent, and who should receive them.

Configure email notifications in Microsoft Defender XDR, including incidents, actions, and threat analytics

Email notifications provide a controlled way to communicate security events beyond the Microsoft Defender XDR interface. A common scenario is when high-severity incidents trigger immediate email notifications to the security operations team, so critical activity is surfaced even when analysts are not actively monitoring the platform.

Notification trigger sources and event types

Email notifications in Microsoft Defender XDR are driven by specific event types that originate from different stages of the security workflow. Each one reflects a different kind of activity within the platform and determines what information is communicated.

One primary trigger source is **incidents**. Incidents represent correlated collections of alerts that have been grouped together based on related activity. When notifications are tied to incidents, they reflect outcomes from the detection pipeline after correlation has already occurred. This makes them suitable for communicating consolidated security events rather than individual detections.

Another trigger source is **automated actions**. These are generated when response activities, such as automated investigation or remediation, are executed within the environment. Notifications based on these events provide visibility into what actions have been taken, allowing stakeholders to understand how the system is responding without needing to inspect the platform directly.

A third trigger source is **threat analytics updates**. These represent intelligence-driven insights. Notifications in this category communicate newly identified threats, trends, or relevant intelligence that may impact the environment. They are not tied to a specific alert or incident but instead provide broader situational awareness.

Configuring these notifications requires selecting the appropriate trigger sources based on what type of information needs to be communicated. For instance, incident-based notifications communicate correlated attack activity, while automated action notifications show which remediation steps have already been taken.

Configuration of notification conditions and severity

Once trigger sources are defined, notification behavior is controlled through conditions that determine when those triggers result in an email. These conditions act as the filtering layer between platform activity and communication, so only relevant events are surfaced.

In the Microsoft Defender portal, go to **Settings > Microsoft Defender XDR**, then **select Email notifications** under **General**.

From there, the configuration depends on the notification type:

- **Incident notifications:** configured from the **Incidents** tab. The rule defines the notification name, recipients, severity filter, device group scope, and whether one notification is sent per incident.

- **Response action notifications:** configured from the **Actions** tab. The rule defines the action source, action type, action status, device group scope, and recipients.
- **Threat analytics notifications:** configured from the **Threat analytics** tab. The rule defines which report updates generate email notifications and who receives them.

Conditions are typically based on attributes such as **severity**, **status**, and **event type**. Severity is one of the most important controls because it aligns notification behavior with impact. High-severity incidents can trigger immediate communication, while lower-severity events may be excluded when they do not require direct action.

Status-based conditions define **when in the lifecycle** a notification is sent. For example, notifications may be triggered when an incident is first created, when it is updated, or when it is resolved. This allows communication to be aligned with progression, ensuring stakeholders are informed at meaningful points rather than at every change.

Event-type conditions further refine notification behavior by limiting which triggers result in communication. Even within the same trigger source, not all events are equally relevant. Filtering by event type ensures that notifications reflect only the specific categories of activity that matter to the intended audience.

These conditions keep notification rules tied to operational value. Severity, status, and event type should give a clear reason for sending the message. Selecting severity-based conditions ensures that only high-impact incidents trigger notifications, avoiding unnecessary alerts for low-priority activity.

Recipient targeting and distribution configuration

After defining when notifications are triggered, the next step is determining **who receives them**. Recipient configuration controls how notification information is distributed and ensures that communication aligns with roles and responsibilities.

Recipients can include individual users, security teams, or distribution lists. The selection of recipients should reflect operational ownership. For example, high-severity incident notifications are typically directed to security operations teams, while broader updates—such as threat intelligence notifications—may be shared with a wider audience including security managers, incident response teams, threat intelligence analysts, IT operations personnel, and other stakeholders responsible for monitoring organizational risk. This alignment ensures that the right people receive the right information without unnecessary exposure.

Recipient targeting is not just about inclusion but also about **scoping**. Notifications should be mapped to specific event types and conditions so that recipients only receive relevant communication. Sending all notifications to all recipients reduces effectiveness, as important signals can become lost in volume. Proper scoping ensures that communication remains focused and actionable. Targeting should also follow operational ownership. Each notification type should have a clear audience so the message reaches the people responsible for acting on it.

Further, distribution configuration also determines how notifications are managed at scale. Using groups or distribution lists allows communication to be handled consistently without requiring individual configuration for each recipient. This supports maintainability and ensures that updates to team structures do not require constant reconfiguration of notification settings.

> Note
>
> **Separation of notifications from detection and incident creation**
>
> As shown in *Table 11.1*, email notifications are communication outputs, not detection controls. They report selected incidents, actions, or threat analytics updates after platform activity has already occurred.
>
> The practical implication is configuration ownership. If the goal is to change who is informed, when they are informed, or which notification type is sent, notification settings are the correct control. If the goal is to reduce alerts, change detection behavior, or alter incident formation, the change belongs in alert tuning, suppression, correlation, or rule configuration.

Configure alert notifications in Microsoft Defender XDR, including tuning, suppression, and correlation

Alerts in Microsoft Defender XDR represent the output of detection logic applied across endpoints, identities, email, and other protected workloads. They are the first indication that suspicious or malicious activity has been identified, and they form the foundation for incident creation and investigation.

Unlike email notifications, alerts are part of the **detection pipeline itself**. They are generated by security controls based on observed behavior and are then evaluated, filtered, and grouped into incidents. This means that how alerts are configured directly affects what is detected, how much noise is produced, and how effectively incidents are formed.

Configuring alert behavior centers on three controls: **tuning**, **suppression**, and **correlation**. Each affects a different part of the alert pipeline and is configured for a different purpose. Together, these controls determine which detection signals become alerts, which alerts are filtered, and how related alerts are grouped before investigation begins.

The distinction between these controls is summarized in *Table 11.2*.

Alert control	What it does	Result	When to use it
Tuning	Adjusts how known alert patterns are handled.	The alert can still be generated, but it may be hidden, resolved, or converted into a behavior.	Use when the activity is expected but still useful in a hunting or investigation context.
Suppression	Prevents known benign activity from surfacing as alerts.	The detection may still occur, but the alert is not surfaced to analysts.	Use for repetitive, low-value signals that do not require triage.
Correlation	Groups related alerts into incidents.	Related alerts are combined into a single investigation unit.	Use when related signals should be investigated together as part of the same activity chain.

Table 11.2 – Comparison of alert controls in Microsoft Defender XDR

These controls are selected based on what needs to happen to the alert output:

- Tuning is used when known activity should be handled differently but must still remain useful for investigation context
- Suppression is used when repetitive benign activity should not surface as an alert
- Correlation is used when related alerts need to be grouped into one incident so analysts can investigate the full activity chain

Alert generation from detection logic sources

Alerts in Microsoft Defender XDR are generated by detection logic that evaluates activity across multiple protected workloads. These detections originate from different services—such as endpoint, identity, email, and cloud applications—and each produces alerts based on its own telemetry and detection capabilities.

Detection logic analyzes events against known threat patterns, behavioral signals, and security rules. When activity meets defined criteria, an alert is created to represent that specific event. This means alerts are not arbitrary—they are the direct result of detection mechanisms identifying something that deviates from expected or safe behavior.

Each alert reflects a **single detection outcome**, tied to a specific workload and activity type. For example, endpoint detections may identify suspicious process behavior, while identity-based detections may flag abnormal sign-in activity. Although these originate from different sources, they are normalized within Microsoft Defender XDR so they can be handled consistently.

> Tip
>
> Understanding where alerts come from is important for configuration. Detection sources determine what types of activity can generate alerts, and therefore what tuning or suppression may be required. If a particular workload produces excessive alerts, it is the underlying detection logic—not the alert itself—that must be adjusted.

Alerts serve as the **input layer for incident creation**. They are later correlated into incidents, but at this stage, each alert represents an independent detection signal. Correctly interpreting alert generation ensures that configuration changes are applied to the right layer of the detection pipeline.

Alert tuning and sensitivity adjustments

Tuning focuses on reducing false positives without weakening detection coverage. In environments with high variability, known or benign activity may still match predefined detection logic. Alert tuning rules handle those matching alerts in a way that reflects expected activity, so analysts are not repeatedly triaging the same low-value pattern.

This often appears when repeated alerts are triggered by known administrative activity, approved tools, or security testing that should not create the same triage workload each time.

In the Microsoft Defender portal, **alert tuning rules** are configured from: **System > Settings > Microsoft Defender XDR > Rules > Alert tuning**.

A rule can be created from the **Alert tuning** page or from an **alert details** page. The **tuning wizard** defines the alert context, the matching conditions, the action to take, and the scope of the rule. **Conditions** can use alert evidence and entity properties, such as files, processes, users, devices, scheduled tasks, or other entities associated with the alert.

Examples of **tuning rules** include hiding alerts generated by a known administrative script, resolving repeated low-risk alerts from an approved tool, or converting matching signals into behavior records when the activity should remain available for hunting but should not create an alert or incident.

Use this distinction when configuring alert behavior:

- **Tuning** adjusts how matching alert output is handled when known activity meets defined conditions.
- **Suppression** prevents matching alerts from surfacing when the activity is expected or operationally acceptable.
- **Correlation** groups related alerts into incidents so analysts can investigate connected activity together.

This is achieved by defining rule conditions and choosing the action applied when an alert matches those conditions. The goal is not to eliminate detection, but to handle known alert patterns in a way that preserves useful evidence while reducing unnecessary triage.

> Tip
>
> Tuning should be reviewed against the investigation outcome it is meant to improve. A useful tuning rule removes repeated low-value triage while preserving the evidence analysts still need for hunting, incident review, and trend analysis.

Alert tuning directly impacts the quality of incidents. Since alerts are later correlated into incidents, poorly tuned alerts lead to noisy or misleading incidents. Effective tuning ensures that the detection pipeline produces alerts that are both accurate and actionable, forming a reliable foundation for investigation and response.

Alert suppression rule configuration

Alert suppression excludes defined conditions when the underlying activity is known, expected, or operationally acceptable. Unlike tuning, which adjusts how detection logic behaves, suppression filters matching activity from the alert output.

Suppression is applied through rules that match specific attributes of activity. These attributes can include entities such as users, devices, processes, or other contextual identifiers associated with the alert. When activity meets the defined suppression criteria, the detection still occurs, but the alert is not surfaced. It is typically used for known benign activity that would otherwise generate repeated alerts. For example, administrative tasks, approved tools, or expected automation can trigger detections that are valid but not actionable. Suppression rules ensure that these do not continuously appear as alerts, allowing analysts to focus on unknown or high-risk activity.

Tip

Suppression rules must be precise. The rule should identify the known benign activity closely enough to exclude only that scenario without filtering unrelated behavior.

Alert correlation into incidents

Alert correlation is the process of grouping related alerts into a single incident, providing a consolidated view of activity that may otherwise appear as separate detection events. Instead of handling each alert in isolation, correlation connects them based on shared attributes and behavioral relationships.

Correlation operates by analyzing attributes such as **entities (users, devices, IPs)**, **timestamps**, and **activity patterns**. When multiple alerts are determined to be related—either through common entities or as part of the same sequence of actions—they are grouped into one incident. This transforms fragmented signals into a structured representation of a potential attack or activity chain. For example, a phishing attack may generate multiple alerts across different services. A user receives a malicious email, clicks a link, signs in from an unfamiliar location, and then accesses sensitive SharePoint content. Individually, these events may appear as separate email, identity, and data access alerts. Correlation groups them into a single incident, allowing analysts to understand that the alerts are part of the same compromise rather than unrelated events.

The purpose of correlation is to reduce noise and improve context. In environments with high alert volume, individual alerts can be difficult to interpret on their own. By grouping them, correlation provides a clearer view of how events are connected, allowing analysts to understand the broader scope of activity rather than isolated detections.

Correlation directly affects incident quality. If alerts are not correctly correlated, incidents may become fragmented, and manual reconstruction of related activity might be required. Over-correlation, however, can group unrelated alerts together, obscuring the true nature of events. Proper correlation ensures that incidents accurately represent related activity without introducing confusion.

Configure Microsoft Defender for Endpoint advanced features

Microsoft Defender for Endpoint includes a set of advanced features that extend the platform beyond its baseline protection and detection capabilities. These features enable additional behaviors such as enhanced detection coverage, deeper response actions, and expanded control over how endpoint protection operates.

Unlike rules or policies, advanced features are **platform-level capability toggles**. They enable or disable specific functionality within the service rather than defining how detections occur or how controls are enforced. This makes them foundational to how the platform behaves, as they determine which capabilities are available for use.

These features directly influence both detection and response outcomes. Enabling or disabling a feature can change how threats are identified, how aggressively protection is applied, or what actions can be taken during an incident. As a result, they shape the overall behavior of endpoint protection rather than targeting a specific detection or policy scenario. For instance, enabling additional detection capabilities can increase visibility into suspicious behavior, but may also increase alert volume if not properly tuned.

Because advanced features are configured independently, they require deliberate alignment with organizational requirements. Enabling all features without consideration can introduce unintended behavior, while disabling key capabilities can reduce visibility or response effectiveness. The configuration of these features must reflect how the organization intends to balance protection, detection, and operational control.

Identification and enabling of advanced features

Advanced features in Microsoft Defender for Endpoint are enabled individually, and identifying which features are available is the first step in configuring the platform's extended capabilities. These features are exposed as discrete settings, each representing a specific capability that can be turned on or off. Examples of advanced features include:

- Tamper protection: Prevents attackers from disabling Defender security settings
- EDR in block mode: Blocks malicious artifacts even when another antivirus product is primary
- Network protection: Blocks access to malicious domains and URLs
- Web protection: Protects users from phishing sites, malicious websites, and unsafe web content through reputation-based controls
- **Potentially unwanted application (PUA)** protection: Detects and blocks unwanted software such as adware and other low-reputation applications
- Real-time protection: Continuously scans files, processes, and system activity to detect and block threats as they occur
- Cloud-delivered protection: Uses Microsoft's cloud intelligence and machine learning to identify and respond to emerging threats more quickly than local signatures alone
- **Attack surface reduction (ASR):** Reduces common attack vectors by blocking behaviors frequently used by malware and attackers, such as malicious Office macros or credential theft techniques

- **Automated investigation and remediation (AIR):** Automatically investigates alerts, determines their impact, and performs approved remediation actions to reduce analyst workload
- Live response: Allows security analysts to remotely connect to a device, collect forensic information, run commands, and perform investigation actions
- Device isolation: Disconnects a compromised device from the network while maintaining management connectivity, helping contain threats during an incident

It is important to grasp what functionality each feature provides and how it fits into the overall endpoint protection model. Some features extend detection capabilities, others enhance response actions, and some introduce additional control over how threats are handled. Because each feature serves a distinct purpose, they must be evaluated independently rather than treated as a single configuration group.

The required features should be enabled based on organizational needs. This determines which capabilities are available within the environment. Enabling a feature does not change detection logic directly, but it allows the platform to perform additional actions or apply extended protection where applicable.

The effect of these features is cumulative. Each enabled capability adds to the overall behavior of the platform, meaning that the combination of features determines how detection and protection operate together. This creates a layered model where multiple capabilities contribute to the final outcome.

However, these effects must be understood before enabling features. Expanding detection coverage can increase alert volume, and enhanced protection behaviors may introduce stricter controls that affect normal operations. Without proper alignment, this can lead to unnecessary alerts or unintended disruption.

Advanced features in Microsoft Defender for Endpoint are configured independently, allowing each capability to be enabled, disabled, or adjusted without affecting others. Each feature represents a distinct control, and its configuration applies only to that specific capability. Features can be adjusted over time as requirements change, without requiring a full reconfiguration of the platform. This supports iterative tuning, where capabilities are refined based on operational feedback, alert volume, or changes in the threat landscape.

Because features operate independently, their combined effect still has to be understood. For instance, Expanding detection coverage while also enabling stronger response capabilities can increase both alert volume and automated action frequency. Analysts need to review these effects together, because each setting may be configured separately but the endpoint experiences them as one protection model.

Configure rules settings in Microsoft Defender for Endpoint

Rules in Microsoft Defender for Endpoint define how detection logic evaluates activity on endpoints. They determine what types of behavior are assessed, how those behaviors are interpreted, and under what conditions alerts are generated. As a result, rules directly shape how threats are identified within the environment.

Unlike advanced features, which enable platform capabilities, rules operate at the **detection layer**. They do not introduce new functionality but instead control how existing detection mechanisms are applied. This makes them central to how signals are translated into alerts.

Configuring rule settings allows organizations to align detection logic with their environment. This includes adjusting how sensitive detections are, determining which behaviors are evaluated, and ensuring that alerts represent meaningful activity. Properly configured rules ensure that the detection pipeline produces relevant and actionable alerts.

Definition of detection rules and logic behavior

Detection rules in Microsoft Defender for Endpoint define how endpoint activity is evaluated to determine whether it represents a threat. Each rule represents a specific set of conditions that are applied to telemetry, allowing the platform to identify behavior that matches known patterns or suspicious characteristics.

Microsoft Defender for Endpoint uses three broad categories of rules.

- **Built-in rules** are Microsoft-authored detections based on behavioral and signature-based signals.
- **Custom detection rules** are analyst-authored rules created from Advanced Hunting queries and configured to run on a schedule. Custom detection rules are created from **Advanced Hunting | Custom detection**.
- **Indicator-based rules** are used to allow, block, or alert on specific indicators such as files, IP addresses, URLs, or certificates.

A rule typically includes the following:

- A KQL query
- A schedule (such as every 1, 3, or 24 hours)
- Alert severity
- Device group scope

Here is an example of a custom detection rule; it detects PsExec usage by non-approved accounts:

```
DeviceProcessEvents
| where FileName == "psexec.exe"
| where InitiatingProcessAccountName != "ITAdmin"
```

A rule can be configured to run every hour, generate a medium-severity alert, and apply only to specific device groups.

Rules operate by analyzing events such as process execution, file activity, network connections, and other endpoint signals. When activity meets the conditions defined by a rule, it is flagged as a detection and can generate an alert. This makes rules the direct link between raw telemetry and actionable security signals.

Each rule is focused on a particular type of behavior. Some rules target specific threat techniques, while others identify broader patterns of suspicious activity. This targeted approach ensures that detection logic is applied in a structured and predictable way, rather than relying on generalized evaluation.

Rule behavior is deterministic; given the same conditions and activity, a rule always produces the same outcome, which is what makes tuning and suppression predictable. Understanding how rules define detection logic ensures that configuration changes are applied at the correct level. Adjusting rules changes how activity is evaluated, directly influencing which behaviors result in alerts and how effectively threats are identified.

Configuration of rule settings and behavior adjustments

Once detection rules are understood, they can be configured to adjust how they behave within the environment. This configuration controls how aggressively rules evaluate activity and whether their outcomes align with expected operational patterns.

Rule settings allow rules to be **enabled, disabled, or adjusted**, depending on their relevance. Enabling a rule activates its detection logic, while disabling it prevents that logic from producing alerts. In addition to simple on/off control, rule behavior can be refined to better match the environment, ensuring that detections are meaningful rather than excessive. For instance, rule behavior can be aligned with real-world activity. In environments where certain behaviors are expected, rules may need to be tuned so that they do not generate unnecessary alerts. This does not remove the detection capability but instead refines how and when the rule evaluates activity to produce an alert.

Tip

Configuration must be applied carefully—overadjustment can reduce visibility into threats, while insufficient adjustment can result in excessive noise.

Effective rule configuration ensures that detection logic remains both accurate and relevant. By controlling how rules operate, organizations can maintain a balance between visibility and signal quality, ensuring that alerts reflect actionable activity rather than expected behavior.

Note

Separation of rules from policy-based enforcement

Table 11.1 establishes the boundary between rules and policies. Rules sit at the detection layer and define how endpoint activity is evaluated. Policies sit at the enforcement layer and define how protection settings are applied to devices.

The practical implication is that alert behavior and endpoint enforcement must be configured in the correct place. Changing a rule affects what activity is detected or surfaced. Changing a policy affects how protection is applied on the endpoint. Treating one as a substitute for the other leads to configuration changes that do not produce the intended result.

Configure custom data collection in Microsoft Defender for Endpoint

Microsoft Defender for Endpoint collects a baseline set of telemetry to support detection and investigation, but this default data set does not always provide full visibility into every environment. Custom data collection extends Microsoft Defender for Endpoint telemetry by allowing additional event sources to be ingested for hunting and detection.

It is configured from **Settings | Endpoints | Advanced features | Custom network indicators/Custom data collection**, or via Intune device configuration profiles for Windows event logs.

The supported sources include the following:

- Windows Event Logs, such as PowerShell Operational or Sysmon if deployed
- Additional registry paths

- Custom file locations
- Network indicators not covered by built-in feeds

Once enabled, collected data becomes available in Advanced Hunting tables such as **DeviceEvents**, **DeviceRegistryEvents**, or **DeviceFileEvents**.

Custom data collection expands the inputs that detection and investigation processes can use. Without sufficient telemetry, certain activities may not be visible, limiting the effectiveness of detection. With expanded data collection, more detailed activity can be analyzed, improving the ability to identify and investigate threats.

> Tip
>
> Additional telemetry should be targeted to the investigation gap it is meant to close. Collecting broad endpoint data without a clear purpose can increase storage, processing, and analysis effort without improving detection outcomes. Targeted collection keeps the evidence useful for analysts while avoiding unnecessary data volume.

Definition of custom telemetry collection scope

Defining the scope of custom telemetry collection determines **what additional data is gathered from endpoints** beyond the default baseline. This step establishes the boundaries of visibility by selecting which types of activity should be captured and made available for analysis.

Scope is defined by identifying relevant data sources and activity types that are not fully covered by standard telemetry. This may include specific process execution activity, command-line arguments, registry modifications, network connections, file operations, event categories, extended logging, or additional signals that provide deeper insight into endpoint behavior. The goal is to ensure that critical activities—especially those relevant to threat detection or investigation—are visible within the platform.

The scope must be **targeted rather than exhaustive**. The scope of collection directly affects detection and investigation capabilities. Activities that are not collected cannot be queried, correlated, or evaluated by detection logic. Conversely, collecting excessive telemetry can increase storage requirements and make analysis more difficult by introducing unnecessary noise. Organizations should therefore balance visibility requirements against operational and performance considerations.

Configuration of data collection settings

Once the scope of telemetry is defined, data collection settings determine *how that data is captured and made available* within Microsoft Defender for Endpoint. These settings translate the defined scope into actual collection behavior on endpoints.

Configuration involves selecting which telemetry types are enabled and ensuring that endpoints are configured to collect and forward that data. This defines the **active data pipeline**, controlling which signals are ingested and retained for analysis. If a data type is not enabled at this stage, it will not be available for detection or investigation.

Data collection settings also control consistency across endpoints. For telemetry to be useful, it must be collected in a uniform way so that detection logic can evaluate it reliably. Inconsistent configuration can result in partial visibility, where some endpoints provide detailed data while others do not, leading to gaps in analysis.

These settings must align with the previously defined scope. Enabling data outside of that scope increases volume without adding value, while failing to enable required data results in missing signals. Configuration therefore acts as the enforcement layer for telemetry decisions.

Changes to data collection settings have a direct impact on what can be analyzed. Enabling additional telemetry increases visibility but may introduce higher data volume, while restricting collection reduces overhead but limits detection capability. Effective configuration ensures that the selected telemetry is both available and usable across the environment.

Availability and usage of collected telemetry in endpoint analysis

Once data collection settings are applied, the value of custom telemetry depends on its availability and usability within analysis workflows. Collected data must not only exist but also be accessible in a form that supports detection and investigation.

Availability means that telemetry is consistently present across endpoints and accessible through the platform's analysis tools. If data is collected inconsistently or is missing from certain devices, investigations become fragmented, making it difficult to reconstruct activity or validate findings. Collected telemetry must also be relevant to the analysis workflow. If analysts cannot access the data consistently, or if the data does not support the investigation question, it does not help them validate activity or determine impact.

Usage refers to how that telemetry is leveraged during detection and investigation. Detection logic relies on collected data to identify suspicious behavior, while investigation workflows use it to trace activity, understand context, and determine impact. The usefulness of telemetry is therefore tied directly to how well it supports these processes.

In practice, telemetry only has value when analysts can use it to answer the investigation question.

Configure security policies for Microsoft Defender for Endpoint, including attack surface reduction (ASR) rules

Security policies in Microsoft Defender for Endpoint define how protection is enforced across devices. They determine which controls are applied, how those controls behave, and which devices or groups are affected. This makes policies the primary mechanism for translating security requirements into enforced behavior on endpoints.

As shown in *Table 11.1*, policies sit at the enforcement layer. They apply configuration settings that control how the platform protects devices, including enabled protections, allowed behavior, and threat-handling settings.

Attack Surface Reduction (ASR) rules are a key component of these policies. They are designed to block or restrict behaviors commonly used by attackers, such as exploit techniques or misuse of legitimate tools. Rather than detecting activity after it occurs, ASR rules act *proactively*, reducing the opportunities for attacks to succeed. For instance, an ASR rule might block the execution of scripts from email attachments to prevent common phishing-based attacks.

> Note
>
> Policies and ASR rules work together to shape endpoint behavior. Policies provide the structure and assignment, while ASR rules enforce specific restrictions within that structure. This ensures that preventive controls are consistently applied across the environment.

Policy definition and assignment to devices and groups

Policy configuration determines how Microsoft Defender for Endpoint protections are applied across managed devices. The policy should make clear which controls apply, where they apply, and how exceptions or operational impact will be handled.

Security policies are first defined by specifying the protection settings that will be enforced and then assigned to the devices or device groups that those settings should apply to. This establishes both *what controls are in place* and *where they are enforced*. Policies may include antivirus settings, ASR rules, EDR settings, device control policies, web protection settings, or firewall configurations. Configuration settings control how protections operate, what actions are allowed or restricted, and how the platform responds to potential threats.

Policies are assigned to devices directly or through device groups, allowing different configurations to be targeted based on factors such as role, risk level, or operational requirements. This is because devices with different roles may require different levels of protection, and policies must reflect those differences to maintain both security and usability. This ensures that controls are aligned with how devices are used rather than applied uniformly across all endpoints. For example, servers may receive a different policy from user workstations, and privileged administrator devices may require stricter controls than standard employee devices. Assigning policies through device groups allows these requirements to be managed consistently at scale.

After assignment, policy deployment should be monitored to ensure devices receive the intended configuration. Devices that fail to receive or apply a policy may operate without the expected protections, creating gaps in security coverage.

The combination of definition and assignment ensures that policies are both **intentional and targeted**. A well-defined policy that is incorrectly assigned will not achieve its purpose, just as a correctly assigned policy with inappropriate settings can introduce risk or disruption.

Configuration of ASR rules within policies

ASR rules are configured within security policies to enforce restrictions on behaviors commonly used by attackers. These rules operate as **preventive controls**, blocking or limiting specific actions at the endpoint before they can be exploited.

Configuration involves selecting which ASR rules are enabled and defining how each rule behaves. Each rule targets a specific technique or behavior, such as misuse of scripting engines, credential theft methods, or unauthorized process activity. Because each rule is independent, they can be configured individually to match the organization's requirements. ASR rules also support different enforcement modes, including block, audit, and disabled. These modes are configured within the policy; their effect on endpoint behavior is covered in the next subsection.

Since ASR rules are applied through policies, their effectiveness depends on correct policy assignment. Once configured and applied, they enforce behavior restrictions consistently across targeted devices, reducing exposure to common attack techniques.

The configuration of ASR rules must consider operational impact. Some rules may affect legitimate processes if applied too broadly, while others provide strong protection with minimal disruption. That impact should be reviewed before enforcement behavior is finalized.

Enforcement behavior of policies and ASR controls

Once policies and ASR rules are configured and assigned, enforcement determines how those controls are applied on endpoints and how they affect user and system activity. This is where configuration translates into **real-world behavior**, shaping how threats are prevented and how normal operations are impacted.

ASR enforcement is driven by the configured mode of each rule. In **block mode**, the behavior is prevented entirely, stopping the action before it can execute. In **audit mode**, the behavior is allowed but recorded, providing visibility but no enforcement. This distinction determines whether the control actively prevents activity or simply observes it.

Enforcement must be consistent across targeted devices to ensure predictable behavior. If policies are not applied uniformly, some endpoints may enforce controls while others do not, creating gaps in protection. Consistent enforcement ensures that security controls operate as expected across the environment.

Further, The impact of enforcement should be reviewed against normal endpoint activity before broad deployment. This keeps ASR behavior tied to the intended protection outcome rather than treating enforcement as a generic on/off decision.

Manage automated investigation and response capabilities in Microsoft Defender XDR

AIR in Microsoft Defender XDR is designed to reduce the manual effort required to analyze and respond to security incidents. It operates by automatically investigating alerts and incidents, determining their validity, and taking appropriate actions based on predefined logic.

AIR sits within the **response layer**, bridging the gap between detection and remediation. While alerts identify suspicious activity and incidents group related signals, AIR evaluates those incidents to determine whether they represent real threats and what actions should be taken. This shifts part of the investigative workload from analysts to the platform. For instance, When AIR automatically analyzes an alert and determines that it represents a real threat, it applies remediation actions without requiring immediate analyst intervention.

The capability operates through a structured process: alerts trigger investigations, the system analyzes related entities and behaviors, and response actions are executed where appropriate. This allows threats to be handled more quickly and consistently, especially in environments with high alert volume.

Automation levels define how AIR behaves, determining whether actions are taken automatically or require approval before execution. This provides control over how much authority is delegated to the platform, balancing efficiency with oversight. Full automation applies actions immediately, while semi-automated configurations require approval, and the correct choice depends on the organization's risk tolerance.

> **Note**
>
> AIR is distinct from orchestration-level automation. It investigates and responds within Microsoft Defender XDR, while automation rules and playbooks coordinate broader incident workflows across systems.

When configured correctly, AIR improves response speed and consistency while reducing analyst workload. However, it must be carefully managed to ensure that automated actions align with organizational expectations and do not introduce unintended consequences.

Automated investigation workflow execution

AIR begins with the execution of an investigation workflow that is triggered by alerts or incidents. This workflow systematically analyzes the detected activity, examining related entities and behaviors to determine whether the activity represents a real threat.

The investigation process expands beyond the initial alert by collecting and evaluating additional context. This includes analyzing related files, processes, users, and devices associated with the activity. By correlating this information, AIR builds a broader view of what has occurred, rather than relying on a single detection signal.

The workflow follows a structured evaluation model. It assesses evidence, determines the likelihood of malicious behavior, and classifies findings based on that analysis. This allows the system to distinguish between benign activity and confirmed threats, reducing the need for manual triage.

As part of this process, AIR generates investigation results that describe what was analyzed and what conclusions were reached. These results provide transparency into the automated process, allowing analysts to understand how decisions were made and what actions may follow.

The execution of this workflow ensures that each alert or incident is evaluated consistently. Instead of relying solely on manual investigation, AIR applies the same analytical process across all relevant events, improving both speed and reliability in identifying threats.

Configuration of automation levels and response controls

Automation levels in Microsoft Defender XDR determine how AIR executes actions after an investigation is completed. While the investigation process itself is automated, these levels control whether response actions are applied automatically or require approval.

Automation levels typically define a spectrum of control. At one end, actions are executed **fully automatically**, allowing the platform to respond immediately when a threat is confirmed. At the other end, actions require **manual approval**, ensuring that analysts review and authorize changes before they are applied. This provides flexibility in how much authority is delegated to the system.

These settings directly affect response behavior. In fully automated configurations, remediation actions such as containment or cleanup are applied without delay, improving response speed. In approval-based configurations, actions are staged and presented for validation, providing greater oversight but introducing latency.

Management and review of automated actions

After AIR executes actions, those actions must be **managed and reviewed** to ensure they were appropriate and effective. This step provides visibility into what the platform has done and allows analysts to validate or adjust outcomes if necessary.

Automated actions are recorded as part of the investigation results, including what action was taken, which entity was affected, and why the action was triggered. This creates a traceable record that allows analysts to understand the reasoning behind each response decision. Note that Reviewing these actions is critical for maintaining trust in automation. Analysts must be able to confirm that actions align with expected behavior and do not negatively impact normal operations. If an action is incorrect or overly aggressive, it may need to be reversed or adjusted.

Management also involves monitoring patterns in automated responses. Repeated actions against similar activity may indicate that detection or configuration needs refinement. This feedback loop allows organizations to improve both detection accuracy and response behavior over time.

This stage ensures that automation remains **controlled and accountable**. While AIR reduces manual effort, it does not remove the need for oversight. Effective management ensures that automated actions support security objectives without introducing unintended consequences.

Configure automatic attack disruption in Microsoft Defender XDR

Automatic attack disruption in Microsoft Defender XDR is designed to *identify and interrupt active attacks in progress*, stopping malicious activity before it can fully execute. Unlike traditional detection and response processes, which identify and remediate threats after detection, attack disruption focuses on *real-time intervention.*

This capability operates at the point where an attack sequence is already underway. It analyzes patterns of activity across multiple signals to determine whether behavior represents a coordinated attack. When such activity is identified, the platform takes immediate action to break the attack chain.

Automatic attack disruption is built into Microsoft Defender XDR, but its behavior depends on licensing, workload deployment, permissions, and automation settings. It can be configured or limited in these ways:

- **Enable or disable:** attack disruption is generally available when the required Defender XDR prerequisites are met. If an organization must opt out, this is done by opening a support case in the Microsoft Defender portal. More commonly, specific users, devices, device groups, or IP addresses are excluded from automatic attack disruption through the automated response exclusion settings.
- **Supported attack scenarios:** disruption is designed for high-confidence, active attack sequences such as ransomware or other sophisticated attacks where Microsoft Defender XDR correlates signals into a single incident and identifies compromised assets used by the attacker.
- **Supported workloads:** coverage depends on deployed Defender products, such as Microsoft Defender for Endpoint, Defender for Identity, Defender for Office 365, and Defender for Cloud Apps. The relevant product must be deployed both to detect the scenario and to execute the automated action.
- **Containment actions:** disruption can automatically contain affected devices and disable compromised accounts through the relevant Defender workload.
- **Prerequisites:** required licensing, deployed Defender workloads, appropriate permissions, standard device discovery for Defender for Endpoint device containment, and required workload-specific prerequisites must be in place before disruption actions can run.

Note

Attack disruption is distinct from device isolation and user containment:

- **Attack disruption** automatically interrupts active attacks by isolating compromised entities (e.g., disabling a user account, stopping a process chain).
- **Device isolation** is a manual or AIR-driven action that restricts network communication.
- **User containment** disables sign-in for compromised identities.

Attack disruption events appear in the **incident timeline** as "Attack Disruption Action Taken," allowing analysts to review what was interrupted and why.

The actions taken during disruption are automated and targeted. They are designed to limit attacker movement, prevent escalation, and reduce impact. Because these actions occur without manual intervention, they provide a rapid response capability that complements other parts of the security workflow.

Configuring attack disruption requires understanding its role within the response pipeline. It is not a replacement for detection or investigation, but an additional layer that intervenes when active attack behavior is identified. When properly configured, it reduces the window of opportunity for attackers by stopping activity before it can progress further.

A common scenario is when automatically disabling a compromised user account stops an attack in progress before further access is gained.

Detection of active attack sequences

Automatic attack disruption begins with identifying **active attack sequences**, rather than isolated suspicious events. This detection focuses on recognizing patterns of behavior that indicate an attacker is progressing through multiple stages of an attack.

Instead of evaluating single events in isolation, the platform analyzes **chained activity across entities and time**. This includes linking actions involving users, devices, processes, and network activity to determine whether they form part of a coordinated sequence. The emphasis is on identifying progression—how one action leads to another—rather than detecting a single anomaly.

Detection of attack sequences relies on recognizing relationships between activities. For example, initial access behavior may be followed by privilege escalation or lateral movement. When these steps are connected, they form a sequence that indicates an active attack rather than unrelated events.

This approach distinguishes attack disruption from standard alerting. Alerts may represent individual detections, but sequence detection identifies **how those detections are connected**, enabling the platform to determine whether an attack is actively unfolding.

Accurate sequence detection is critical. If activity is not correctly linked, the platform may fail to recognize an ongoing attack. Conversely, incorrectly linking unrelated activity can result in unnecessary disruption. Effective detection ensures that only genuine attack sequences trigger disruption actions.

By focusing on behavior over time and across entities, this mechanism allows the platform to identify active threats at the point where intervention can prevent further progression.

Execution of automated disruption actions

Once an active attack sequence is identified, Microsoft Defender XDR executes **automated disruption actions** to interrupt the attacker's activity. These actions are applied immediately, targeting the specific entities involved in the attack to prevent further progression.

Disruption actions are focused on **containment and interruption**, rather than investigation. They are designed to break the attack chain by restricting the attacker's ability to continue operating. This may involve limiting access, isolating affected components, or blocking specific behaviors associated with the attack sequence.

These actions are applied automatically based on the platform's determination that an attack is in progress. There is no requirement for manual approval at this stage, as the goal is to reduce response time and minimize impact. The immediacy of execution is what differentiates disruption from other response mechanisms.

Execution is also **targeted rather than broad**. Actions are applied to the specific entities involved in the attack, such as a compromised user or device, rather than affecting the entire environment. This ensures that disruption limits attacker activity while minimizing disruption to legitimate operations.

Because these actions occur in real time, they must be precise. Incorrect execution can impact normal activity, while delayed execution can allow the attack to progress. The effectiveness of disruption depends on accurate detection and controlled, targeted action.

Separation of disruption from investigation workflows

Automatic attack disruption operates independently from investigation workflows, and understanding this separation is critical to using it correctly. Disruption is designed to **interrupt active attacks immediately**, while investigation workflows—such as Automated Investigation and Response (AIR)—focus on analyzing and validating what has occurred.

Disruption acts at the point of **active threat execution**, where rapid intervention is required to stop attacker activity. It does not perform detailed analysis or build a full understanding of the incident before acting. Instead, it relies on detection of attack sequences and applies targeted actions to break that sequence.

Investigation workflows, in contrast, operate after detection to evaluate evidence, determine the scope of the threat, and guide remediation. These workflows prioritize accuracy and context, often involving deeper analysis of entities, timelines, and relationships. This process takes more time and may include human oversight.

Because these processes serve different purposes, they must not be treated as interchangeable. Disruption is **speed-focused and preventive**, while investigation is **analysis-focused and**

corrective. Attempting to use investigation mechanisms to stop active attacks introduces delay, while relying on disruption to fully analyze incidents results in incomplete understanding.

Both capabilities work together within the response pipeline. Disruption limits immediate impact by stopping the attack, while investigation follows to validate findings, assess scope, and complete remediation. Maintaining this separation ensures that each function operates effectively without interfering with the other.

Configure and manage device groups, permissions, and automation levels in Microsoft Defender for Endpoint

Device groups, permissions, and automation levels define how endpoints are organized, accessed, and acted upon within Microsoft Defender for Endpoint. Together, they control the structure of the environment and how response capabilities are applied across different sets of devices.

Device groups provide the organizational layer, allowing endpoints to be grouped based on attributes such as role, function, or risk profile. This grouping is used to scope policies, control visibility, and apply different configurations across the environment. Rather than treating all devices uniformly, groups enable targeted management. For example, grouping high-risk devices separately allows stricter policies and automation settings to be applied without affecting lower-risk systems.

Permissions define who can access and operate on those devices. They control visibility into endpoint data and determine which actions users can perform. This ensures that access to sensitive information and response capabilities is restricted based on role, maintaining proper operational boundaries.

Automation levels determine how response actions are executed for the devices within each group. These settings define whether actions are applied automatically or require approval, directly affecting how quickly and autonomously the platform can respond to threats on those endpoints.

Device groups determine which devices analysts can see and what automation level applies to each group. They can be configured under **Settings | Endpoints | Device groups** and support the following:

- **Role-based access control (RBAC)**
- Automation levels (None, Semi, Full)

Automation levels control how **Automated Investigation and Response** (**AIR**) behaves:

- **None** – AIR runs in audit-only mode; no remediation actions are taken
- **Semi** – AIR investigates automatically but requires analyst approval for remediation
- **Full** – AIR investigates and remediates without approval

- Assignment based on tags, OS, domain, or device name patterns

Misalignment between these can lead to overexposure, restricted visibility, or inappropriate response actions. Configuring and managing these elements ensures that endpoint security operations are structured, controlled, and aligned with organizational requirements, enabling effective protection without compromising governance or oversight.

Device group creation and classification logic

Device groups in Microsoft Defender for Endpoint are created to organize endpoints into logical segments that reflect how those devices are used and managed. This classification determines how policies, visibility, and response behaviors are applied across the environment.

Group creation is based on defining criteria that separate devices into meaningful categories. These criteria can include attributes such as device role, operating system, location, or risk profile. The goal is to group devices in a way that aligns with operational requirements rather than treating all endpoints as a single set.

Classification logic determines how devices are assigned to these groups. This logic must be consistent and predictable so that devices are placed in the correct group as they are onboarded or as their attributes change. Accurate classification ensures that the correct controls and configurations are applied automatically.

The structure of device groups directly affects how security controls are scoped. Policies and automation settings are often applied at the group level, meaning that incorrect grouping can lead to inappropriate enforcement or response behavior. For example, grouping high-risk and low-risk devices together may result in overly restrictive or insufficient controls.

Effective group design gives enough structure to target policies and automation settings while keeping the classification model simple enough to maintain consistently.

Configuration of permissions and access control

Permissions in Microsoft Defender for Endpoint define who can access endpoint data and what actions they are allowed to perform. This control ensures that operational capabilities are aligned with roles, preventing unauthorized access while enabling analysts to perform required tasks.

Access control is implemented through role-based permissions, where users are assigned specific roles that determine their level of visibility and authority. These roles control actions such as viewing alerts, investigating devices, or executing response actions. The configuration of these permissions establishes clear operational boundaries within the environment.

Permissions are also scoped to device groups. This means that access is not only defined by role, but also by which devices a user can interact with. For example, a user may have full investigative capabilities but only within a specific group of devices. This combination of role and scope ensures that access is both functional and restricted.

Proper configuration of permissions is essential for maintaining security and operational integrity. Overly permissive access can expose sensitive data or allow unintended actions, while overly restrictive access can limit the ability to respond effectively to threats. The goal is to align permissions with responsibilities so that users have exactly the access they need—no more, no less.

Assignment and management of automation levels

Automation levels in Microsoft Defender for Endpoint define how response actions are applied to devices within each group, controlling whether remediation occurs automatically or requires approval. These settings are assigned at the device group level, allowing response behavior to vary based on the characteristics and risk profile of different endpoints.

Assignment of automation levels determines the **degree of autonomy** the platform has when responding to threats. Devices in groups configured for full automation will have response actions applied immediately, while devices in groups requiring approval will pause actions until they are reviewed. This ensures that response behavior aligns with the sensitivity and operational impact of each group.

Management of these levels involves continuously evaluating whether the assigned behavior is appropriate. High-risk or critical systems may require stricter control with approval-based responses, while less sensitive systems may benefit from faster, fully automated remediation. Adjusting automation levels allows organizations to refine how quickly and aggressively the platform responds.

As discussed earlier, automation levels directly influence how AIR operates on endpoints. The same investigation process may result in different outcomes depending on the assigned level—either immediate action or staged approval. This makes automation levels a key control point for balancing response speed and oversight.

Automation should be applied consistently and appropriately across device groups. Misaligned settings can either delay response to active threats or introduce unintended actions without sufficient review.

Create and configure automation rules in Microsoft Sentinel

Automation rules in Microsoft Sentinel control how incidents are handled as they are created and updated. They sit within the **incident management layer**, shaping how alerts—once correlated into incidents—are processed, assigned, and prioritized.

Automation rules manage the workflow around incidents, ensuring that handling is consistent and aligned with operational processes. This includes applying tags, assigning ownership, updating status, and controlling how incidents move through the lifecycle. They are triggered by incident events, such as creation or modification. When conditions are met, predefined actions are applied automatically. This allows organizations to standardize how incidents are handled without requiring manual intervention for routine tasks.

These rules are essential in environments with high alert volume. Without them, incident handling becomes inconsistent and time-consuming, as analysts must manually apply the same actions repeatedly. Automation rules ensure that incidents are processed in a structured and predictable way.

Incident settings control how alerts are grouped into incidents. Located under **Microsoft Sentinel | Settings | Incident settings**, these options include:

- **Alert grouping** (by tactics, entities, or time window)
- **Incident creation options** (one incident per alert rule vs. grouped incidents)

Proper configuration reduces noise and ensures related alerts are investigated together.

Trigger conditions and incident-based execution

Automation rules in Microsoft Sentinel are executed based on defined trigger conditions tied to incident events. These conditions determine when a rule runs and which incidents it applies to, forming the decision layer that drives automated workflow behavior.

Triggers are typically based on incident lifecycle events, such as when an incident is created, updated, or closed. When one of these events occurs, the platform evaluates the rule conditions to determine whether the rule should be applied. This ensures that automation is responsive to changes in incident state rather than operating on a fixed schedule.

Conditions refine this behavior further by filtering incidents based on attributes. These attributes can include severity, incident classification, associated entities, or other contextual properties. By combining triggers with conditions, rules can be precisely targeted, for example, applying only to high-severity incidents or those involving specific workloads. Execution occurs immediately when both the trigger event and conditions are satisfied. This allows rules to apply actions at the right point in the incident lifecycle, ensuring that handling is consistent from the moment an incident is created or updated.

If trigger conditions are too broad, rules may apply to too many incidents, creating unnecessary or conflicting actions. If too restrictive, important incidents may not be processed as intended. Effective configuration ensures that rules execute only when relevant, aligning automation with operational priorities.

Configuration of rule actions for incident management

Once trigger conditions are met, automation rules in Microsoft Sentinel apply actions that modify how an incident is handled. These actions do not investigate or remediate threats; instead, they shape the workflow around the incident to ensure consistent processing.

Rule actions include operations such as **assigning ownership**, **applying tags**, **updating status**, and **setting classification or severity adjustments**. These actions standardize how incidents are managed, ensuring that similar types of incidents are handled in the same way every time they occur.

Assignment actions direct incidents to the appropriate analysts or teams, aligning responsibility with expertise. Tagging provides additional context, allowing incidents to be categorized or filtered based on attributes such as threat type or affected system. Status updates control the lifecycle of the incident, ensuring it progresses through defined stages such as active, in progress, or closed.

These actions are applied automatically at the point of rule execution, reducing the need for manual handling of routine tasks. This ensures that incidents are immediately structured and routed correctly as soon as they are created or updated. However, actions must be configured carefully. Conflicting or overlapping rules can result in inconsistent handling, such as multiple assignments or incorrect status changes. Clear and targeted action configuration ensures that each rule contributes to a predictable and controlled workflow.

Separation of automation rules from response execution

Table 11.1 establishes the boundary between automation rules and playbooks. Automation rules manage incident workflow in Microsoft Sentinel, such as assignment, tagging, status updates, classification changes, and playbook invocation. Playbooks execute response actions through Logic Apps.

Automation rules are configured under **Microsoft Sentinel | Automation | Automation rules**. Each rule includes the following:

- **Trigger:** when an incident is created or updated
- **Conditions:** severity, tactics, alert provider, entity type, incident title, tags
- Actions which include:
    - Assign owner
    - Change severity
    - Change status
    - Add tags
    - Run a playbook
    - Close incident with classification

Automation rules run *before* playbooks and can call playbooks as part of their action set.

> **Tip**
>
> Workflow control and response execution should not be configured as the same thing. Use automation rules when the incident lifecycle needs to be organized or routed. Use playbooks when an action needs to interact with users, systems, resources, or external services.

Create and configure Microsoft Sentinel playbooks

Playbooks in Microsoft Sentinel automate response actions using workflows built on Azure Logic Apps. They execute actions that directly interact with systems, users, and resources. Playbooks operate at the **response execution layer**, where actions such as containment, notification, enrichment, or integration with external services are performed. They are triggered either automatically—through automation rules—or manually by analysts during an investigation.

Each playbook represents a defined workflow that sequences actions based on conditions and logic. This allows complex response processes to be automated, reducing manual effort and ensuring that actions are applied consistently across incidents. For example, a playbook can automatically send notifications, enrich incident data, and trigger response actions across multiple systems when an incident is created.

Playbooks are not limited to Microsoft Sentinel. Because they are built on Logic Apps, they can interact with a wide range of systems and services, enabling cross-platform response and integration. This allows organizations to extend response capabilities beyond a single tool, coordinating actions across their environment.

To function correctly, a playbook requires the following:

- A **managed identity** with permissions to perform actions (e.g., isolate device, disable user, send email)
- A **trigger**, typically "When an incident is created" or "When an alert is created"
- **Connectors**, such as:
    - Microsoft Defender for Endpoint
    - Microsoft Entra ID
    - Office 365 Outlook
    - Teams
    - Azure Resource Manager

Playbooks should be tested using the **Run Trigger | Run with payload** feature to validate logic before production use.

Because playbooks operate as execution mechanisms, designing them well requires clear decisions about what actions to automate, in what sequence, and under what conditions.

Playbook creation using Logic Apps

Playbooks in Microsoft Sentinel are created as workflows using Azure Logic Apps. This means that each playbook is defined as a sequence of steps that execute actions based on triggers, conditions, and connectors.

Creation begins with defining the **workflow structure**, which includes the trigger, the sequence of actions, and any conditional logic that determines how the workflow progresses. The trigger defines when the playbook runs, while the actions define what it does once executed.

Logic Apps provides a wide range of **connectors** that allow playbooks to interact with services both inside and outside the Microsoft ecosystem. These connectors enable actions such as sending notifications, updating records, querying data sources, or interacting with external systems. This makes playbooks highly flexible, as they can integrate with multiple platforms within a single workflow.

While connectors define which service each playbook step interacts with, the action can only run if the connection has the required permissions. For Microsoft Sentinel actions, the playbook can authenticate by using a managed identity, which gives the Logic App its own identity in Microsoft Entra ID. That identity is then assigned the required access to the Sentinel workspace or target resource, so the playbook can update incidents, read data, or call external services without relying on a user's credentials.

The design of the workflow determines how effectively the playbook performs its function. Actions must be sequenced correctly, and conditions must be defined to ensure that the workflow behaves as intended. Poorly structured workflows can result in incomplete or incorrect execution, while well-designed workflows provide consistent and reliable automation.

> **Note**
>
> Because playbooks are built on Logic Apps, they inherit its execution model. Each step runs in sequence, with outputs from one step feeding into the next. This allows data to be passed through the workflow, enabling more complex logic and decision-making.

Triggering mechanisms for playbook execution

Playbooks in Microsoft Sentinel are executed based on defined triggers that determine *when the workflow runs*. These triggers connect playbooks to incidents and events, ensuring that response actions are applied at the appropriate point in the incident lifecycle.

Playbooks can be triggered automatically through *automation rules*. In this model, when an incident meets specific conditions, the automation rule invokes the playbook. This allows response actions to occur without manual intervention, ensuring consistent and timely execution.

They can also be triggered *manually* by analysts during investigation. This provides flexibility, allowing playbooks to be executed on demand when additional context or judgment is required. Manual execution is often used when automation is not appropriate or when a specific action needs to be applied selectively.

The trigger mechanism determines how tightly playbooks are integrated into the response workflow. Automated triggers provide speed and consistency, while manual triggers provide control and precision. Both approaches are used depending on the scenario and the level of risk associated with the action.

Trigger configuration should reflect where the playbook fits in the incident lifecycle. High-severity incidents may invoke a playbook automatically so response steps begin immediately, while lower-severity incidents may leave execution to the analyst when more judgment is needed.

Execution of response actions across systems

Once triggered, playbooks in Microsoft Sentinel execute **response actions that operate across multiple systems**, using Azure Logic Apps to coordinate those actions in a structured workflow.

Execution involves running a sequence of actions that interact with different services, platforms, or data sources. These actions can include notifying users, updating records, enriching data, or initiating response steps in external systems. The ability to operate across systems is what allows playbooks to extend response beyond a single platform.

Each action within the playbook is executed in order, with outputs from earlier steps used by subsequent ones. This enables workflows to adapt dynamically, using data gathered during execution to inform later actions. However, Cross-system execution requires reliable integration. Playbooks depend on connectors and permissions to interact with external services, and failures in these integrations can interrupt execution. Ensuring that connections are properly configured and authorized is essential for consistent operation.

Because each step in the workflow passes its output to the next, and because connectors allow those steps to span multiple platforms, a single playbook can coordinate actions that would otherwise require separate tools and manual handoffs. For example, a playbook can update a ticketing system, notify stakeholders, and apply containment actions in response to a single incident.

> **Tip**
>
> Because playbooks can affect multiple systems, their impact must be controlled. Actions should be targeted and appropriate to the incident, as overly broad or incorrect execution can introduce unintended consequences. Proper design ensures that actions are applied only where needed and in the correct sequence.

Summary

This chapter covered how automation is configured across Microsoft Defender XDR, Microsoft Defender for Endpoint, Microsoft Sentinel, and related response workflows. You looked at email notifications, alert tuning, suppression, and correlation, and how these settings affect what analysts receive, investigate, and act on.

You also covered advanced features, rule settings, custom data collection, security policies, and ASR rules in Microsoft Defender for Endpoint. These controls define which endpoint capabilities are available, how telemetry is collected, and how preventive controls are applied to devices.

The chapter then moved into automated response. You reviewed AIR, automatic attack disruption, device groups, permissions, automation levels, Microsoft Sentinel automation rules, and playbooks. Together, these mechanisms show how automated handling, response execution, and cross-system coordination are configured without losing analyst oversight.

Throughout this book, you have explored the core security operations capabilities measured in the SC-200 exam, including threat detection, investigation, hunting, incident response, data collection, analytics, and automation across Microsoft security solutions. Automation brings these capabilities together by reducing manual effort, accelerating response times, and helping analysts focus on higher-value investigative work. Understanding how these technologies work individually and how they operate together as an integrated security operations platform is essential both for success in the SC-200 exam and for performing effectively in a modern SOC.

Exam Readiness Drill – Chapter Review Questions

Apart from mastering key concepts, strong test-taking skills under time pressure are essential for acing your certification exam. That's why developing these abilities early in your learning journey is critical.

Exam readiness drills, using the free online practice resources provided with this book, help you progressively improve your time management and test-taking skills while reinforcing the key concepts you've learned.

HOW TO GET STARTED

- Open the link or scan the QR code at the bottom of this page
- If you have unlocked the practice resources already, log in to your registered account. If you haven't, follow the instructions in *Free Benefits with Your Book* section in this book's *Preface* and come back to this page.
- Once you log in, click the START button to start this chapter's quiz
- We recommend attempting a quiz multiple times till you're able to answer most of the questions correctly and well within the time limit.
- You can use the following practice template to help you plan your attempts:

Working On Accuracy		
Attempt	**Target**	**Time Limit**
Attempt 1	40% or more	Till the timer runs out
Attempt 2	60% or more	Till the timer runs out
Attempt 3	75% or more	Till the timer runs out
Working On Timing		
Attempt 4	75% or more	1 minute before time limit
Attempt 5	75% or more	2 minutes before time limit
Attempt 6	75% or more	3 minutes before time limit

The above drill is just an example. Design your drills based on your own goals and make the most out of the online quizzes accompanying this book.

Link to this Chapter's Quiz

You need to unlock the online practice resources to access the link below. Check the *Free Benefits with Your Book* section in the *Preface* for detailed instructions on how to do this. You only need to unlock the resources once.

Open Quiz `https://packt.link/sc200js-ch11` or scan the QR code

12

Unlock Your Exclusive Benefits

Your copy of this book includes the following exclusive benefits:

Online Exam-Prep Tools

Ace your certification exam with exam-ready online resources

DRM-Free PDF Version

Download DRM-free PDF and ePub copies of this book.

7-Day Packt Library Access

Get 7-day unlimited access to 8,000+ books and videos. No credit card required.

Available for first-time Packt+ trial users only.

Next-Gen Reader Access

Read this book on Packt Reader with progress sync, dark mode and note-taking.

Follow the guide below to unlock them. The process takes only a few minutes and needs to be completed once.

Unlock this Book's Free Benefits in 3 Easy Steps

Step 1

Keep your purchase invoice ready for *Step 3*. If you have a physical copy, scan it using your phone and save it as a PDF, JPG, or PNG.

For more help on finding your invoice, visit `https://www.packtpub.com/en-us/unlock?step=1`.

> Note
>
> **Note**: If you bought this book directly from Packt, no invoice is required. After *Step 2*, you can access your exclusive content right away.

Step 2

Scan the QR code or go to `packtpub.com/unlock`.

On the page that opens (similar to *Figure 12.1* on desktop), search for this book by name and select the correct edition.

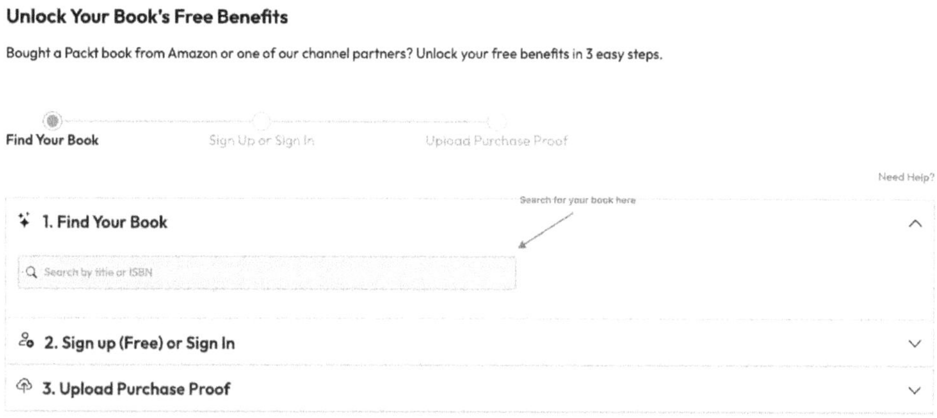

Figure 12.1: Packt unlock landing page on desktop

Step 3

After selecting your book, sign in to your Packt account or create one for free. Then upload your invoice (PDF, PNG, or JPG, up to 10 MB). Follow the on-screen instructions to finish the process.

Need Help

If you get stuck and need help, visit `https://www.packtpub.com/unlock-benefits/help` for a detailed FAQ on how to find your invoices and more. This QR code will take you to the help page.

Note

Note: If you are still facing issues, reach out to `customercare@packt.com`.

Other Books You May Enjoy

If you enjoyed this book, you may be interested in these other books by Packt:

Microsoft Defender for Endpoint in Depth

Paul Snow, Ru Campbell, Ian Hoyle, Joe Anich, Justen Graves

ISBN: 978-1-83702-611-1

- Explore the current Defender for Endpoint architecture and capabilities
- Clarify how next-gen protection, ASR, and EDR work together
- Prepare a deployment plan that fits your estate, risk, and existing tools
- Roll out Defender for Endpoint to production in staged, testable phases
- Protect mobile devices using Defender for Endpoint and MTD
- Tune alerts, exclusions, and policies for different scenarios and assets
- Support SecOps investigations using incidents, hunting, and device data
- Diagnose common health, connectivity, and performance issues in live estates

Unified SecOps Playbook

Jose Lazaro, Marcus Burnap

ISBN: 978-1-83763-286-2

- Deploy Microsoft Sentinel with RBAC, governance, and financial planning
- Align security programs with Zero Trust and global frameworks
- Automate assessments with ScubaGear, Maester, and Azure DevOps
- Build secure Sentinel foundations with Entra ID, PIM, and management groups
- Onboard customers and partners via Azure Lighthouse and GDAP
- Master the Sentinel workflow backbone: KQL, detections, automation, MITRE ATT
- Accelerate rollouts using FastTrack deployment and CI/CD pipelines
- Harness Security Copilot for AI-assisted detection and investigation

Packt is searching for authors like you

If you're interested in becoming an author for Packt, please visit `authors.packtpub.com` and apply today. We have worked with thousands of developers and tech professionals, just like you, to help them share their insight with the global tech community. You can make a general application, apply for a specific hot topic that we are recruiting an author for, or submit your own idea.

Share your thoughts

Now you've finished *Microsoft Security Operations Analyst Exam Ref SC-200 Guide-Second Edition*, we'd love to hear your thoughts! Scan the QR code below to go straight to the Amazon review page for this book and share your feedback or leave a review on the site that you purchased it from.

https://packt.link/r/1836204418

Your review is important to us and the tech community and will help us make sure we're delivering excellent quality content.

Index

A

B

C

S

T

www.ingramcontent.com/pod-product-compliance
Lightning Source LLC
LaVergne TN
LVHW060028210926
848481LV00013B/3814
9781836204411